Whatever has been is what will be,
and whatever has been done is what will be done.
There is nothing new beneath the sun.

ECCLESIASTES 1:9

THE PATH TO TYRANNY

A HISTORY OF FREE SOCIETY'S DESCENT INTO TYRANNY

SECOND EDITION

MICHAEL E. NEWTON

ELEFTHERIA PUBLISHING

Published by Eleftheria Publishing
www.eleftheriapublishing.com

SECOND EDITION
Second Printing

ISBN-10: 0-9826040-1-7
ISBN-13: 978-0-9826040-1-4
Library of Congress Control Number: 2010-927867

Printed in the United States of America

Front cover background:
      Course of Empire: Consummation (3rd in series) by Thomas Cole, 1836.
      Accession no. 1858.3
      Collection of The New-York Historical Society
Back cover background:
      Course of Empire: Destruction (4th in series) by Thomas Cole, 1836.
      Accession no. 1858.4
      Collection of The New-York Historical Society

CONTENTS

CHAPTER ONE
FREE SOCIETIES AND TYRANNIES

F reedom has been the utmost desire of mankind for thousands of years, with many even valuing it above life itself. Yet, once it is obtained, many sacrifice it for promises of wealth and equality. A prescient few predict that this will lead to disaster, but most people are too enamored by the utopian promises to listen to these "reactionaries." Following the "progressive" leaders, the population is surprised when their man-made paradise turns into tyranny.

A golden age of wealth and freedom has caused mankind to forget the lessons of history. George Santayana warned, "Those who cannot remember the past are condemned to repeat it."[1] To prevent a repeat of history, we must study the causes of free society's descent into tyranny.

FREE SOCIETY AND GOVERNMENT

Free societies establish governments to protect the rights of man, especially the inalienable rights of "life, liberty, and the pursuit of happiness."[2] James Madison wrote, "If men were angels, no government would be necessary."[3] Because men are imperfect, government is needed to protect the people's rights from those who would violate them. Nearly two thousand years ago, Rabbi Chanina said, "Pray for the integrity of the government; for were it not for the fear of its authority, a man would swallow his neighbor alive."[4] Although government is necessary to protect man's essential rights, it infringes upon the people's rights and liberty when it expands beyond its basic role. Thomas Paine writes, "Government, even in its best state, is but a necessary evil; in its worst state, an intolerable one."[5] A small government designed to protect the people's rights is "a necessary evil." A large government taking the people's money and spending it as it sees fit is "an intolerable one."

U.S. Supreme Court Justice Oliver Wendell Holmes said, "Taxes are what we pay for civilized society."[6] Although taxes are necessary to fund the government, this does not mean one should overpay. A high rate of taxation is a sign that government has grown too large or that the tax system is being used to redistribute wealth.

Taxation though is not a perfect gauge of the size of government or its meddling in society. Many governments receive a large income stream from oil or mineral rights, which enables them to maintain low tax rates while still operating a large government. The population enjoys the benefits given to them by the large government, not realizing that the government's income stream should belong to them. Therefore, though it is important to consider the tax system, it is even more important to look at the level of government spending.

Collectivists believe that political freedom can be maintained even as economic freedom is restricted. They believe that the government can centrally control the economy while leaving people's civil and political rights untouched. This is impossible. Over two hundred years ago, the Founding Fathers of the United States realized that private property was necessary to protect the other rights of man. In 1787, John Adams wrote in *A Defence of the Constitutions of Government of the United States of America*:

> "The moment the idea is admitted into society that property is not as sacred as the laws of God, and that there is not a force of law and public justice to protect it, anarchy and tyranny commence. If "Thou shalt not covet" and "Thou shalt not steal" were not commandments of Heaven, they must be made inviolable precepts in every society before it can be civilized or made free."[7]

Banning private property or placing numerous restrictions on its use results in a number of economic problems. Without private property, there is no way to gauge supply and demand and efficiently allocate resources.* Private property also incentivizes hard work and penalizes misuse of resources. Beyond its economic necessity, private property is required to ensure the other rights of mankind. Freedom of press, religion, and speech are insecure if society owns all the printing presses, television and radio stations, churches, temples, assembly halls, and even the street corners. In theory, society could collectively own everything and still allow free speech, free press, and freedom of religion, but it will do so only as long as the administering government is not threatened by allowing such freedoms. Once the government becomes unpopular and its position becomes vulnerable, there will be nothing to stop government officials from seizing the printing presses and closing the churches, temples, and assembly halls, which they already control. When it comes time to overthrow an unresponsive and corrupt government, the people, deprived of all their property, will have no means with which to fight.

Free speech and free press are even more important than physical weapons in the fight against despotic government. As Edward Bulwer-Lytton wrote, "The pen is mightier than the sword."[8] The battle to maintain free society is an ideological battle more than a physical one. When a party within free society advocates some "progressive" agenda, supporters of liberty must renew society's desire for freedom by reminding them of its incalculable value. Even when free society is being physically threatened by a military coup or invasion, often the people must be roused to defend their freedom. Frederick Douglass said, "Liberty is meaningless where the right to utter one's thoughts and opinions has ceased to exist. That, of all rights, is the dread of tyrants. It is the right which they first of all strike down."[9] If the government has already curtailed free speech, the defense of freedom becomes much more difficult, if not impossible.

---

* This is known as the economic calculation problem. It was first proposed by Ludwig von Mises in his 1920 article "Economic Calculation in the Socialist Commonwealth." Friedrich Hayek further developed this idea, most notably in his 1937 "Economics and Knowledge" and his 1945 "The Use of Knowledge in Society."

In addition to encouraging free speech, a free society should per-
mit each person to practice religion freely, as long as no harm is done
to others. In reality, a person can believe whatever one wants and the
government has no ability to stop one's thoughts and beliefs. However,
a large government may have the power to restrict religious practice,
especially if it involves public gatherings. This freedom of religion,
though, does not preclude an official state religion. England is officially Anglican, Germany is officially Lutheran, and the Netherlands is
officially Reformed, yet each guarantees freedom of religion to its
citizens.

Free society must also be democratic. A society in which government possesses force of law and arms but does not answer to the
people is not a free one. An unaccountable government may grant the
people all the rights of free society, but can just as easily take them
away. In free society, the people select their representatives and kick
out corrupt and ineffective politicians through the election process. In
1914, John Basil Barnhill said in a debate about socialism, "Where the
people fear the government you have tyranny. Where the government
fears the people you have liberty."* Democratic elections keep government officials in fear of their constituents.

Therefore, a free society must have all or most of the following:
elected officials representing the people, small government, private
property, and freedom of speech, press, and religion. As government
grows and infringes upon these aspects of liberty, society becomes less
free and moves closer to tyranny.

TYRANNY

Tyranny must first be defined before its causes and effects can be
analyzed. The word comes from the ancient Greek *tyrannos*, meaning

---

* This quote, or a variant of it, is often misattributed to Thomas Jefferson. ("When
governments fear the people, there is liberty...(Quotation)," *Thomas Jefferson
Encyclopedia*.)

"absolute ruler." With time, the definition of *tyrannos* changed from "absolute ruler" to "illegitimate, cruel, and oppressive ruler." Today, the dictionary definition of *tyrant* is "an absolute ruler unrestrained by law or constitution" and *tyranny* is "oppressive power" especially as "exerted by government."

In ancient Greece, Aristotle defined tyranny as "a kind of monarchy which has in view the interest of the monarch only."[10] He adds, "A tyrant, as has often been repeated, has no regard to any public interest, except as conducive to his private ends; his aim is pleasure."[11] As a result, the people were forced to serve the tyrant instead of the monarch serving the people. In today's more democratic world, in which few genuine monarchs remain, a tyrant of this nature is much less likely. Instead, there is the twentieth century concept of totalitarianism, which is "centralized control by an autocratic authority," whereby a single individual or a select group controls the country. Ancient tyranny and modern totalitarianism are the same because both call for centralized control of people's lives by a single ruler or group. Although totalitarian regimes supposedly have the people's interest in mind, their primary goal is the consolidation of power and they act just like the tyrannies of old. There should be little doubt that Hitler and Stalin, acting as heads of totalitarian regimes for the supposed benefit of the German and Russian peoples, were just as powerful, evil, and despotic as the tyrants of ancient Greece and Rome.

The twentieth century autocrats did not call themselves tyrants and most avoided the totalitarian label, as well. Instead, the supporters of totalitarianism called their systems communism, fascism, Nazism, or Maoism, each of which sounded good at the time, but today are shunned. Friedrich Hayek explains, "Fascism and Communism are merely variants of the same totalitarianism which central control of economic activity tends to produce."[12]

Because the various forms of collectivism are no longer popular, the collectivists instead advocate public welfare, social justice, government compassion, consumer protection, progressivism, liberalism, environmentalism, and a whole host of other pleasant sounding programs. They use this new terminology to make their collectivism sound more appealing, just as others have in the past. Nevertheless, this use of government power to direct or coordinate society is a form of tyranny, because there can be no greater tyranny than an individual or group controlling the lives of an entire population, even if popularly elected.

Tyranny today may appear suddenly, through foreign invasion for example, but it most often works its way insidiously through the political system. Collectivists hide their agenda and adamantly deny that they favor socialism or big government. They advocate numerous pleasant sounding programs, each of which is innocuous on its own. Even though humanity has survived for thousands of years without these government programs, the people are convinced by politicians and interest groups that they are necessary and their costs will be minimal. However, the true purpose of these proposals is the redistribution of wealth, increased regulation, and other forms of government intervention.

By its very nature, government wishes to grow larger as politicians almost always seek more power. At some point, though, government becomes so powerful that it is controlling, either directly or indirectly, the whole economy and, therefore, controlling the lives of each individual by deciding where they work, where they live, how much they earn, and what they consume.

By supporting an endless number of "good" causes, free society gradually becomes collectivist and tyrannical. The Russians did not choose tyranny, but they did choose a communist system that led to tyranny. The Germans did not choose a brutal dictatorship, but it was the inevitable outcome of their choice of a National Socialist (Nazi) government that promised to enrich the Aryans by coordinating the economy and purging the nation of undesirable people, especially the Jewish capitalists.

Upton Sinclair, author of *The Jungle*, socialist, and a founder of the consumer protection movement, wrote to six-time presidential candidate Norman Thomas of the Socialist Party of America in 1951: "The American People will take Socialism, but they won't take the label... Running on the Socialist ticket I got 60,000 votes, and running on the slogan to "End Poverty in California" I got 879,000... There is no use attacking it by a front attack, it is much better to out-flank them."[13] The last half century of American history has proven Upton Sinclair correct. The United States government has grown dramatically and enacted one socialist idea after another, yet the American people continue to deny the collectivism that is all around them.

More than two thousand years ago, the Greek historian Polybius warned that "democracy in its turn is abolished and changes into a rule of force and violence" as the people grow more "accustomed to feed at the expense of others and to depend for their livelihood on the property of others."[14] This is just as true today as it was then.

THE PATH TO TYRANNY

This book focuses on free societies that embrace centralized control of the economy and, as a direct result, descend into tyranny. This is most relevant to today with the record number of free democratic nations embracing big government. To avoid tyranny, free society must return to its small government principles.

Fortunately, societies with big governments can avoid the descent into tyranny by reversing course. Often, societies will temporarily choose big government during a time of crisis. After the crisis is over, society will scale back the government, returning it to its original small size. For example, the United States government grew dramatically during World War I and again during World War II, but was able to scale it back after each war had ended. In ancient Greece and in the Roman Republic, the people could select a dictator to lead them into battle against an enemy, expecting him to cede power after the enemy was defeated. Societies must be careful, though, because many politicians and temporary dictators want to keep the power they gained during the crisis. Additionally, these temporary powers and dictators establish dangerous precedents for the future. Only by quickly reducing the size and power of government, can societies avoid tyranny and remain free.

Additionally, not all tyrannies come about through big government. The most obvious exceptions are external invasions and military coups. In these cases, one need not ask why the tyrant chose to take over because a tyrant always seeks to expand his control. It is more important to investigate how to prevent invasion by foreign tyrants and forestall internal coups by potential tyrants. A free society with a small government is more likely to resist tyranny because people already living under a big government controlling many aspects of their lives will be less resistant to a new one that is only slightly more controlling. Additionally, control over a large government with its vast amounts of wealth and power is very alluring to a tyrant, whereas potential tyrants are less interested in controlling a small and decentralized government. Therefore, the best way to prevent invasion and coup is to maintain a small and decentralized government with a strong defense, a well-armed population, and the courage to defend one's rights and liberty.

While free societies often descend into tyranny because of the choices they make, the people never actually choose tyranny. Instead, demagogues and ideologues promising freedom, equality, and wealth lead them to it. Today, politicians promise the right to high quality education, the right to free or affordable health care and housing, and many more so-called rights. These are not genuine rights. They are benefits at the expense of others. The rights to private property, free speech, and freedom of religion are true rights because they have no cost. The "rights" to education, housing, and health care cost the providers who must supply them for free or at a discount, or they must cost other taxpayers to reimburse the providers. As a result of the government providing these new "rights," the people have fewer choices as the government rations goods and services, businesses are burdened with more regulation, and costs rise as more bureaucracy is added to the system. Instead of the greater freedom and wealth promised, the people are poorer and become slaves to the government.

Each chapter in this book will be a study of a different society, focusing on the freedom it had, how and why it chose centralized control of the economy, how a select group of individuals warned the people about the ill effects of government control, how the people ignored these warnings, and how each society descended into tyranny as a result; thus showing how choosing big government and centralized control of the economy turns free societies into tyrannies.

In the last chapter, the United States will be examined. The causes of how Americans maintained their freedom for well over two hundred years will be investigated and the current direction of the country will be evaluated. Furthermore, by using the examination of the U.S. as a baseline, the reader can evaluate the situations in other countries and determine how free they are and how close they are to tyranny. Studying the history of free societies descending into tyranny and evaluating the current situation will enable the reader to recognize tyranny as it approaches and continue the eternal fight for freedom.

CHAPTER TWO

ANCIENT GREECE

T he liberty enjoyed by much of the world today is a direct descendant of the freedom and equality born in ancient Greece. The ideas of democracy, elections, constitutions, and popular assemblies all originated in ancient Greece. Yet, the free Greek city-states often lost their rights and freedom after an external hostile takeover, internal political coup, or when the population sought the benefits of centralized government. Their new ruler, unbound by any laws or constitution, was given the name *tyrannos*, or tyrant.

THE BIRTH OF FREEDOM

Around the year 1600 BC, the Greeks first arrived in the Aegean. They formed city-states, each ruled by a king claiming to be a god or chosen by the gods. The king would build his palace on the tallest hill in the city, the acropolis, for defensive reasons. The common people either worked their own land and paid taxes to the king or worked for the king on his land or in his palace.

Starting about 1100 BC, Greece suffered a three hundred year "Dark Age." During this era, the population of Greece declined and cities were abandoned and left in ruin. The cause of this decline is still being debated, but speculation includes natural disasters, economic failure, and internal conflict.[1] The ancient Greeks believed that the Dorians invaded Greece, pushing out the native Mycenaeans.[2] Others claim that Greece's Dark Age was caused by the "Sea People," a mysterious group of sea-faring people wielding iron weapons who attacked much of the eastern Mediterranean.[3]

Through natural population growth and immigration, Greece began growing again around the year 800 BC, with the increased population leading to the development of new cities and rebuilding of old
ones. The Greeks modified Phoenician script into the Greek alphabet.
With the new immigrants, many of whom had contacts in their places
of origin, and the adoption of Greek as the common spoken and
written language, commerce expanded in the region. A new mercantile
class grew wealthy and they desired a larger role in the administration
of the government. To appease the merchants, the kings slowly distributed power downward. First, the king took on some of the leading
citizens as advisors. Later, a council was created, made up of members
from elite families. Later yet, an assembly of all the citizens was formed,
further weakening the king and distributing power to the people.[4]

These governments survived and thrived for a long time, as long as
the king and aristocrats performed well and put the public interest at
the same level or ahead of their own. However, too often the government and its leaders were corrupt, causing the people to rebel. A new
leader would emerge, castigating those in power and issuing promises
to the people. The people would overthrow the old government and
install this leader as the new ruler. With the support of the people and
amid the chaos of revolution, the new ruler frequently turned into a
tyrant.[5]

With the growing population of Greece, land and food became
scarce. The poor threatened to revolt rather than starve, forcing the
ruling elite into action. To prevent their overthrow, the kings and
aristocrats had two ways to appease the people: conquer a foreign
land, enslave its people, and promote the local poor to a higher class
or create a more equal society through political, economic, and social
change. Sparta adopted the first method whereas Athens chose the
second.

To help deal with a shortage of land and to improve the welfare of
the Spartan poor, Sparta conquered Messenia, among other territories,
in the eighth century BC. Sparta indentured the locals and forced
them to give over half their produce. Spartans, even the previously

poor, were now able to live off the production of the Messenians. Free from working the land, all Spartans, rich and poor alike, were required to serve in the army to defend against foreign invasion and to fight the Messenians if they decided to revolt. In fact, the Messenians revolted at least twice, but did not regain their independence until Sparta was defeated by Thebes at the Battle of Leuctra in the fourth century BC. The requirement that all people, regardless of economic or social status, serve in the army created a new kind of equality among the Spartans that helped develop their idea of freedom. Though this freedom for Spartan citizens was hypocritical with their enslavement of the Messenians and their very structured life dedicated to the state and military training, these ideas of liberty and equality were firmly planted among the Spartans who would go on to defend them to great fame in the war against the Persians.

After selecting Solon, the rich hoped to persuade him to favor them whereas the poor hoped to sway him toward them. Solon found a middle path, helping the poor without violating the rights of either side. Solon rejected the idea of isomoiria, equal distribution of the land, which the poor desperately wanted. But he did restore the freedom of enslaved Athenian farmers, shook off the burden of heavy debt from the poor,* and prohibited lending with the debtor's person

Athens experienced a similar land shortage and threat of revolt by the poor, but decided to reform its society and pursue commercial trade instead of conquering and enslaving. At the beginning of the sixth century BC, the Athenians chose Solon, the "lawmaker of Athens," to lead them and resolve their ongoing disputes. Plutarch writes, "At this point, the wisest of the Athenians cast their eyes upon Solon. They saw that he was the one man least implicated in the errors of the time; that he was neither associated with the rich in their injustice, nor involved in the necessities of the poor. They therefore besought him to come forward publicly and put an end to the prevailing dissensions."[6]

---

* The Greek word used is *seisachtheia*, meaning "shake off the burden," and it is generally understood that Solon cancelled all debts. However, others claim that

as collateral. In other words, he restored the people's freedom but avoided most of the people's demands for wealth redistribution.

Solon also implemented a series of economic reforms to help lift the economy and enrich both the rich and the poor. He encouraged fathers to teach their sons a trade by enacting "a law that no son who had not been taught a trade should be compelled to support his father."[7] He encouraged immigration by extending citizenship to those "who removed to Athens with their entire families to ply a trade."[8]

After Solon implemented his reforms, the people constantly came to him "with praise or censure of them, or with advice to insert something into the documents, or take something out. Very numerous, too, were those who came to him with inquiries and questions about them, urging him to teach and make clear to them the meaning and purpose of each several item."[9] Annoyed by all the questions and the constant desire to change his system, he bought a ship, obtained a ten year leave of absence, and left Greece. Not long after Solon's reforms were in place, the same old disputes between rich and poor reappeared and, after years of political disorder, Peisistratos captured the Acropolis and installed himself as tyrant. Solon had returned to Athens and opposed Peisistratos' rise to power, but even Solon could not stop his ascension. Although Solon's reforms lasted only thirty-one years before Peisistratos' tyranny, the ideas he helped develop, those of

---

Solon merely lowered the interest rate or devalued the drachma, thus making debts smaller in real terms. Plutarch (*Parallel Lives* Solon 15.4-5) writes, "Some writers, however, and Androtion is one of them, affirm that the poor were relieved not by a cancelling of debts, but by a reduction of the interest upon them, and showed their satisfaction by giving the name of "disburdenment" to this act of humanity, and to the augmentation of measures and the purchasing power of money which accompanied it. For he made the mina to consist of a hundred drachmas, which before had contained only seventy-three, so that by paying the same amount of money, but money of lesser value, those who had debts to discharge were greatly benefited, and those who accepted such payments were no losers. But most writers agree that the "disburdenment" was a removal of all debt, and with such the poems of Solon are more in accord." Aristotle writes in *The Athenian Constitution* (Section 1 Part 6), after describing Solon's complete cancellation of all debts, that he is "bound to consider this accusation to be false."

freedom, rule of law, a legal constitution, equal protection under the law, and opposition to tyranny, survive to this very day.

Both Sparta's expansion and Athens' reforms helped develop the Greek concept of freedom, each in its own way. A third dynamic also fostered liberty in ancient Greece. The rapid population growth in Greece created waves of migration to hundreds of colonies all around the Mediterranean, primarily to Italy, Sicily, and Asia Minor. With the old monarchies, a king would gain little benefit from a far flung province whose people would be hard to rule over, but whose defense would be costly.* However, the merchant class would profit from the increased trade, as would members of the middle and lower classes who could establish their own farms or businesses in the new colonies. Though linked to their mother cities for trading purposes, the Greek colonies were generally left alone by the mother city and were told to govern and defend themselves; the glaring exception being Corinth's control of Corcyra and the subsequent war between them. With little government intervention in their economies, many of these colonies prospered and their people enjoyed the freedom of living on the frontier far away from the bigger government back home.† These

---

* To conclude *The Wealth of Nations*, Adam Smith similarly wrote about the expense of Great Britain's defense of its colonies. After detailing the cost of defending the American colonies, Adam Smith concludes that Britain's empire is not worth the expense unless the colonies pay higher taxes, to which the colonists objected and were already rebelling against. "If any of the provinces of the British empire cannot be made to contribute towards the support of the whole empire, it is surely time that Great Britain should free herself from the expense of defending those provinces in time of war, and of supporting any part of their civil or military establishments in time of peace, and endeavour to accommodate her future views and designs to the real mediocrity of her circumstances." (Smith, *The Wealth of Nations* 1028.)

† Similarly, colonial United States received an influx of immigrants from the overcrowding in England. The new American frontiersmen, enjoying their new political, economic, and religious freedom, created the most free and powerful country the world has ever seen. The ancient Greek colonies around the Mediterranean, often composed of refugees escaping the expanding and often enslaving city-states, such as Messenians fleeing Sparta's growing empire, had the same desire for freedom.

colonists helped move the idea of freedom off the Greek peninsula and spread it to a much wider audience around the Mediterranean, including Italy where it undoubtedly helped Rome develop their own free republic.

The rights granted to Athenians, Spartans, and the colonists planted the idea and desire for freedom among the other Greeks and even many non-Greeks who had close contact with them through trade. Even the city-states that ended in tyranny helped foster the desire for freedom as their citizens despised their tyrants and wished for a freer society. But this concept of freedom was still new and not understood by everybody. For example, Solon had to fight with both the wealthy and the poor to establish the first roots of freedom in Athens. It was not until the threat of Persian invasion came to Greece that freedom became paramount, as the Greeks were no longer fighting one Greek city-state against another, with little difference whether Chalkis or Eretria controlled the Lelantine Plain, for example. The war with Persia was between east and west, between slavery and freedom. The Greeks were fighting to defend their own land; not just the land of the Greek people or their city-state, but their own pieces of earth on which they farmed and lived. While the Persians fought in a foreign land as slaves to their kings, the Greeks fought as free individuals defending their way of life.

ELEUTHERIA

The Greek concept of freedom, eleutheria in the ancient Greek, did not develop overnight. Over the course of centuries, the ancient Greeks created new ideas, tested them, and abandoned or updated them. They wrote constitutions and formed new political systems while the philosophers of the time debated these new concepts. In many respects, the Greek world revolved around the ongoing struggle between freedom and slavery on an individual basis and between liberty and tyranny on a communal basis. In fact, one of Zeus' many names was Zeus Eleutherios, which means Zeus the liberator, and the Greeks celebrated a festival in Zeus' honor called Eleutheria to celebrate the victory over the Persians at Plataea in 479 BC, adding a religious nature to this idea of freedom.[10]

In his discussion of democracy, Aristotle writes, "One principle of liberty is for all to rule and be ruled in turn."[11] He adds, "the majority must be supreme, and that whatever the majority approve must be the end and the just. Every citizen, it is said, must have equality."[12] Using this principle, it is easy to understand how the Spartans could view themselves as free yet continue to own slaves and live very structured lives dedicated to military training. Provided that the majority of citizens approved of the slavery of non-citizens and supported its militaristic state, it was "just" to compel the minority into military service and the non-citizens into slavery. As long as the Spartan citizens were equal and lived by majority rule, Spartans could consider themselves free, under Aristotle's initial principle.

However, this unlimited form of direct democracy creates mob rule, what is now called the tyranny of the majority.[*] Aristotle calls democracy a perversion of constitutional government in the interest of the needy.[13] In ancient Greece, this democracy often led to tyranny, not just of the majority, but also to tyranny of a single ruler chosen by the majority to lead them.

Plato warned about the evils of democracy from its birth to its death. He argues that, from the start, democracy involves killing and exiling its enemies. "And a democracy, I suppose, comes into being when the poor, winning the victory, put to death some of the other party, drive out others, and grant the rest of the citizens an equal share in both citizenship and offices."[14]

The result of this democratic uprising, Plato argues, is anarchy, mockingly calling democracy "a delightful form of government,

---

[*] The term "tyranny of the majority" originated with Alexis de Tocqueville in *Democracy in America*. (Tocqueville, *Democracy in America* 292.) However, Polybius, the Greek historian who lived from 203-120 BC, used the expression "cheirokratia," loosely translated as "mob rule," to describe this unlimited direct democracy, arguing that mob rule was a result of "the licence and lawlessness" of democracy. (Polybius, *Histories* 6.4.9.)

anarchic and motley, assigning a kind of equality indiscriminately to equals and unequals alike!"[15] But he contends that the end of democracy is tyranny as demagogues prey on the people's lust for wealth. "Well, then, the insatiate lust for wealth and the neglect of everything else for the sake of money-making was the cause of its undoing."[16] Plato insists that this "climax of popular liberty... is attained in such a city when the purchased slaves, male and female, are no less free than the owners who paid for them."[17] "And so the probable outcome of too much freedom is only too much slavery in the individual and the state... from the height of liberty, I take it, the fiercest extreme of servitude."[18]

Plato's preferred form of government is the philosopher king, but all monarchies, if their power is maintained, descend into tyranny as rulers become corrupted by power or are succeeded by evil men. Fortunately, Aristotle lists a second principle of liberty: "A man should live as he likes. This, they say, is the privilege of a freeman, since, on the other hand, not to live as a man likes is the mark of a slave. This is the second characteristic of democracy, whence has arisen the claim of men to be ruled by none, if possible, or, if this is impossible, to rule and be ruled in turns; and so it contributes to the freedom based upon equality."[19]

This second principle is in many ways a contradiction of his first principle. The first includes "all to rule and be ruled in turn" whereas the second is "to be ruled by none." The first says "the majority must be supreme" whereas second says "a man should live as he likes." The first principle leads to the tyranny of the majority whereas the second results in anarchy. It is only by balancing the two principles that a free society can be maintained without falling into tyranny or anarchy.

Small Government and Taxation

Greek history books are filled with political intrigues, battles, invasions, and the development of Greek philosophy. Very little, though, is written about the economic history of Greece. This is partly because the economy was generally left to its own devices as the government interfered very little in the day-to-day economic affairs of the people. The primary purpose of a city-state's government was protection from external enemies and law breakers, not management of the economy. Internally, the government's job was limited to protecting the people's rights and property, defining and enforcing standard weights and measures, and issuing coins of consistent weight to encourage trade. Even in terms of defense, most city-states did not have a permanent paid army or hired mercenaries, but an army made up of citizens. Because of this hands-off approach to economic life, ancient Greece enjoyed a capitalist economic system and prospered for many centuries, despite the many wars that hurt trade and consumed much wealth.[20]

Because of the government's limited size, income taxes were generally low in the free city-states of Ancient Greece. Some cities imposed property taxes on houses, slaves, livestock, and wine to fund the general operations of government, but not all cities had these. Instead of income and property taxes, Athens instituted indirect taxes including taxes on use of the marketplace, imports and exports, and on foreigners who moved to the city. Later, the Athenian government received most of its revenue from its silver mines. Similarly, Thasos received its funds from a gold mine it owned.

The very wealthy often volunteered or were required to build or maintain public works. These quasi-taxes were call liturgies. If entirely voluntary, as they originally were, it was seen as a way of giving back to the community and also to gain fame and popularity.* In most places though, these liturgies became a required tax. Even when forced to give funds for public works, this method was more free, competitive, and efficient than the government taking the money and doing as it wishes. Projects would be assigned to wealthy individuals who could spend as little or as much as they liked to complete their assignments.[21] This encouraged the wealthy to supervise the construction and maintenance of their projects to ensure their success. Further-

---

* This is similar to the philanthropy of Andrew Carnegie and John D. Rockefeller at the beginning of the 20th century in the United States.

more, to gain honor, the wealthy would often spend more than required and publicly boast about their generosity.[22] This was an effective way to fund annual festivals or build and supply naval ships without creating large government bureaucracies. The liturgy system encouraged the rich to support the community in exchange for honor.[23]

Unfortunately, the Greek city-states often needed extra funds to defend themselves against other city-states or foreign powers. To hire soldiers, build ships, and purchase equipment, a special tax called the eisphora was placed on the very wealthy. When the war was over, this tax was repealed and the low tax environment resumed.[24] This system of low and temporary taxes, liturgies on the wealthy, and laissez-faire government helped the Greeks create a large and prosperous commercial network.

Private Property

Private property was probably the most important right to the ancient Greeks. Most Greeks were farmers, making a good plot of land essential. Furthermore, citizenship was based on land ownership. Therefore, Greek citizens staunchly defended their private estates to ensure not just their homes and incomes, but also their rights as citizens, including the right to vote and freedom of speech.

Much of what is known about early Greek law comes from the Gortyn Code, which was inscribed in the fifth century BC on the walls of a building in Gortyn in southern Crete. The Gortyn code established a system of property rights and also set down rules of inheritance. Inheritance is a very important but often overlooked aspect of private property, determining who receives all or part of an estate upon the owner's death. Alexis de Tocqueville writes in *Democracy in America*: "I am astonished that commentators of old and new have not attributed to the laws of inheritance a greater influence on the progress of human affairs... Through the impact of these laws, man exerts an almost godlike power over the future of his fellow man."[25] In general, there are two methods of distributing the property of the deceased: primogeniture, in which the firstborn, often limited to the firstborn son, inherits the entire estate, and partible inheritance, in which the estate is subdivided.

Primogeniture creates a wide divide between the wealthy and the poor, with the aristocracy gaining political power along with their wealth. Tocqueville writes, "When framed in a certain way, this law unites, draws together, and gathers property and, soon, real power in the hands of an individual."[26] Conversely, partibility results in no landed aristocracy, greater equality, and decentralization of power, making it more difficult for an aspiring despot to gain power and create a tyranny. Tocqueville explains, "If directed, however, by opposite principles and launched along other paths, its effect is even more rapid; it divides, shares out, and disperses both property and power."[27]

Ancient Greece adopted partible inheritance, which helped further promote freedom and equality. According to the Gortyn Code, when a man died, his property was split evenly among all his children, though sons received twice as much as daughters. If a woman died, the children received the inheritance, not the husband, though he acted as a trustee until he died or remarried. Unlike in Gortyn, in most of ancient Greece, it appears that inheritance was divided equally among the sons with the daughters receiving nothing.[28]

The concept of wills, bestowing one's property as he sees fit upon his death, also existed in ancient Greece, though it was often allowed only when one had no sons. Plutarch gives high praise to Solon for introducing wills to Athens, giving men more control over their own property: "He was highly esteemed also for his law concerning wills... by permitting a man who had no children to give his property to whom he wished, ranked friendship above kinship, and favour above necessity, and made a man's possessions his own property."[29]

The silver mines at Laurion and Thorikos were a special case of public ownership. They were owned by Athens as a city-state, not by private individuals. Instead of dividing the revenue among the Athenians as the people initially preferred, in 483 BC, Themistocles "dared to come before the people with a motion that this division be given up, and that with these moneys triremes be constructed for the war against Aegina... The result was that with those moneys they built a hundred triremes, with which they actually fought at Salamis against Xerxes."[30] Although Athens used its silver to build ships, called triremes, to defend against Aegina and the Persians, it later used this wealth and sea power to secure an empire. Athens, the defender of liberty, had become the conqueror. The triremes, previously the tools of freedom, became the tools of tyranny. But once people experience freedom, they are loathe to give it up. A number of city-states, often supported by Sparta or Persia, rebelled against Athens, resulting in the Peloponnesian War that lasted nearly thirty years and ended with the defeat and subjugation of Athens. One can see here how easily tyranny can be created by a government with vast wealth, a steady stream of revenue, and a military inclination. It seems likely that Athens and Greece would have been better off if the silver mines had been privately owned or the revenue from them divided among the people.

Slavery

In discussing freedom in ancient Greece, one must look not just at how much liberty the free people had, but also how they treated their slaves. In fact, the slaves in ancient Greece had significantly more rights and freedom than most enslaved people elsewhere in the world. In many respects, the slaves in Greece were also better off than many other free people, who often lived at the whim of the country's monarch, worked on the king's land, paid exorbitant taxes, and were drafted into his army to fight foreign enemies in distant lands. Whereas most countries granted its citizens no rights at all and required strict obedience to the king and the religion, the slaves in Greece were granted a number of rights.

With thousands of city-states, each with its own government and constantly evolving laws, the rights and conditions of slaves varied by time and location. In general, the freer the society, the more rights the slaves had. Conversely, more tyrannical societies gave their slaves fewer rights and treated them harshly. Because ancient Greece spent most of its years as a free society, only later descending into tyranny, the slaves were generally treated well. Though they had no political rights, the law protected slaves to a certain extent by limiting the use of force against them. Euripides writes, "For among you the same law holds good for slave and free alike respecting bloodshed."[31] Xenophon concurs, "Another point is the extraordinary amount of license granted to slaves and resident aliens at Athens, where a blow is illegal, and a slave will not step aside to let you pass him in the street... The Athenian People is no better clothed than the slave or alien, nor in personal appearance is there any superiority... We have established an equality between our slaves and free men; and again between our resident aliens and full citizens."[32]

Slaves could win their freedom by fighting bravely in battle along-side freemen. Slaves were allowed to own property and allowed to operate their own businesses, if their masters permitted, which many did for a share of the profit. Furthermore, slaves could purchase their freedom, which made economic sense if the master received a payment larger than the future value of his slave's work. The master could also choose to free his slave. Initially, there was little incentive to do so, but it became somewhat popular and a kind of custom to free slaves. The Sophists, Stoics, and Cynics believed that all people, including barbarians and slaves, were born equal and free, and argued for the elimination of slavery.[33] Epicurus, for example, taught women and slaves in his school, showing that all humans are equal and have the capacity for advanced intellectual pursuits. As a result, many slave owners freed their slaves. However, a freed slave could never be equal to his master because he would join the population of resident aliens, known as metics, and would not become a citizen.[34] Slaves were also allowed to marry other slaves and, at least in Gortyn, were even allowed to marry free people.

Slave-owners had little interest in injuring their slaves and losing the valuable work they performed. In fact, finding the most produc-tive use of their skills would benefit the slave owners greatly. Although most slaves did household jobs or worked in the fields, some took on professions.[35] In fact, slaves could perform any job except for politics.

It is difficult to estimate how many slaves were in ancient Greece. Of course, the number varied by time and location, but it is generally estimated that slaves made up a quarter to a half of the population.[36] Most slaves in Greece were barbarians who were purchased from their tribes, taken by pirates, or captured as prisoners of war.[37]

There is no denying that many slaves were treated harshly, especially the slaves who worked in the silver mines of Laurion, which produced much of the wealth of Athens. The silver in the mines contained dangerously high levels of lead and the men working there would die from lead poisoning after just a few years. Therefore, the most honest and productive slaves were assigned to other tasks, while criminals and barbarians were sent to the mines for what turned into a death sentence.[38]

Nevertheless, slaves were protected by the law and were generally treated well. Slaves fought alongside freemen in battle and performed the same jobs as them. Thus, the slaves in Greece were treated relatively well. Although the slaves in ancient Greece were by no means free, they were freer than slaves in other places at that time. Just compare the rights of these slaves, including some protection under the law and the rights to own property, run a business, and get married, to the lack of rights of the Israelites in Egypt or, more recently, the Africans in the southern United States and the Caribbean. Furthermore, the slaves in ancient Greece were in many respects better off than free people living in most of the ancient world who enjoyed no protection from their own monarchs and aristocrats. The average Persian or Babylonian, drafted into the army to fight for the king, was in many respects less free than the Greek slaves. Whereas the Greek slaves were able to win their freedom for bravery in battle, no such reward was granted in the areas of the world which, at that time, had no concept of freedom for anybody, regardless of class.

For hundreds of years, the free Greeks and even the slaves saw their freedom and rights increase. In their desire for wealth and empire, the Greeks began treating the slaves more harshly. Athens was using tens of thousands of slaves in its silver-mines at Laurion in deplorable conditions.[39] Thucydides reports twenty thousand slaves fleeing from

Decelea in 413 BC after Sparta conquered the area.[40] With the advent of the Greek empires and their tyranny, slaves lost many of their rights.

Freedom of Speech

Initially, the ancient Greeks developed the idea of isegoria, equality of speech. Technically, this did not mean that a citizen had free speech; it meant that each person's words had a value equal to that of all other citizens.[41] This meant that all citizens were allowed to speak in the Assembly and that nobody's opinion was more valuable than another's. The lower class had just as much a right to speak as the upper class, as long as they too were citizens, but non-citizens, such as slaves, did not have any such right.

Isegoria was later supplemented by parrhesia, meaning "to speak everything" or freedom of speech. It may seem like a semantic difference, but it is not. Regarding speech, isegoria means equality whereas parrhesia means freedom. This is quite similar to the two principles of liberty proposed by Aristotle. Isegoria, equality of speech, matches with the first principle of majority rule. Parrhesia, freedom of speech, matches the second principle of rule by none.

The idea of parrhesia eventually overtook isegoria because it was free from any political system. Isegoria was obviously tied to democracy with its notion of equality. Parrhesia, though, was independent of the political system and people could demand it even in times of monarchy, oligarchy, or tyranny.

A good example of freedom of speech appears in the time of Dion in Syracuse during the fourth century BC. Plutarch writes, "Now, there was a certain Sosis, a man whose baseness and impudence gave him renown in Syracuse, where it was thought that abundance of liberty could only be shown by such license of speech as his."[42] Sosis "rose in an assembly and roundly abused the Syracusans for not comprehending that they had merely exchanged a stupid and drunken tyrant for a watchful and sober master."[43] Though this Sosis was a known trouble-maker, even he was granted free speech and allowed to criticize the ruler of Syracuse in the assembly, thus demonstrating the "abundance of liberty" they had. Unfortunately, Sosis was condemned to death after he falsely accused Dion of attacking him.[44] Nevertheless, this demonstrates just how far freedom of speech went in ancient Greece, enabling even men of "baseness and impudence" to speak freely.

Freedom of Religion

Though many think that the trial of Socrates and his execution for his disbelief in the Greek pantheon of gods demonstrates Greece's religious intolerance, in truth, the Greeks had more freedom of religion than is commonly known. Even though the Greeks generally believed in a pantheon of gods, they disagreed on which was the primary god to worship. Some gods had their own areas of dominion, such as Poseidon ruling the seas and Hyperion the sun. Additionally, some cities were associated with specific gods. Athens belonged to Athena and was named after her. Delphi and Delos were linked to Apollo, Olympia worshipped Zeus, and Aphrodite was connected with Corinth.

But not all Greeks believed in the official pantheon. A number of Greek philosophers were agnostic, atheist, or monotheist,[45] and they often spoke and wrote about their beliefs. Xenophanes (570–480 BC), for example, criticized the idea that the gods had forms similar to humans and argued that the acts of the gods were really natural phenomenon. He believed that "God is one, supreme among gods and men, and not like mortals in body or in mind."[46] Xenophanes added that God "sets in motion all things by mind and thought"[47] and knows everything that is occurring, but he did not see God actively meddling in the world as most Greeks believed. Other famous Greek heretics include Pythagoras, Anaxagoras, Protagoras, Diagoras of Melos, Plato, Aristotle, Epicurus, and Zeno of Citium.[48]

The most famous case of heresy against the Greek pantheon belongs to Socrates. In 399 BC, Socrates was charged with disbelieving in the official Greek pantheon. Socrates was put to death on these charges and for corrupting the youth of Athens. But Socrates had also angered most of Athens for praising Sparta while the two were at war with each other, insulting the intellectuals of Athens by claiming he was the wisest man alive, criticizing the leaders of Athens, arguing against democracy, and because one disciple, Critias, became one of the Thirty Tyrants that Sparta installed in Athens and another student, Alcibiades, betrayed Athens and joined Sparta, though he later rejoined Athens but was exiled after his defeat in the Battle of Notium. It may have been a crime to preach the disbelief of the ancestral gods, but no other person is known to have been executed for this, even though others openly preached it. Instead of this being a restriction on the people's freedom of religion, it was the tyranny of the majority that caused the execution of Socrates, an evil of democracy that Socrates warned about. But this was Athens in 399 BC, an Athens that had already become a tyrant city, had just lost its primacy after losing the naval battle of Notium in 406 BC against Sparta, and had surrendered to Sparta in 404 BC in the face of starvation, thus ending the Peloponnesian War.[49] Athens was teetering between democracy and tyranny and when the democrats took power after overthrowing the Thirty Tyrants, they charged, tried, and executed Socrates for teaching his religious beliefs, which he had been espousing for years. However, his opposition to democracy and his alleged support of the pro-Spartan Thirty Tyrants may have been the real cause of his execution.

A few others were charged for their religious beliefs, including Diagoras of Melos and Anaxagoras, both in Athens in the fifth century BC, but none other than Socrates is known to have been executed. In these cases, as well, there may have been other circumstances leading to the accusations, including misplaced loyalty, with Anaxagoras accused of siding with the Persians[50] and Diagoras coming from Melos, an enemy of Athens.[51] Again accusations of supporting the enemy and politics, more than religion, may have been the causes of these persecutions.

As is evident, these Greek philosophers were often causing trouble. According to Plato, Socrates said at his trial, "For if you put me to death, you will not easily find another, who, to use a rather absurd figure, attaches himself to the city as a gadfly to a horse, which, though large and well bred, is sluggish on account of his size and needs to be aroused by stinging. I think the god fastened me upon the city in some such capacity, and I go about arousing."[52] It is no surprise that many of the city's leaders wanted to be rid of Socrates and his constant "stinging."

Although the philosophers of ancient Greece debated religion and got into trouble for their controversial statements, the common people appeared to have much more freedom regarding their religious practices and beliefs. Many Greeks were not satisfied with the official pantheon of gods and created their own mystery religions.[53] Even slaves were allowed to keep their religions, which they had brought with them after being conquered, kidnapped, or sold into slavery.[54] Even though Greece had its official pantheon of gods, each city chose its own god to worship and each individual chose his own religious belief, whether it be the belief in one god, no god, his city's god, or one of the mystery religions. Even with a set pantheon of gods and common beliefs, other religions and practices were widely tolerated and not uncommon.

THE ADVANTAGES OF TYRANNY

Despite all the benefits of freedom and constitutional democracy, there are, in fact, a few significant advantages to tyranny. At times, those advantages might, in the minds of the people, outweigh the disadvantages.

The Greeks often chose a temporary dictator, normally a battle proven general, to lead them in their defense against an external enemy, whether it be another city-state or Persia. An army needs discipline and a single commander-in-chief to succeed. An army cannot be debating and questioning orders during the middle of a battle. Unfortunately for the Greeks, too many of these temporary commanders did not cede power after their victories and went on to become permanent tyrants.

Another advantage to tyranny is that it is much quicker to make political decisions. A democracy must debate every bill before approving it, creating delays. An absolute ruler, though, can decide quickly without needing to consult others.

In addition to the military and political benefits to a single decider instead of a democratic vote on each strategy and move, there are economic benefits as well. To complete a major construction project in a democratic society requires much debate, cost-benefit analysis, and approval from various government agencies. In contrast, a government with an absolute ruler could approve a project immediately. Currently, it is taking a long time to rebuild the World Trade Center site, as each party and interest group expresses its opinion of the rebuilding plan. In contrast, the dictatorial central government of China approves and completes projects much more quickly, despite objections from many parties. For example, the Chinese are building the Three Gorges Dam, with little resistance, despite the forced relocation of over a million residents, objections from environmentalists, and charges of corruption.

In ancient Greece, Demosthenes, a strong opponent of tyranny and enemy of Philip II of Macedon and Alexander the Great, marked the benefits of an absolute ruler and the disadvantages of democracy. Regarding Philip II of Macedon, Demosthenes wrote, "For the swift and opportune movements of war he has an immense advantage over us in the fact that he is the sole director of his own policy, open or secret, that he unites the functions of a general, a ruler and a treasurer, and that he is always at the head of his army."[55] This praise is in contrast to Demosthenes' description of how Athens acted against Philip: "For at present our system is a mockery, and, by Heaven, I do not believe that even Philip himself would pray that Athens might act otherwise than she is acting. You are behind your time and waste your money; you look round for someone to manage the business and then quarrel with him; you throw the blame on one another."[56] Demosthenes certainly preferred the freedom of democracy to the tyranny of an absolute ruler, but he did not hide the advantages of tyranny and the disadvantages of democracy. Consequently, many Greek city-states adopted the more organized and responsive tyranny over the more decentralized and deliberate democracy.

The advantages of big government and tyranny are evident in the silver mines at Laurion and Thorikos. On the recommendation of

Themistocles, instead of distributing the money to the citizens, the Athenians chose to use the revenue from its silver mines to build a fleet of naval ships to fight the Aeginetans, with whom Athens had been battling for many years, and to prepare for a possible Persian invasion. One cannot criticize the Athenians here for choosing to build up their defense in the face of such large military threats. However, they chose to sacrifice much of their wealth and freedom by giving control of the military and much of the economy to Themistocles and the Athenian government. Although they did not directly choose tyranny, they were attracted to the organizational skills of big government and placed their faith in its hands. The Greeks chose well, in the short term, as Themistocles and the Athenian navy defeated both the Aeginetans and the Persians. Soon thereafter, Themistocles was accused of taking bribes, fell out of favor, and was ostracized, yet the Athenian navy he created went on to establish an empire, sparking the Peloponnesian War. Choosing an absolute ruler and the organizational skills of a large government is often advantageous in a time of crisis, but the difficult part is rolling back the large government and tyranny after the emergency has ended, which Athens was unable to do.

IDENTIFYING THE TYRANTS

Over the centuries, the Greek city-states saw dozens if not hundreds of tyrants seize power. Herodotus lists more than fifty tyrants,[57] but Thucydides lists just one tyrant in his *History of the Peloponnesian War*.[58] Most likely, the two had very different definitions of tyranny. Tyranny originated from the Greek word *tyrannos*, meaning absolute ruler. However, later philosophers, most notably Aristotle, redefined tyranny to include only evil absolute rulers. Aristotle writes, "For tyranny is a kind of monarchy which has in view the interest of the monarch only."[59] He writes more fully, "The idea of a king is to be a protector of the rich against unjust treatment, of the people against insult and oppression. Whereas a tyrant, as has often been repeated, has no regard to any public interest, except as conducive to his private ends; his aim is pleasure, the aim of a king, honor. Wherefore also in their desires they differ; the tyrant is desirous of riches, the king, of what brings honor. And the guards of a king are citizens, but of a tyrant mercenaries."[60] Thus, one must evaluate each monarch to determine whether he was interested in himself or in helping his people, a determination that is not always obvious.

There is an additional form of tyranny not strictly linked to an individual tyrant: the tyrant city. Although it was still a democracy, Athens became a tyranny as it oppressed its neighbors and created an empire in the latter half of the fifth century BC.[61] Thucydides reports that Pericles told the Athenians: "For what you hold is, to speak somewhat plainly, a tyranny."[62] Cleon told them: "Your empire is a despotism and your subjects disaffected conspirators, whose obedience is insured not by your suicidal concessions, but by the superiority given you by your own strength and not their loyalty."[63] The tyranny of the majority had overtaken democratic Athens.

PRECONDITIONS FOR TYRANNY

Tyranny only appears where it is worthwhile for an ambitious man to seize power. A poor village offers little to potential tyrants, but a wealthy metropolis attracts power-hungry men. Therefore, tyranny in ancient Greece increased as the economy grew and the people prospered. A potential tyrant not only wants wealth for himself to live a life of luxury, he needs it to pay off the mercenaries he hired to gain power and protect him from his enemies. Aristotle wrote, "As of oligarchy so of tyranny, the end is wealth; (for by wealth only can the tyrant maintain either his guard or his luxury)."[64]

Wealth is not the only desire of tyrants. A tyrant also desires power over others. This becomes especially true when the tyrant's popularity declines and the people start rebelling against him. At this point, the tyrant could easily leave with his army of mercenaries and the wealth stolen from the people, but instead he tries to maintain his power and punish the rebels. Plutarch gives an example: "For since Dionysius now despaired of his cause and fiercely hated the Syracusans, he wished to make their city as it were a tomb for his falling tyranny. So his soldiers... resorted to the speediest destruction and annihilation of everything by burning... As the Syracusans fled, some were overtaken and slain in the streets, and those who sought cover in their houses were driven out again by the fire, many buildings being now ablaze and falling upon those who were running about."[65]

A potential tyrant needs a political opportunity to accommodate his rise to power. When the government is unpopular, the people will demand change, thinking that "anything else will be better than this." At this point, a demagogue convinces them that the government, whether it is a democracy, oligarchy, or monarchy, is poorly run and corrupt and that he will fix the nation and bring prosperity to all. Such an appeal is likely to gather much support and could bring him to power.

Another opportunity for the potential tyrant to gain power is during the threat of foreign invasion. When facing invasion from a foreign nation or another city-state, an absolute ruler is often more efficient than the debating and dissent that goes with democracy. An ambitious and successful military leader positions himself to be selected by the people to lead them to victory over their enemies. However, this leader, with the support of both his army and the people, can quickly install himself as a tyrant, especially if he defeats the enemy and his popularity increases even further. Dionysius I of Syracuse did just this by earning fame fighting Carthage starting in 409 BC, being elected commander of the entire military in the continuing war against Carthage in 406 BC, seizing power, and becoming tyrant in 405 BC.

GAINING POWER

When the conditions are right for an ambitious man to install himself as tyrant, he has a number of tools to help him in his quest. Popularity, most often earned for successful military or political service, helps one gain and keep power. It is much simpler for a popular political or military leader to seize power or convince the people to give it to him than it would be for an unknown to do so. Aristotle makes creating a tyranny sound like an easy task: "In any of these ways an ambitious man had no difficulty, if he desired, in creating a tyranny, since he had the power in his hands already, either as king or as one of the officers of state. Thus Pheidon at Argos and several others were originally kings, and ended by becoming tyrants; Phalaris, on the other hand, and the Ionian tyrants, acquired the tyranny by holding great offices."[66]

Of course, convincing the people to appoint or elect somebody absolute ruler is much easier to do when that candidate is a good liar. Some tyrants see themselves as public servants trying to help the people, but either fail at their task or become corrupted by their power. However, many, if not most, lie to gain power. They promise to defeat the enemy, though they have no plan or means to do so. They promise to give the people more wealth and rights, but then do just the opposite. Aristotle calls them demagogues: "Panaetius at Leontini, Cypselus at Corinth, Peisistratus at Athens, Dionysius at Syracuse, and several others who afterwards became tyrants, were at first demagogues."[67]

Many of the tricks these demagogues used in ancient Greece are still being used today. Demagogues, then and now, impugn the current government, the wealthy, and other men of power. Aristotle writes, "History shows that almost all tyrants have been demagogues who gained the favor of the people by their accusation of the notables. At any rate this was the manner in which the tyrannies arose in the days when cities had increased in power."[68]

Today, class warfare is often used to collect votes, but this is nothing new. In the 360s BC at Sicyon, Euphron attacked the rich[69] and argued that his "government was to be on terms of full equality."[70] Euphron delivered on some of his promises and the people paid "him pious honours as the founder of their city,"[71] but he accomplished this only by killing or exiling his enemies, taking their property, acting generously to his mercenaries, and bribing his allies.[72] In Athens in 461 BC, Pericles promised full redistribution of wealth with "allotments of public lands, festival-grants, and distributions of fees for public services,"[73] though he never delivered.

A man cannot become tyrant and stay there without assistance from others. Possessing allies is certainly helpful but, with their own agendas and self-interest, allies can change sides. Instead, potential tyrants hire mercenaries, who are paid soldiers with no intrinsic interest in whether a city is free or enslaved and care only about getting paid. These mercenaries were often brought from far away so that they have no friends or relatives in the area, nothing to disturb their loyalties. Aristotle writes that this is one of the identifying marks of a tyrant: "Another mark of a tyrant is that he likes foreigners better than citizens, and lives with them and invites them to his table; for the one are enemies, but the Others enter into no rivalry with him."[74] Xenophon notes that Euphron used foreign mercenaries to gain and keep power, making "some of these mercenaries faithful to him by treating them generously, and took others into his pay, sparing neither the public nor the sacred funds."[75]

Another mark of a tyrant is how he treats his opponents. In free societies, opponents are tolerated, often have a place in government, and are an important check on those in power. But tyrants cannot stand opposition, constantly afraid of seeing their power slip away. Aristotle makes this point: "From democracy tyrants have borrowed the art of making war upon the notables and destroying them secretly or openly, or of exiling them because they are rivals and stand in the way of their power; and also because plots against them are contrived by men of this class, who either want to rule or to escape subjection."[76] According to Xenophon, in fourth century BC Sicyon, Euphron "treacherously put to death some of his fellow-officials and banished others, so that he brought everything under his control and was manifestly a tyrant."[77] According to Diodorus Siculus, "he sent forty of the wealthiest Sicyonians into exile."[78] In third century BC Sparta, Agis IV deposed his co-monarch, Leonidas, who had been blocking his land redistribution and debt abolition proposal.[79] Over two thousand years later, many governments continue to oppress, exile, and kill their political opponents, an obvious demonstration of their tyranny.

USING AND ABUSING POWER

Though the people of ancient Greece often chose tyranny on the hope of increased freedom, equality, and wealth, the tyrant most often delivered the exact opposite. It is not just that the tyrant lies to the people and uses his position for personal wealth and power, but he must, in fact, oppress the people to maintain his position. A ruler who is popular need not fear being overthrown, but no ruler can remain popular forever. Peisistratos in the sixth century BC is considered a popular tyrant, yet he was twice removed from office and exiled from Athens. According to Niccolo Machiavelli, it is safer for the tyrant to be feared than to be popular: "From this arises an argument: whether it is better to be loved than to be feared, or the contrary. The answer is that one would like to be both one and the other. But since it is difficult to be both together, it is much safer to be feared than to be loved, when one of the two must be lacking."[80]

Aristotle writes that a tyrant maintains power using three categories of oppression: "These are, (1) the humiliation of his subjects; he knows that a mean-spirited man will not conspire against anybody; (2) the creation of mistrust among them; for a tyrant is not overthrown until men begin to have confidence in one another; ... (3) the tyrant desires that his subjects shall be incapable of action, for no one attempts what is impossible, and they will not attempt to overthrow a tyranny, if they are powerless."[81]

Aristotle notes that one method of humiliating the people and making them powerless is to impoverish them.[82] A populace with little money is too busy working and trying to scrounge up a living to focus its attention on organizing a revolt. Furthermore, without means, it is much more difficult for potential rebels to gather the tools necessary for a revolution, such as weapons and promotional materials. By taking away all the people's money, the people are made poor, thus making it more difficult to rebel, while the tyrant and his cronies become wealthy.

The primary means of taking the people's wealth was through taxes. Aristotle explains, "Another practice of tyrants is to multiply taxes, after the manner of Dionysius at Syracuse, who contrived that within five years his subjects should bring into the treasury their whole property."[83] Another means was by looting, simply taking the money and property of a supposed enemy. After taking power over the city of Sicyon, Euphron "availed himself of the property of all those whom he banished for favouring the Lacedaemonians,"[84] "found the shrines full of offerings both of silver and of gold, and left them empty of all these treasures,"[85] and "sent forty of the wealthiest Sicyonians into exile, first confiscating their property, and, when he had secured large sums thereby, he collected a mercenary force and became lord of the city."[86]

The tyrant also builds grand public works, acting as if he is helping the people, but his real goal is to impoverish them and keep them occupied. Aristotle gives some examples: "The people, having to keep hard at work, are prevented from conspiring. The Pyramids of Egypt afford an example of this policy; also the offerings of the family of Cypselus, and the building of the temple of Olympian Zeus by the Peisistratidae, and the great Polycratean monuments at Samos; all these works were alike intended to occupy the people and keep them poor."[87]

Another method of keeping the people busy, distracted, and loyal is with war. Whenever a country is attacked or is under threat of attack, patriotism rises, at least initially. Aristotle writes, "The tyrant is also fond of making war in order that his subjects may have something to do and be always in want of a leader."[88] Throughout Greek history, tyrants rose to power when the city-state was under attack or threat of attack. Once in power, these tyrants continued to make war by finding new enemies after each was defeated or peace was made with them.

Warfare is an effective method of keeping the people too busy to conspire against the tyrant. With the military training and soldiers leaving home to fight battles far away, much of the population is either preoccupied or absent and therefore unable to plot against the tyrant. Additionally, with so many people leaving their regular jobs to train and fight, the rest of the population has to increase its workload to make up for the lost workers, thus leaving them with less free time.

During much of Greek history, the various city-states lived at peace with each other. This was less conducive to tyranny, so the tyrants created wars. After the war with the Persians ended in 448 BC, the Greeks could have lived in peace. Instead, Athens decided to build an empire. Thucydides explains that the members of the Delian League, which Athens dominated, were forced to "pay their share of the expense in money instead of in ships, and so to avoid having to leave their homes. Thus while Athens was increasing her navy with the funds which they contributed, a revolt always found them without resources or experience for war."[89] Athens also forced the city-states it subjugated to adopt its religion, coinage, and legal structure.[90]

Although many Athenians supported conquering the rest of the Greeks, some objected. Pericles, leader of Athens from 461 to 429 BC, had to convince the people that an empire would not just be good for Athens, but would help the rest of the Greeks. According to Thucydides, Pericles said, "In generosity we are equally singular, acquiring our friends by conferring not by receiving favors. Yet, of course, the doer of the favor is the firmer friend of the two, in order by continued kindness to keep the recipient in his debt; while the debtor feels less keenly from the very consciousness that the return he makes will be a payment, not a free gift. And it is only the Athenians who, fearless of consequences, confer their benefits not from calculations of expediency, but in the confidence of liberality."[91] Pericles thus argued that Athens was conquering its neighbors as a favor to them.

By making war noble and by using a small share of the confiscatory taxes to build public works when the real goal is to enrich the tyrant and impoverish the people, the tyrant twists his evil intention into laudatory sounding objectives. This propaganda is yet another tool the tyrant uses to maintain power. The tyrant must appear to be good and generous while acting brutally and selfishly. He accomplishes this by appearing to fight wars to spread freedom and wealth, when the real goal is to conquer and enslave. He erects buildings for the public's benefit to hide the money he has taken for himself through high taxes and looting. The tyrant grants the people a constitution, even though it will be totally ignored. The tyrant uses imagery to rally support, creating symbols and flags to engender patriotism. The tyrant hides reality with pleasant sounding words. The tyrant appears to be good while he acts with evil intent.

DETERIORATION OF LEADERSHIP

After the people choose a ruler for themselves in the hope that he will fulfill his promises, lead them to victory over their enemies, and increase their wealth, sometimes the ruler actually succeeds. Of course, the demagogues who lie to gain power have no interest in succeeding for the people. But some rulers are well intentioned leaders who honestly believe that their absolute rule would be best for the people, and some of these succeed in their task. However, his successor, whether it be his son, a chosen heir, or another ambitious politician, may lack his skills, experience, or incorruptibility. As a result, many good rulers are not succeeded by others like them, but by evil tyrants instead.

Pericles' political career saw many ups and downs. Though many Athenians saw Pericles as a brutal tyrant and he was constantly accused of financial mismanagement, he was re-elected many times. The situation after he died made the Athenians miss what they had. Plutarch writes, "The progress of events wrought in the Athenians swift appreciation of Pericles and a keen sense of his loss. For those who, while he lived, were oppressed by a sense of his power and felt that it kept them in obscurity, straightway on his removal made trial of other orators and popular leaders, only to be led to the confession that a character more moderate than his in its solemn dignity, and more august in its gentleness, had not been created."[92] Though they felt oppressed by Pericles, his successors made them realize that Pericles was "moderate" and "august." Both Thucydides and Aristophanes wrote negatively about Pericles' successor, Cleon,* though each may have held a grudge against him.[93] This is a risk of installing an absolute ruler, even a good one, because his successor can do great harm with the powers granted to him.

Another example is Peisistratos, a popular tyrant of Athens in the sixth century BC, and his son Hippias. Herodotus congratulates Peisistratos on a job well done: "Pisistratus ruled the Athenians, disturbing in no way the order of offices nor changing the laws, but governing the city according to its established constitution and arranging all things fairly and well."[94] Aristotle agrees: "Such was the origin and such the vicissitudes of the tyranny of Pisistratus. His administration was temperate, as has been said before, and more like constitutional government than a tyranny. Not only was he in every respect humane and mild and ready to forgive those who offended, but, in addition, he advanced money to the poorer people to help them in their labours, so that they might make their living by agriculture."[95]

Hippias assumed power in 527 BC after the death of Peisistratos, his father. Hippias was not the good man and ruler his father was. Herodotus writes, "Hippias, their tyrant, was growing ever more bitter in enmity against the Athenians because of Hipparchus' death,"[96] even though the murder of Hipparchus, Hippias' brother, had no political motive.[97] Thucydides agrees: "After this the tyranny pressed harder on the Athenians, and Hippias, now grown more fearful, put to death many of the citizens, and at the same time began to turn his eyes abroad for a refuge in case of revolution."[98] Aristotle also agrees: "After this event the tyranny became much harsher. In consequence of his vengeance for his brother, and of the execution and banishment of a large number of persons, Hippias became a distrusted and an embittered man."[99] Even if a man worthy to be absolute ruler is found, there is no guarantee his successor will also be worthy. It is best to avoid

---

* Thucydides, *The Peloponnesian War* 3.36.6 calls Cleon "the most violent man at Athens." See Aristophanes throughout *The Knights* and *The Wasps*.

absolute rulers entirely because the consequences of all that power concentrated in one man will eventually result in an evil ruler and great harm to the people.

Furthermore, once tyranny is established, it is difficult to abandon. Most often, upon the death or overthrow of one tyrant, another tyrant takes his place. Aristotle points out that "a tyranny often changes into a tyranny, as that at Sicyon changed from the tyranny of Myron into that of Cleisthenes."[100] Sian Lewis gives an even more impressive example: "When one looks before a tyrant such as Pittacus or Cypselus to see what kind of government they replaced, one tends to find not aristocracies or monarchies, but an infinite regress of tyrants, each apparently overthrown by a successor in the name of liberty: at Mytilene, for instance, Pittacus overthrew the tyrant Myrsilus, who had in turn overthrown Melanchrus, and before Melanchrus we hear of Megacles, who put down the rule of the club-wielding Pentheli-dai."[101]

This succession of one tyrant followed by another makes it all the more important to avoid the first tyrant. Plutarch reports that Solon "uttered the famous saying, that earlier it had been easier for them to hinder the tyranny, while it was in preparation; but now it was a greater and more glorious task to uproot and destroy it when it had been already planted and was grown."[102]

THE DEFENDERS OF LIBERTY

When tyranny was taking over, either through demagoguery, succession, or invasion, there were a few who recognized this and defended the institutions of liberty. These men dedicated their lives, and sometimes their deaths, to fighting tyranny.

In addition to writing the law of Athens, Solon fought against tyranny. Solon was offered to be made tyrant of Athens by the people in 594 BC. He immediately rejected the idea, saying, according to Plutarch, "that a tyranny was a lovely place, but there was no way down from it."[103] Later in life, while opposing Peisistratos' rise to power in 561 BC, "Solon, although he was now a very old man, and had none to support him, went nevertheless into the market-place and reasoned with the citizens, partly blaming their folly and weakness, and partly encouraging them still and exhorting them not to abandon their liberty... No one had the courage to side with him, however, and so he retired to his own house, took his arms, and placed them in the street in front of his door, saying: "I have done all I can to help my country and its laws.""[104] His whole life, Solon fought for liberty and opposed tyranny.

Demosthenes, a superb orator and statesmen, was one of the first and most vocal opponents of Philip of Macedon. In 352 BC, Athens temporarily stopped Philip at Thermopylae, but Philip continued fighting and he became stronger with each military victory. For the next ten years, Demosthenes spoke constantly against Philip, but soon realized that Athens would not be strong enough to oppose him. Athens sued for peace and an agreement was sworn between Athens and Philip. Demosthenes continued his opposition to Philip, but had little success gaining allies. After a disagreement between Philip and Athens, Demosthenes demanded action arguing it is "better to die a thousand times than pay court to Philip."[105] After Athens renounced the peace treaty, Philip began his march south toward Athens while Demosthenes led the opposition, building alliances with other city-states in the area, most notably with Thebes. After Philip's victory over Thebes and Athens at Chaeronea, where Demosthenes fought as a hoplite, a citizen soldier, Philip occupied Thebes but spared Athens. When Philip was assassinated in 336 BC, Demosthenes attempted yet again to form alliances and encouraged the territories under Macedonian control to rebel. But Philip's son Alexander quickly went to Thebes, which immediately submitted to him. Thebes and Athens rebelled yet again upon mistakenly hearing that Alexander was dead, at which Alexander destroyed the city of Thebes and placed Athens under Macedonian control. When Alexander the Great died in 323 BC, Demosthenes again tried to rally the people to seek independence, but Antipater, Alexander's successor in Greece and Macedon, defeated the Athenians in battle, forced them to dissolve their government, and Demosthenes committed suicide before he could be arrested and most likely executed.

Demosthenes stood up for his principles, but the Macedonian army was too powerful for Athens. Demosthenes must have had little military training or skill, which explains why he fought as a regular soldier instead of a commander and why he ran away when the battle began. Plutarch writes, "Up to this point, then, he was a brave man; but in the battle he displayed no conduct that was honourable or consonant with his words, but forsook his post, cast away his arms, and ran away most disgracefully, nor was he ashamed to belie the inscription on his shield, as Pytheas said, whereon was written in letters of gold, "With good fortune.""[106] Had Demosthenes been more militarily inclined, he might have taken a different approach in his opposition to Philip and Alexander, other than outright battle against a much stronger army.

In addition to his opposition to the growing Macedonian empire, Demosthenes fought bigger government, higher taxes, and political corruption. Two of his works, *Against Androtion* and *Against Leptines*, were attacks on people who tried raising taxes, though he also accused Androtion of corruption. He also fought corruption in his *Against Timocrates* and *Against Aristocrates*.

In addition to the politicians who opposed tyranny in ancient Greece, many of the philosophers, men who had little desire for power and focused their lives on being and doing good, also fought for freedom and opposed tyranny. Aristotle wrote voluminously about the evils of tyranny. For example, Aristotle wrote that "a tyrant, as has often been repeated, has no regard to any public interest, except as conducive to his private ends."[107] He called the tyrants demagogues and accused them of killing opponents and seeking wealth.[108] He also listed the ways tyrants oppress the people: they raise taxes, impoverish the people, and are fond of joining and starting wars.[109]

Socrates spent his life fighting for freedom of speech and freedom of religion and became a martyr for these causes. Plato writes that Socrates argued against democracy and its tyranny of the majority.[110]

Socrates was also accused by the Athenians of siding with Sparta,[111] but that does not reconcile with his refusal to bring Leon of Salamis for execution to the Thirty Tyrants, who were installed by Sparta upon Athens in 404 BC after Sparta overthrew the democratic Athenian government.[112] Through his actions, which often upset those in power, it is obvious that Socrates uncompromisingly believed in freedom, taught it to his students, publicly defended it, opposed both the democrats and tyrants who wished to restrict freedom, and sacrificed his life rather than relinquish his freedom. Socrates could easily have adopted the famous quote "Give me liberty or give me death" as his motto. Or in the modern Greek, "Eleftheria i thanatos,"* meaning "liberty or death," which was the motto of the Greeks in their battle for independence against the Ottomans in the 1820s.

Plato expresses the same sentiment, attacking the tyrant, the democratic nature of his rise to power, and the promises of wealth redistribution: "And is it not true that in like manner a leader of the people who, getting control of a docile mob, does not withhold his hand from the shedding of tribal blood, but by the customary unjust accusations brings a citizen into court and assassinates him, blotting out a human life, and with unhallowed tongue and lips that have tasted kindred blood, banishes and slays and hints at the abolition of debts and the partition of lands."[113]

Thucydides, the famous historian, also philosophized about tyranny: "Again, wherever there were tyrants, their habit of providing simply for themselves, of looking solely to their personal comfort and family aggrandizement, made safety the great aim of their policy, and prevented anything great proceeding from them."[114]

These defenders of liberty argued for constitutional government. Constitutions were popular in ancient Greece, establishing rule of law, guaranteeing the rights of the people, and limiting the power of the government or ruler. With a constitution, the ancient Greeks hoped that tyrants would not be able to rise to power. The constitution, if

---

* The modern eleftheria comes from the ancient eleutheria.

supported and defended by the people, makes changing the governmental system and its powers much more difficult.

Unfortunately, constitutions are often ignored by the leaders and the people. Therefore, the risk of tyranny remains even with this legal document. To grant themselves new "rights," the people change, ignore, violate, or throw out the constitution. But when a constitution is easily changed or discarded, it does little to restrict the rise of tyranny. Though the Greek philosophers and orators worked on developing systems to restrict tyranny, no system or piece of paper can protect mankind from tyranny. Only through constant vigilance can tyranny be avoided. As a result, ancient Greece experienced cycles of freedom and tyranny, never able to maintain the freedom it loved so much.

CHAPTER THREE
ANCIENT ROME

A s ancient Greece sacrificed its freedoms and began its economic and cultural decline, Rome adopted a republican form of government, implemented rule of law, created a system of checks and balances, and guaranteed the rights of its people. As a result, Rome became the most powerful republic and then the most powerful empire the world had ever seen. The Roman Republic thrived for well over four hundred years and the Roman Empire endured for another five hundred.

The Roman Republic was epitomized by the Senate, becoming the model for all legislative bodies to follow. Traditionally believed to have been created in 753 BC by Romulus, it survived the falls of the Roman Kingdom, the Roman Republic, and even the Roman Empire. Though its powers and functions varied over its long history, the Roman Senate survived for nearly two thousand years, finally disappearing in the thirteenth century, during the Fourth Crusade. The United States Senate, at an age of 220 years, is just a baby compared to the Roman version.

But the Roman Senate comprises just one-third of the story of ancient Roman politics. The history of Rome centers on the relationship between the Roman Senate, the people of Rome, and the executives, whether they be the initial kings, the consuls that followed, or the emperors thereafter. Each of these three power centers had their own strengths, but the separation of powers and system of checks and balances created what the Romans had hoped would be an everlasting system. Though Rome surpassed all other nations in terms of wealth, power, and longevity, the people's desire for increased government intervention in the economy and strong executives to administer it led to tyranny, economic decline, military weakness, and the fall of Rome.

FROM FOUNDATION TO FREEDOM

According to Virgil's *Aeneid*, Aeneas led the defeated Trojans to Italy, where they settled in Latium and founded Alba Longa, mother city of Rome. According to legend, Aeneas' descendants, Romulus and Remus, founded Rome on April 21, 753 BC. Romulus then killed his brother Remus, named the city Rome, and became its first king.

Legend says that Rome was ruled by seven kings, starting with Romulus in 753 BC and ending with Lucius Tarquinius Superbus, who was expelled from Rome in 510 BC. The king had absolute power and served as the head of all three branches of government, the commander-in-chief, and the chief priest. A Senate did exist, established by Romulus, but it only served as an advisory council and, at most times, had little power or authority. However, the Senate became very important and powerful after the death of a king, upon which the Senate was tasked with nominating a candidate to be the next king, to be voted on by the people. By controlling the nomination process, the Senate held most of the power during this interval.

The last of the seven kings, Lucius Tarquinius Superbus, was an evil man: a murderer, plunderer, and a tyrant. After Superbus' son raped a patrician Roman, the victim's relative, Lucius Junius Brutus, led a revolt against Superbus in 510 BC. Brutus called the Senate into session, listed a whole litany of charges against Superbus, and Superbus was banished from Rome.[1]

After overthrowing the king, the first act of Lucius Junius Brutus, founder of the Roman Republic, "was to secure the people, who were now jealous of their newly-recovered liberty, from being influenced by any entreaties or bribes from the king. He therefore made them take an oath that they would not suffer any man to reign in Rome."[2]

To replace the king, two consuls would be elected to one-year terms, each with veto power over the other's actions. The consuls initially had all the same powers as the prior kings, but with veto power over each other and a short one-year term, they became much weaker than the kings. According to Livy, the Roman historian (59 BC-17 AD), this was "the origin of liberty" in Rome "because the consular authority was limited to one year."[3]

The consuls, though elected by the people, were nominated by the Senate, thus giving the Senate most of the power after the kingship was overthrown. The Senate was composed of only the richest Romans, leaving the poor and middle class disenfranchised and dissatisfied. At various times over the next few hundred years, the lower and middle classes threatened to revolt or secede from Rome and start a new town. To appease the people, power was distributed to them and, as a result, the people obtained better guarantees of their freedoms. The position of praetor was created, receiving the consul's judicial powers. Next, the censor was created with authority over the census and the Republic's finances. Then, the people of Rome were given two tribunes, later increased to ten, to defend their rights against the Senate and consuls.

This distribution of power is described by Polybius, the Greek historian (203-120 BC), in his discussion on the Roman constitution: "Now the first of these to come into being is monarchy, its growth being natural and unaided; and next arises kingship derived from monarchy by the aid of art and by the correction of defects. Monarchy first changes into its vicious allied form, tyranny; and next, the abolishment of both gives birth to aristocracy. Aristocracy by its very nature degenerates into oligarchy; and when the commons inflamed by anger take vengeance on this government for its unjust rule, democracy comes into being; and in due course the licence and lawlessness of this form of government produces mob-rule to complete the series."[4]

This is exactly what happened in Rome. Rome started with a king. Lucius Tarquinius Superbus made himself into a tyrant and was overthrown, giving power over to the Senate. The Senate became corrupt, thus becoming an oligarchy. The people revolted or threatened to, forcing the Senate to cede some of its power or risk losing all of it. Thus Rome became more democratic. Later, mob rule took over with Tiberius Gracchus in 133 BC, leading Rome back to monarchy and tyranny with Julius Caesar and the emperors.

The key, therefore, to maintaining peace, prosperity, freedom, and stable government is to create a system balancing monarchy, aristocracy, and democracy, each with checks on the other two. But as power was being distributed downward to the people, Polybius warned that giving the people too much power would result in mob rule followed by a new tyranny: "And hence when by their foolish thirst for reputation they have created among the masses an appetite for gifts and the habit of receiving them, democracy in its turn is abolished and changes into a rule of force and violence. For the people, having grown accustomed to feed at the expense of others and to depend for their livelihood on the property of others, as soon as they find a leader who is enterprising but is excluded from the houses of office by his penury, institute the rule of violence; and now uniting their forces massacre, banish, and plunder, until they degenerate again into perfect savages and find once more a master and monarch."[5]

Just twenty-four years after the kings were overthrown and the Republic was founded, the people were already using their power to vote themselves benefits at the expense of others. In 486 BC, the Romans concluded a treaty with the Hernici, a people living east of Rome, and took much of their land. Spurius Cassius Vecellinus promised to distribute that land to the plebeians, who were middle and lower class Romans, to garner their support. Livy writes, "A treaty was concluded with the Hernici, two-thirds of their territory was taken from them. Of this Cassius intended to give half to the Latins and half to the Roman plebs. He contemplated adding to this a quantity of land which, he alleged, though State land, was occupied by private individuals. This alarmed many of the patricians, the actual occupiers, as endangering, the security of their property… Cassius had courted popularity amongst the allies by including them in the distribution and had thereby sunk in the estimation of his fellow-citizens. To recover their favour he gave orders for the money which had been received for the corn from Sicily to be refunded to the people. This offer the plebeians treated with scorn as nothing else than the price of a throne. Owing to their innate suspicion that he was aiming at monarchy, his gifts were rejected as completely as if they had abundance of everything."[6]

This time, the people saw through the lies of the demagogue and Spurius Cassius Vecellinus was tried and executed. However, "the attractiveness of the Agrarian Law, though its author was removed, was in itself sufficient to make the plebeians desire it, and their eagerness for it was intensified by the unscrupulousness of the senate, who cheated the soldiers out of their share of the spoil which they had won that year."[7] Already, just a few years after becoming a republic, the Roman people were learning how to use the power of government to enrich themselves at the expense of others. The rich and poor fought over this land from Hernici for years, but neither side could achieve victory. A number of times, the poor were ready to revolt, but an external enemy would cause the rich and poor to reunite.[8] This shows the effectiveness of the system Brutus set up. Though it looked like the rich had the upper hand, controlling the Senate and the nomination of the consuls, the people had strength in numbers. In the end, they were evenly matched and a fair balance was found.

The distribution of power after the fall of the Roman Kingdom and creation of the Roman Republic created a complex system in which each group had checks and balances on the others. Polybius writes, "none of the principles should grow unduly and be perverted into its allied evil, but that, the force of each being neutralized by that of the others, neither of them should prevail and outbalance another, but that the constitution should remain for long in a state of equilibrium like a well-trimmed boat, kingship being guarded from arrogance by the fear of the commons, who were given a sufficient share in the government, and the commons on the other hand not venturing to treat the kings with contempt from fear of the elders, who being selected from the best citizens would be sure all of them to be always on the side of justice; so that that part of the state which was weakest owing to its subservience to traditional custom, acquired power and weight by the support and influence of the elders."[9]

In many ways, the foundation and prosperity of the Roman Republic was one of circumstance and trial and error. The Romans did not create a constitution with separation of powers and checks and balances based on well-studied principles and ideas. Instead, it evolved out of the various groups seeking more power and political rights. Polybius explains, "the Romans while they have arrived at the same final result as regards their form of government, have not reached it by any process of reasoning, but by the discipline of many struggles and troubles, and always choosing the best by the light of the experience gained in disaster have thus reached…the best of all existing constitutions."[10] Though this evolutionary process resulted in a confusing tangle of political offices and elections, it limited the concentration of power, enabling the free market to work so that Rome could grow over the next 450 years into the greatest city on the Italian peninsula and in the world.

SENATUS POPULUSQUE ROMANUS

After the monarchy was overthrown in 510 BC, the Senate took control over the administration of Rome. It never had total control like the kings before it, but it was certainly the most powerful institution in Rome at the time. Polybius explains the power vested with the Senate: "In the first place it has the control of the treasury, all revenue and expenditure being regulated by it. For with the exception of payments made to the consuls, the quaestors are not allowed to disburse for any particular object without a decree of the senate… Similarly crimes committed in Italy which require a public investigation, such as treason, conspiracy, poisoning, and assassination, are under the jurisdiction of the senate. Also if any private person or community in Italy is in need of arbitration or indeed claims damages or requires succour or protection, the senate attends to all such matters. It also occupies itself with the dispatch of all embassies sent to countries outside of Italy for the purpose either of settling differences, or of offering friendly advice, or indeed of imposing demands, or of

receiving submission, or of declaring war; and in like manner with
respect to embassies arriving in Rome it decides what reception and
what answer should be given to them. All these matters are in the
hands of the senate, nor have the people anything whatever to do with
them. So that again to one residing in Rome during the absence of the
consuls the constitution appears to be entirely aristocratic; and this is
the conviction of many Greek states and many of the kings, as the
senate manages all business connected with them."[11]

After looking at the Senate, it appears that it had all the power in
Rome, but as Polybius explains, this was not so: "After this we are
naturally inclined to ask what part in the constitution is left for the
people, considering that the senate controls all the particular matters I
mentioned, and, what is most important, manages all matters of
revenue and expenditure, and considering that the consuls again have
uncontrolled authority as regards armaments and operations in the
field. But nevertheless there is a part and a very important part left for
the people. For it is the people which alone has the right to confer
honours and inflict punishment, the only bonds by which kingdoms
and states and in a word human society in general are held together...
It is by the people, then, in many cases the offences punishable by a
fine are tried when the accused have held the highest office; and they
are the only court which may try on capital charges... Again it is the
people who bestow office on the deserving, the noblest regard of
virtue in a state; the people have the power of approving or rejecting
laws, and what is most important of all, they deliberate on the question of war and peace. Further in the case of alliances, terms of peace,
and treaties, it is the people who ratify all these or the reverse. Thus
here again one might plausibly say that the people's share in the
government is the greatest, and that the constitution is a democratic
one."[12]

A balance of power had been established between the Senate and
the people. If one looks at the Senate alone, "the constitution appears
to be entirely aristocratic." But if one looks at the power of the people,
it seems like the "constitution is a democratic one." This is one of the
many balances within the government of the Roman Republic.

The people were represented by three assemblies: the Assembly of the Centuries represented the soldiers, the Assembly of the Tribes represented the various geographical regions, and the Plebeian Council, which was an assembly of land owning non-patrician Roman citizens. Different powers were assigned to each assembly, thus limiting the control any one man, group, economic class, or geographic region could acquire over the government and people.

The third branch of the Roman government, the executive branch, was made up of magistrates who were charged with maintaining order. Magistrates, elected by the people of Rome, had the power of coercion, but were otherwise limited. In Rome, citizens had the right to *provocatio*, which was a form of due process enabling Roman citizens to appeal the magistrate's decision. Additionally, magistrates had checks on each other. For each magisterial office, there would be two magistrates, each with veto power over the other. Additionally, higher ranking magistrates could overrule lower ranking ones. Furthermore, terms were limited, thus reducing the ability of magistrates to use their power for personal gain. For example, consuls, the most powerful magistrates, were elected to one-year terms and had to wait another ten years before serving in that post again. Polybius detailed the powers of the consuls: "It is they who consult the senate on matters of urgency, they who carry out in detail the provisions of its decrees. Again as concerns all affairs of state administered by the people it is their duty to take these under their charge, to summon assemblies, to introduce measures, and to preside over the execution of the popular decrees. As for preparation for war and the general conduct of operations in the field, here their power is almost uncontrolled; for they are empowered to make what demands they choose on the allies, to appoint military tribunes, to levy soldiers and select those who are fittest for service. They also have the right of inflicting, when on active service, punishment on anyone under their command; and they are authorized to spend any sum they decide upon from the public funds, being accompanied by a quaestor who faithfully executes their instructions."[13] Polybius also points out "that if one looks at this part of the administration alone, one may reasonably pronounce the constitution to be a pure monarchy or kingship."[14] Thus, the executive branch acts as a check on both the Senate and the popular assemblies, which in turn check the power of the magistrates.

Polybius sums up the balance of power between the Senate, the people, and the executive magistrates: "Such being the power that each part has of hampering the others or co-operating with them, their union is adequate to all emergencies, so that it is impossible to find a better political system than this... For when one part having grown out of proportion to the others aims at supremacy and tends to become too predominant, it is evident that...none of the three is absolute, but the purpose of the one can be counterworked and thwarted by the others, none of them will excessively outgrow the others or treat them with contempt. All in fact remains in statu quo, on the one hand, because any aggressive impulse is sure to be checked and from the outset each estate stands in dread of being interfered with by the others. . . ."[15] Charles de Secondat Montesquieu, the French political thinker (1689-1755), also salutes the Roman system: "The government of Rome was admirable. From its birth, abuses of power could always be corrected by its constitution, whether by means of the spirit of the people, the strength of the senate, or the authority of certain magistrates."[16]

Only ten years after the creation of the Roman Republic in 510 BC, the Romans adopted the idea of a temporary dictator to lead the military in war. Marcus Tullius Cicero (106-43 BC) writes, "Scarcely ten years after the first consuls, we find the appointment of the Dictator in the person of Titus Lartius. And this new kind of power, namely, the dictatorship, appears exceedingly similar to a reproduction of the monarchical royalty. All his power, however, was vested in the supreme authority of the senate, to which the people deferred; and in these times the greatest exploits were performed in war by brave men invested with supreme domination, whether dictators or consuls."[17] Only to be declared in time of war, the dictator would hold office for six months, during which time he would have absolute power over the country and its citizens, after which the previous government would be restored. A more famous example is that of

Lucius Quinctius Cincinnatus, who was elected dictator in 458 BC, ordered the people to join the army, defeated the Aequians, and yielded power just sixteen days after receiving it. In 439 BC, he again became dictator, suppressed a revolt by the plebeians, yielded power, and returned to his farm. How fortunate the Romans were to have found a man who twice yielded power even as he stood at the head of a huge army and was immensely popular.

Unfortunately, the Romans became more enchanted with the idea of a dictator to solve their problems, even non-military ones. In 81 BC, Lucius Cornelius Sulla Felix was appointed dictator by the Senate with the approval of the people. The Romans were not at war and no set time limit was placed on Sulla's dictatorship, unlike the dictators who preceded him, such as Cincinnatus. Sulla instead was chosen solely to create a new constitution. This yielding of power by both the Senate and the people was a precursor to Julius Caesar's dictatorship just three decades later and the emperors not long after that.

Sulla sided with the Senate in the long standing battle for power between the senatorial aristocracy and the plebeian population. Sulla reformed the Plebeian Council and took away from the tribunes the power of initiating legislation. Sulla also revoked the tribune's right to veto acts of the Senate and gave control of the courts back to the Senate. But Sulla did more than just rearrange the government and give power back to the Senate. Sulla was vicious, executing thousands of his opponents and seizing the estates of his enemies.[18] Even though Sulla was a brutal tyrant, after about a year, Sulla resigned his dictatorship and the constitutional government took over again. Nevertheless, Montesquieu writes, "The whim that made him give up the dictatorship seemed to restore life to the republic. But, in the frenzy of his successes, he had done things that made it impossible for Rome to preserve its liberty."[19] According to Montesquieu, Sulla "gave the lands of citizens to the soldiers, and made them forever greedy; from this moment onward, every warrior awaited an occasion that could place in his hands the property of his fellow citizens."[20]

Sulla's shifting of power away from the people upset them and they sought a leader to take power away from the Senate. Sulla had set a bad example. First, Sulla established the precedent that one can become dictator during peace time and with no time limit. Second, Sulla encouraged class warfare between the citizens and the soldiers. Third, Sulla's resignation convinced the people and Senate that any dictator, even a tyrant, would voluntarily resign his office. Fourth, if a dictator can give power to the Senate, the people believed another dictator could give the people more power. Just thirty years later, the people would support Julius Caesar, hoping that he would take power away from the Senate, give it to the people, and then resign from office. Instead, they got a dictator who took power for himself and never resigned.

ROMAN LIBERTY

Even in the days of the kingdom, Romans were not totally indentured to their kings. In fact, the kingship of Rome was not even a hereditary office. After the death of the king, the Senate nominated a new king and the people voted for or against his assumption of power. When the kingship was overthrown in 510 BC, the Romans became even more free and liberty increased, with the term liberty coming from the Latin *libertas* meaning freedom. In 445 BC, Canuleius, a tribune of the plebs, proposed allowing intermarriage between patricians and plebeians. In his speech to the Senate arguing for his bill, according to Livy, Canuleius summarized the idea of liberty in Rome: "The hope of attaining high office be granted to men of ability and energy, that it be open to them to be associated with you in taking their share of the government, and - which is the essence of equal liberty - to rule and obey in turn, in the annual succession of magistrates."[21] The republican system of government that developed in Rome, with its checks and balances, ensured that all Romans had the same rights and all had a say in the administration of governmental affairs. These concepts of equal protection under the law and the democratic republic are the foundations of Western society, government, and liberty.

The Twelve Tables and Property Rights

In 462 BC, to help the people know and follow the law, a plebeian named Terentilius proposed establishing and writing down the laws of Rome. In 450 BC, ten men, the Decemvirate, were chosen to write the legal code. After researching the laws and governmental system of the Greek city-states, the Decemvirate wrote twelve tables of laws on tablets and posted them in the Roman Forum for all to see. The Twelve Tables is mostly concerned with property rights and damages to people and property. Thanks to this establishment of property rights and legal protection, Rome enjoyed a capitalist system of private property and free trade.

Half of the Twelve Tables deals with property rights. Table II regards theft of private property. Table III deals with lending property and interest. Table V discusses inheritances. Table VI is about "ownership and possession," VII pertains to property damage, and VIII is "concerning the laws of real property."[22]

Many of the laws in the Tables remain to this day: "Stolen property shall always be his to whom it formerly belonged; nor can the lawful owner ever be deprived of it by long possession, without regard to its duration; nor can it ever be acquired by another, no matter in what way this may take place."[23] As is true today in most countries, stolen goods always belong to the owner, not the thief or one who purchases it from the thief. This obviously requires the buyer to determine the ownership of land or a good before making a major purchase, or risk losing his money and the purchased item.

According to Roman law, the owner has total control of the disposal of his property through a will: "No matter in what way the head of a household may dispose of his estate, and appoint heirs to the same, or guardians; it shall have the force and effect of law."[24]

Even accidental damage is a crime, for which reparation must be made.[25] Intentional property crimes are often punishable by death.[26] This is severe by modern standards, but nobody can deny that Rome had property rights. Of course, it was the rich who had the property and the poor likely committed most of the property crimes. However, most of the crimes listed in the Twelve Tables were destruction of property, such as cutting down trees, burning buildings, or stealing goods, not stealing food for survival. When the Tables do mention food stolen for the thief's use, it adds: "which the owner of the land has laboriously obtained by plowing and the cultivation of the soil."[27] In this case, the thief is not just stealing private property, but also the owner's time and hard work.

The Twelve Tables also established contractual law, even when verbalized and not written: "When anyone contracts a legal obligation with reference to his property, or sells it, by making a verbal statement or agreement concerning the same, this shall have the force and effect of law."[28]

Fraud was also banned, with execution the punishment for its violation: "When a patron defrauds his client, he shall be dedicated to the infernal gods."[29] Property rights applied not just to land and goods, but also to information. The concept of caveat emptor, buyer beware, did not apply if the seller lied.

The Twelve Tables also dealt with zoning laws: "A space of two feet and a half must be left between neighboring buildings."[30] This gap gave each owner access to his building, helped prevent fires, and also created a level of privacy that is not available in connected houses.

Possibly most important of all were the limits on government intervention in economic matters and equality before the law: "No privileges, or statutes, shall be enacted in favor of private persons, to the injury of others contrary to the law common to all citizens, and which individuals, no matter of what rank, have a right to make use of."[31] "The same rights shall be conferred upon, and the same laws shall be considered to have been enacted for all the people residing in and beyond Latium, that have been enacted for good and steadfast Roman citizens."[32] As long as these laws were followed, the people had nothing to fear from government and could conduct their lives and business free from government interference.

By instituting a system of private property, laying out punishments for violating the rights of others, limiting the use of government for personal gain, and conferring equal rights to all Romans, the Twelve

Tables established economic freedom and equal opportunity, which helped Rome become the most prosperous city in the world.

The Roman Economy and Free Trade

Ancient Rome's economy was primarily based on agriculture, notably grains, grapes, and olives. Rome relied on its slaves to help produce the food needed to feed the Roman people, including the many who served in the Roman legions and, therefore, were not producing any goods or services of their own. Close to the Mediterranean, many Romans earned a living fishing. Industry and manufacturing were a relatively small part of the economy. Rome had its share of textile, pottery, and glass manufacturers in addition to blacksmiths who made both farming tools and weapons. In the surrounding areas and overseas, mining and quarrying were significant industries. Mines in Italy and in the countries conquered by Rome produced the copper, iron, lead, and tin used to make weapons and tools. Quarrying, especially the marble of Italy and Greece, provided stone to build both private and public buildings. Starting in the second century BC, Rome mined gold and silver in Spain, which was brought back to create coins and jewelry.

Rome built an extensive trading network around the Mediterranean, importing grains from Egypt, for example, and exporting olive oil and wine. Travel by land, especially with heavy goods, was slow and expensive, but the Italian peninsula was surrounded by the Mediterranean and Adriatic Seas, making shipping a cheaper and faster way to send goods. Rome was not unique in this as Phoenicia, Greece, and Carthage all used the Mediterranean to trade and travel. However, by controlling much of the territory from Spain to the Middle East, Rome was able to create a single giant free enterprise zone within which goods could be traded freely.

Much of the wealth of Rome was acquired by conquering and plundering, but clearly not enough to feed a million people in Rome and millions more elsewhere. Furthermore, Rome must have had a source of grain before conquering Egypt in 30 BC, a source of silver and gold before conquering Spain in the second century BC, and a source of industrial metals before conquering Britannia in 55 BC and again in 43 AD. Before Rome became a military superpower and conquered these territories, it was already an economic superpower. The Roman Republic relied on internal growth and free trade to develop its economy. Only after this economic success and the sacking of Rome in 387 BC by the Celts of Gaul did Rome develop its military and expand its territory. Rome did not unify the Italian peninsula until 275 BC, 235 years after the Republic was formed. The Roman Empire would not control the whole Mediterranean and much of Europe until a few centuries later. Although the expansion of Rome and the plundering of the defeated certainly added to the Roman treasury, this only occurred in the latter half of the Roman Republic and, more so, during the Roman Empire. Until then, the free trade, private property, and easy shipping enabled Rome to prosper.

Taxation in the Roman Republic

The Roman Republic kept taxes low for much of its history as the government had little role in daily matters except for the military and coinage. Rome initially had no income or sales taxes. Government revenue was collected by charging small custom duties on imports and exports.* Even in the late Republic and early Empire, as the role of government increased and the size of the military grew with the empire, taxes remained low. Julius Caesar imposed a one percent sales tax. Augustus kept the one percent sales tax on most items, but increased the sales tax on slaves to four percent. The government also collected a tax equal to one percent of a man's wealth, rising to three percent during times of war.[33]

The government increased its spending, and therefore its taxes, as it started sponsoring public games and festivals. These were not very big or expensive initially, but grew into exorbitant contests and celebrations toward the end of the Republic and during the Empire. For example, gladiator fighting did not start until 310 BC and were

---

* Suetonius, *The Lives of the Twelve Caesars* Vespasian 1.2 reports a tax on imports and exports equal to one fortieth, or 2.5 percent, of the value.

not held in Rome until 246 BC when just three pairs of slaves fought. By 183 BC, 120 gladiators fought. In 65 BC, Julius Caesar increased the number to 640 gladiators.[34] Initially, gladiator contests were privately sponsored, often by politicians seeking the people's votes. With the fall of the Republic, the emperors became the sole providers of gladiatorial contests.[35] The Colosseum, famed for its gladiator contests, was not built until 80 AD. Thus, these huge building projects, expensive public festival and games, and the rising tax burden to fund them did not occur until the end of the Republic and after the Roman Empire had taken over.

The Roman government had other sources of income in addition to taxes. Much of the revenue during the late Republic and during the Empire came from plundering conquered territories. For example, the gold and silver from Spanish mines after their capture in the second century BC provided much of the government's revenue. But when the empire stopped growing, it lost a major source of revenue, though the costs to defend its acquisitions remained. Therefore, taxes had to be raised and Rome devalued its coinage, becoming two of the major causes of the decline and fall of the Roman Empire.

Slavery

Rome and the Roman controlled lands had a large number of slaves who primarily worked on their masters' farms and within their households as servants. Estimates are that one-quarter to one-third of the population consisted of slaves during the late Republic and early Empire.[36] The early Republic had fewer slaves and the Romans only became dependent on them as the Republic conquered foreign territories starting in the third century BC. In fact, Rome allowed most of the conquered to remain free, only requiring them to pay tribute to Rome. However, these territories often already had slaves and Rome neither freed the slaves nor enslaved the free. Dionysius of Halicarnassus, a Roman historian in the first century BC, writes, "There was yet a third policy of Romulus... it being, in my opinion, the best of all political measures, as it laid the most solid foundation for the liberty of the Romans and was no slight factor in raising them to their position of supremacy. It was this: not to slay all the men of military age or to enslave the rest of the population of the cities captured in war or to allow their land to go back to pasturage for sheep, but rather to send settlers thither to possess some part of the country by lot and to make the conquered cities Roman colonies, and even to grant citizenship to some of them."[37] Therefore, the Roman Republic enslaved very few people as it annexed territory and expanded its empire.

Although Rome did not enslave people as it annexed territory, it did enslave those who actively fought the expanding Roman empire. As a result, many territories put up no resistance, preferring to live under Roman rule as free citizens rather than fight a losing battle and be enslaved.

Another early source of slaves were debtors who could not pay off their creditors, but this debt bondage was made illegal in 326 BC.[38] Additionally, the Twelve Tables states, "If anyone commits a theft during the day, and is caught in the act, he shall be scourged, and given up as a slave to the person against whom the theft was committed."[39] Also, fathers were allowed to sell their sons, but not daughters, into slavery.[40]

Slaves in Rome were not citizens and had few rights. They were the property of their owners and did not even have the right to marry. However, in a dispute about if one is a slave or not, the Twelve Tables says, "Where anyone demands freedom for another against the claim of servitude, the Praetor shall render judgment in favor of liberty."[41] Of course, this did not help an already established slave, but it prevented unethical men from forcibly enslaving others.

Slaves were not always treated well in Rome. Seneca, a Roman Stoic who lived from 4 BC to 65 AD, admonished "the treatment of slaves, towards whom we Romans are excessively haughty, cruel, and insulting."[42] The slaves assigned to the galleys and mines lived in terrible conditions and often had short lives. Furthermore, many of the gladiators were slaves who fought and died to entertain the people. Although gladiators were able to win their freedom, few did so and, as a result of the terrible conditions and high probability of death,

Spartacus the gladiator led the slaves to revolt against Rome in 73 BC. In fact, Spartacus' war was the third major slave revolt during the Roman Republic. The first slave revolt took place in 135 BC with another in 104 BC. Interestingly, there were no major slave revolts before these, as slavery on a large scale came to Rome late in the republican era as Rome was already descending toward dictatorship, empire, and tyranny.

Seneca and the Stoics advocated better treatment of slaves, arguing that they are human beings and that they will work harder and accept their slavery if they are treated well. Most Romans agreed with Seneca, at least from a practical standpoint, and slaves were generally treated the same as hired help, by whose side they often worked. Many slaves even worked in professions or as tutors to their masters' children. Rome was more a culture than a race. An African in Rome could have been a slave or a trader. A Latin could be a Roman citizen, or a slave because his father sold him, his ancestors were slaves, he fought against Rome in battle, or he failed to pay his debts. This ethnic diversity further advanced the idea of equality, which encouraged many Romans to free their slaves. As far back as 450 BC, masters were already freeing their slaves. The Twelve Tables states, "Where a slave is ordered to be free by a will, upon his compliance with a certain condition, and he complies with the condition; or if, after having paid his price to the purchaser, he claims his liberty, he shall be free."[43] The freeing of slaves was so prevalent that it became a big economic and social problem and laws were passed to restrict manumission. In 357 BC, a law was enacted, Lex Manlia, which created a five percent tax on the manumission of slaves. The tax was a big revenue generator,[44] attesting to the already popular idea that slaves should be freed. Freeing slaves became a bigger problem under the Roman Empire. Lex Fufia Caninia, passed in 2 BC, limited the number of slaves a master could free. Lex Aelia Sentia, passed in 4 AD, required the master to be twenty years old and the slave at least thirty in order to free the slave. Additionally, slaves could buy their own freedom and that of other slaves, if they saved up enough money by working extra for his master or somebody else. Freed slaves, however, formed a lower class of citizens, but their children enjoyed full Roman citizenship, with all the rights of a Roman including the right to vote and hold office.

It is interesting that the three societies most closely associated with freedom, Greece, Rome, and the United States, initially had the institution of slavery. Possibly, the juxtaposition of the free citizens living alongside slaves lit a fire among each society's citizens to defend its freedom at all costs. As Cicero said in the first century BC, "Liberty is rendered even more precious by the recollection of servitude."[45]

Freedom of Speech

Rome had nearly unlimited freedom of speech. Any citizen could go to the street corner and speak his mind, but he was not allowed to speak slander. He could yell that Rome needs this or Rome should do that, but could not say the consul is a crook or this senator is a cheat without risking prosecution. Slander and libel were punishable by death as the Twelve Tables states, "When anyone publicly abuses another in a loud voice, or writes a poem for the purpose of insulting him, or rendering him infamous, he shall be beaten with a rod until he dies."[46] It is likely, though, that this punishment was rarely carried out. In fact, Rome had no way to stop a citizen from speaking publicly. The Roman Republic had no state police force and, until late in the Republic, the army was not allowed in Rome itself. There simply was nobody available to patrol the streets and arrest somebody for speaking his mind.

That the only law regarding speech in the Twelve Tables was against slander, demonstrates that other speech, even political speech, was freely allowed. Seneca, Cicero, and Cato admonished the Roman people and politicians for their actions without repercussion, until the dictators and emperors took over. Rome also had freedom of the press with notices freely posted announcing news and upcoming events, an early form of the newspaper. Authors wrote satires, tragedies, and comedies, often mocking the Roman people or its leadership. Livy, Plutarch, Suetonius, Cassius Dio, and other historians detailed the history of Rome, both the good and bad. By all appearances, the Romans were free to speak and publish as they pleased.

In the political arena, ancient Rome is renowned for its open and free debate. Within the popular assemblies, there was no place for debate; they were only for voting. However, the assemblies were preceded by informal meetings in which discussions of political matters were allowed and encouraged. All citizens, even women, could speak at such assemblies. In the Senate, all senators could speak, usually proceeding in order of rank.

In addition to using words, whether spoken or printed, the Romans also used action to express their opinions. The plebeians of Rome often went on strike or seceded, both being a form of non-violent protest, to show their disapproval of an act of government or to demand more political rights.

Cicero equates freedom of speech with liberty, noting that when Julius Caesar took away the right to speak from the nobles as well as the people, they were reduced to slavery.[47] But until the time of the Caesars and the Empire, the Romans enjoyed their freedom of speech, which was essential to the their participation in government.

Freedom of Religion

The Roman Empire is known for its persecution of Christians prior to Constantine's declaration of religious tolerance with the Edict of Milan in 313. However, this persecution only occurred under the emperors starting with Nero, whereas the Roman Republic was very tolerant of other religions. Montesquieu writes, "Just as the old Romans strengthened their empire by permitting every kind of religion in it, so was it subsequently reduced to nothing by amputating, one after the other, the sects which were not dominant."[48]

Ancient Rome was polytheistic, believing in many gods, but these religious beliefs were constantly changing. The Romans added new deities depending on the needs of the day, whether it was for good crops in early agricultural Rome, production of goods in urban Rome, or warfare in the late Roman Republic and in the Empire. Additionally, each assimilated territory added their own gods into the mix. The Twelve Tables states, "Where a family adopts private religious rites every member of it can, afterwards, always make use of them."[49]

Furthermore, in the late Republic, the ideas of Epicureanism, Stoicism, Cynicism, and other alternative philosophies with varying religious views attracted followers. For example, Lucretius, the poet and Epicurean from the first century BC, writes: "For all the gods must of themselves enjoy Immortal aeons and supreme repose, Withdrawn from our affairs, detached, afar: Immune from peril and immune from pain, Themselves abounding in riches of their own, Needing not us, they are not touched by wrath They are not taken by service or by gift."[50] Unlike the official Roman religion, Lucretius believed that gods did not interact with man and they could not be influenced by human actions. Not only did Lucretius believe this, he was able to publish it with no fear of religious persecution.

Furthermore, Rome was a large commercial center with traders traveling to and from the city and many merchants from all around the Mediterranean setting up businesses in Rome. These merchants and traders each brought their own religious beliefs and practices with them. Not interested in managing the private affairs of individuals but very interested in the accumulation of wealth through trade, the Roman government tolerated the many and varied religions and cults.

THE ROAD TO EMPIRE

As the Roman Republic conquered the rest of Italy and much of the Mediterranean in the third and second centuries BC, the economic situation of the poor plebeians worsened. Conscripted into the army instead of tending to their farms and houses, the condition of the plebeians' land and buildings deteriorated as they spent many months fighting overseas. Soldiers returning from the front and farmers from the deteriorating countryside flooded into Rome looking for work and, joining the popular assemblies, voted for whichever candidate promised them the most assistance.

The populace realized that, with their growing numbers, they and not the Senate were the true power in Rome. Of course, the politicians realized this as well and sought their support. In 133 BC, Tiberius Gracchus was elected tribune with a promise to limit how much land anybody could own. The aristocrats obviously opposed this proposal and Marcus Octavius, another tribune, vetoed the law. Tiberius Gracchus had Octavius impeached by the Plebeian Council, thus eliminating the very important check that one tribune had on another. The Roman constitution could thereby be ignored by simply impeaching any politician that dared to oppose the will of the people.

When peaceful methods of advancing the people's agenda of redistribution of land and wealth failed, a conspiracy was launched to use more violent methods. In 63 BC, under the leadership of Lucius Sergius Catiline, opposition consuls and senators were to be assassinated, thus enabling Catiline to enact his reforms. Cicero, the famed orator and powerful senator, discovered the plot and the conspirators were executed. As a result, the Senate's reputation was restored and the populist movement disbanded. However, this did not stop the people from voting benefits for themselves at the expense of the rich nor did it stop politicians from pandering to the people.

In 60 BC, to counter the power of the Senate, Julius Caesar joined with Marcus Licinius Crassus and Gnaeus Pompeius Magnus, known as Pompey, to form the First Triumvirate. Crassus and Pompey were extremely popular for restoring the tribunes that Sulla had stripped of most of their powers, while Caesar was an accomplished general and popular war hero. The powerful Senate was blocking any further reforms, so a secret agreement was made between Caesar, Crassus, and Pompey to promote Caesar as the next consul, thus giving them immense power within the government.

Caesar, Crassus, and Pompey immediately promoted the cause of the people by proposing a bill to distribute public lands to the people. Plutarch writes that Caesar "proposed laws which were becoming, not for a consul, but for a most radical tribune of the people; for to gratify the multitude he introduced sundry allotments and distributions of land."[51] The Senate blocked the bill, so Caesar went straight to the people. "Stationing Crassus on one side of him and Pompey on the other, he asked them if they approved his laws. They declared that they did approve them, whereupon he urged them to give him their aid against those who threatened to oppose him with swords. They promised him such aid, and Pompey actually added that he would come up against swords with sword and buckler too. At this impulsive and mad speech, unworthy of the high esteem in which Pompey stood and unbecoming to the respect which was due to the senate, the nobility were distressed but the populace were delighted."[52] Caesar thus ingratiated himself among the poor who would receive free land, though it would cost the Roman government a quarter of its revenue. Caesar may have believed in this legislation, but his encouragement of taking up arms was most certainly against the constitution and traditions of Rome. The Roman Republic had taken another step toward dictatorship and tyranny. The checks and balances between the people, Senate, and magistrates had disappeared. The people voted for magistrates who would give them increased benefits at the expense of the rich while the magistrates used the people to gain wealth and power.* The Senate was thus powerless against the joint power of the people and the consuls.

The First Triumvirate lasted seven years, ending with the defeat and death of Crassus in 53 BC at Carrhae in battle against the Parthians. After the death of Crassus, Pompey and the Senate worked together to counter Caesar's growing popularity and power. In 49 BC, Caesar crossed the Rubicon with his single legion of troops, in effect declaring war on Rome. Pompey and the Senate fled, even though they had two legions, leaving Rome undefended. Though the Romans disapproved of Caesar crossing the Rubicon with his legion, considering it an act of treason, they also feared and respected him. By this time, the people so hated the Senate that they preferred a tyrant. In fact, there were three potential tyrannies competing for power: the tyranny of mob rule, the tyranny of the corrupt aristocratic Senate, and the tyranny of a military dictator, whether it be Julius Caesar or Pompey. Caesar's invasion of Rome and the Senate's retreat made the people's selection quite easy. Plutarch notes, "However, the Romans gave way before the good fortune of the man and accepted the bit, and regarding the monarchy as a respite from the evils of the civil wars,

---

* Pompey and Crassus headed the commission to distribute the land.

they appointed him dictator for life. This was confessedly a tyranny, since the monarchy, besides the element of irresponsibility, now took on that of permanence."[53]

The people reluctantly accepted Caesar as the new dictator, but hoped he would continue his policies of helping the poor by redistributing the land and wealth of the rich. Upon taking power, "in the effort to surround himself with men's good will as the fairest and at the same time the securest protection, he again courted the people with banquets and distributions of grain, and his soldiers with newly planted colonies, the most conspicuous of which were Carthage and Corinth."[54] To maintain power and quell resistance, he also courted favor with the aristocracy: "As for the nobles, to some of them he promised consulships and praetorships in the future, others he appeased with sundry other powers and honours, and in all he implanted hopes, since he ardently desired to rule over willing subjects."[55] Julius Caesar gave money to the poor and honors to the rich to maintain his power and popularity.

Unfortunately for the Romans, Julius Caesar's primary concern was Julius Caesar and not the well being of Rome or its people. John Dickinson, who was Professor of Law at the University of Pennsylvania, writes in his *Death of a Republic: Politics and Political Thought at Rome 59-44 B.C.*, "To Caesar the art of government meant the promotion of any measure, however inconsistent with his previous or even present professions, that promised to advance the next in his plans; his only long-range objective which can be definitely identified was the enhancement of his power. For this he indulged in a lifetime of double talk, professing slogans of democracy, while debasing and destroying the powers of the electorate, and insisting on constitutional technicalities, while persistently undermining the constitution. In the end, his prescription for government turned out to be a surprisingly simple one: to reduce its mechanism to the simplest and most primitive of all institutional forms, personal absolutism, and to employ it for one of the simplest and most primitive of all purposes, foreign conquest."[56] Caesar tried to control everything. Caesar repressed free speech by imprisoning and killing his political opponents. Caesar even had himself declared dictator in perpetuity in 44 BC, a very unpopular move that led to his assassination not long afterwards.

Julius Caesar was an excellent orator who could sway the hearts of the people to his side, often with lies. To gain the support of the people, he told them that he would distribute food and money to them, a very popular promise among the hungry poor. He spoke softly with the Senate, saying he wished to govern with them and not against them. Whether his words were lies or he just over-promised, Caesar's popularity declined when his promises went unfulfilled. Caesar promised to pay his soldiers handsomely for backing him, but money was short and he could not deliver. Just as in ancient Greece, a tyrant needs his mercenaries or army to back him and they must be bought with money. Without the pay they were promised, Caesar's army rebelled. Caesar's legions stopped fighting for him and demanded that they be released from service and paid what they were due.

Upon becoming dictator, Caesar drew up grandiose plans to con-quer new countries, divert the Tiber River, drain the marshes, con-struct new harbors, and even change the calendar. His new calendar worked very well, but was still a source of ridicule as a sign of Caesar's desire to control everything. Plutarch writes, "However, even this furnished occasion for blame to those who envied Caesar and disliked his power. At any rate, Cicero the orator, we are told, when some one remarked that Lyra would rise on the morrow, said: "Yes, by decree," implying that men were compelled to accept even this dispensation."[57]

THE REPUBLICANS

As a result of Caesar's growing unpopularity among the patricians, conspiracies were formed against him. The Roman historian Sueto-nius (70-130 AD) reports, "Therefore the plots which had previously been formed separately, often by groups of two or three, were united in a general conspiracy, since even the populace no longer were pleased with present conditions, but both secretly and openly rebelled at his tyranny and cried out for defenders of their liberty."[58] Caesar made many enemies in his rise to power. Many were people he insulted, others were people who wished for power, and some simply saw the worsening economic and social conditions. A few, though, believed in republicanism and wished to restore the balance of power between the senate, the people, and the magistrates that existed in the Republic. But Caesar made many allies through demagoguery and bribery, and the republicans found themselves fighting a losing battle.

The republicans opposed the growing power of Caesar but, more generally, they opposed the increasing centralization of power. They also opposed the mob rule that was taking over Rome. These men argued for and often fought in battle for the republican form of government, fearing what Rome would be like under a dictator. Marcus Tullius Cicero and Cato the Younger are the most famous defenders of the Roman Republic and two of Caesar's most adamant and politically powerful opponents. Both paid the ultimate price for their defense of republicanism and freedom.

Cicero was one of the most powerful men in the Senate and Rome. Julius Caesar asked Cicero to join his alliance with Pompey and Crassus, but Cicero declined, fearing it would hurt the Republic. During the civil war between Caesar and the Senate led by Pompey, Cicero tried to play both sides. Some argue he was trying to stay in favor with whoever emerged victorious, but Cicero's speeches and writings show that he was always working to maintain the Republic regardless of who won.

When Julius Caesar was assassinated, Cicero as leader of the Senate and Mark Antony as consul and leader of those who supported Caesar became the two leaders of Rome. Cicero opposed Antony and made a series of speeches against him, known as Philippics for the similarity of his speeches to those of Demosthenes against Philip of Macedon. Mark Antony formed the Second Triumvirate with Octavian, Julius Caesar's heir, and Marcus Aemilius Lepidus, a former consul and strong supporter of Julius Caesar. They immediately sought to exile or kill their political opponents, especially Cicero. Cicero was captured on his way to the coast, where he had hoped to escape to Macedonia. Cicero's capturers "cut off his head, by Antony's command, and his hands — the hands with which he wrote the Philippics."[59]

In addition to his fight against the two Triumvirates, Cicero produced a number of books and many of his speeches were recorded.
Through his words, Cicero continues to fight for liberty, including
private property. Cicero saw no problem with private property, even
the vast accumulation of it, as long as it was done legally and morally:
"Still, I do not mean to find fault with the accumulation of property,
provided it hurts nobody, but unjust acquisition of it is always to be
avoided."[60] He further argues that the primary responsibility of
government is to defend people's property: "The man in an administrative office, however, must make it his first care that everyone shall
have what belongs to him and that private citizens suffer no invasion
of their property rights by act of the state... The chief purpose in the
establishment of constitutional state and municipal governments was
that individual property rights might be secured. For, although it was
by Nature's guidance that men were drawn together into communities,
it was in the hope of safeguarding their possessions that they sought
the protection of cities."[61] Cicero adds, "For, as I said above, it is the
peculiar function of the state and the city to guarantee to every man
the free and undisturbed control of his own particular property."[62]

Cicero fought against the demand to redistribute land and wealth:
"Now, there are many — and especially those who are ambitious for
eminence and glory — who rob one to enrich another; and they
expect to be thought generous towards their friends, if they put them
in the way of getting rich, no matter by what means. Such conduct,
however, is so remote from moral duty that nothing can be more
completely opposed to duty."[63] Cicero also opposed welfare: "To
conclude, the whole system of public bounties in such extravagant
amount is intrinsically wrong; but it may under certain circumstances
be necessary to make them; even then they must be proportioned to
our ability and regulated by the golden mean."[64] Presumably, those
"certain circumstances" are emergencies, such as famines or great
fires.

The people of Rome, like many Greeks before, supported the abolition of debts. On this subject, Cicero writes, "And what is the meaning

of an abolition of debts, except that you buy a farm with my money; that you have the farm, and I have not my money?"[65] Cicero also fought against political corruption: "For to exploit the state for selfish profit is not only immoral; it is criminal, infamous."[66]

Cicero's defense of freedom, republicanism, small government, and private property was unwavering. He played the political game, sometimes siding with a political opponent hoping to influence him to support his positions. Though Cicero's political strategies failed to ensure the freedom of the Roman Republic, he lived and died fighting for what he believed was right and good. Furthermore, Cicero's works survive whereas the tyrants of the Roman Empire have long since passed away.

A second defender of the Roman Republic against the dictators and tyrants of the first century BC was Cato the Younger (95-46 BC). Unlike Cicero who tried to work with his opponents, Cato was a very stubborn man who vehemently opposed corruption, demagoguery, and immorality. Even as a young man during the dictatorship of Sulla, Cato "asked his tutor why no one slew this man. "Because, my child," said the tutor, "men fear him more than they hate him." "Why, then," said Cato, "didst thou not give me a sword, that I might slay him and set my country free from slavery?'"[67]

After serving in the army, Cato returned to Rome and entered politics, where he focused on taxes and wasteful government spending. He immediately prosecuted Sulla's mercenaries: "There were many persons whom the famous Sulla had rewarded for killing men under proscription, at the rate of twelve thousand drachmas... Cato, however, called each one of these to account for having public money in his possession by unjust means, and made him give it up, at the same time rebuking him with passionate eloquence for his illegal and unholy act. After this experience they were at once charged with murder, were brought before their judges condemned beforehand, one might say, and were punished."[68]

Though he was a conservative, favoring the rule of the Senate instead of democracy and its mob rule, Cato quickly became one of the most popular politicians in Rome. His actions were not guided by a quest for popularity, but for his desire to do good. Plutarch writes, "He used to be the first to reach the senate and the last to leave it; and often, while the other senators were slowly assembling, he would sit and read quietly, holding his toga in front of the book. He never left the city when the senate was in session... For it was neither for the sake of reputation, nor to gain riches, nor accidentally and by chance, like some others, that he threw himself into the management of civic affairs, but he chose a public career as the proper task for a good man, and thought that he ought to be more attentive to the common interests than the bee to its honey."[69]

When Caesar, Pompey, and Crassus created the First Triumvirate, Cato was an immediate opponent. Cato already had public disagreements with Caesar: one over whether to execute the Catiline conspirators, which Cato supported but Caesar opposed, and another when it was discovered that Caesar was having an affair with Cato's sister. Cato opposed Caesar's first major proposal to distribute public lands to the people: "No one spoke against the law except Cato, and him Caesar ordered to be dragged from the rostra to prison."[70] When the rest of the Senate opposed Cato's imprisonment, though they disagreed with his position, Caesar was forced to free Cato. Even as Caesar attacked free speech and imprisoned his leading opponent in plain view of the entire public, the people continued to support him: "Cato warned the people that they themselves by their own votes were establishing a tyrant in their citadel."[71] But the people refused to listen to reason, too enamored with all the free land and wealth they would be given in return for their vote.

About ten years later, in 49 BC, Cato led the Senate in passing a resolution ending Julius Caesar's army command, which had already expired, and ordering him to return to Rome. As a civilian, though, Caesar would no longer be immune to prosecution for his actions. Caesar proposed giving up all his commands save for one legion but Cato, being the stubborn man he was, refused the offer. Caesar took his legion and crossed the Rubicon, thus declaring war on the Roman

Senate. The Senate fled and Caesar chased after them. Seeing that Caesar had won and not wanting to live in a world led by a tyrant nor wanting to be caught and executed by Caesar's assassins, "Cato drew his sword from its sheath and stabbed himself below the breast... His servants...saw that he was smeared with blood, and that most of his bowels were protruding, but that he still had his eyes open and was alive; and they were terribly shocked... When Cato recovered and became aware of this, he...tore his bowels with his hands, rent the wound still more, and so died."[72]

These two men, Cicero and Cato, warned the Romans of the approaching tyranny, but the populace was captivated by the demagogues who promised them land redistribution and wealth. The people got their dictators and land redistribution, but the Roman Republic died along with Cicero and Cato.

ESTABLISHING AN EMPIRE

Through his redistribution of land and attacks on political opponents, Caesar became very unpopular within the Senate. However, Caesar remained popular with the people, for a while, before this popularity also waned after many of his promises went unfulfilled. Worse yet, he was slow in rewarding his soldiers, causing them to rebel and demand their release and payment. A tyrant without his mercenaries is vulnerable and the Senate sensed this. On March 15, the Ides of March, in 44 BC, Julius Caesar was stabbed twenty-three times[73] by a group of senators led by Marcus Junius Brutus, descendant of Lucius Junius Brutus who had led the expulsion of Lucius Tarquinius Superbus and created the Roman Republic.

The senators had hoped that killing Caesar would solve Rome's problems, but the problem was not just Caesar the dictator, it was also the people's desire to use government as a tool to redistribute land and wealth. Caesar's popularity rose after his assassination when, according to Suetonius, "To the people he left his gardens near the Tiber for their common use and three hundred sesterces to each man."[74] The

Senate hoped that with Caesar's death, power would be restored to them and the Roman Republic would be reborn. Instead, by killing the champion of the people, the Senate became even more hated.

The people looked for a new dictator to represent them. The obvious choice was Gaius Octavian, Julius Caesar's great-nephew, whom he adopted and gave three-quarters of his estate along with his name in his will.[75] Gaius Octavian, Mark Antony, and Marcus Aemilius Lepidus formed an alliance known as the Second Triumvirate. Opposing them were the republicans Marcus Junius Brutus and Gaius Cassius, who had assembled an army to take back Rome. The hopes of the republicans were shattered when the Second Triumvirate defeated them at the Battle of Philippi. Despite their alliance, Antony and Octavian were already positioning themselves to become the new ruler. Antony set up base in Egypt, fell in love with Cleopatra, and had an affair with her, even though he was married to Octavian's sister. In 31 BC, Octavian's forces defeated those of Antony and Cleopatra on the Ionian Sea near Actium. Octavian consolidated his power and invaded Egypt, upon which Mark Antony and Cleopatra committed suicide. Octavian thus became the first Emperor of Rome and the Senate gave him the new title of Augustus, meaning "the venerable one."

Augustus played the demagogue by reforming the Senate but he gave it little real power, keeping most of it for himself, though he never took on the title of dictator. The real source of Augustus' power was his popularity among the public, the loyalty of the military, and his vast wealth obtained through territorial conquest. The Senate was powerless against Augustus' military legions and popular support, forcing them to bend to his will. Most important, Montesquieu explains, "Augustus (this is the name flattery gave Octavius) established order — that is, a durable servitude. For in a free state in which sovereignty has just been usurped, whatever can establish the unlimited authority of one man is called good order, and whatever can maintain the honest liberty of the subjects is called commotion, dissension, or bad government."[76]

As the new Emperor, Augustus grew the size of government. Suetonius writes, "To enable more men to take part in the administration of the State, he devised new offices: the charge of public buildings, of the roads, of the aqueducts, of the channel of the Tiber, of the distribution of grain to the people, as well as the prefecture of the city, a board of three for choosing senators, and another for reviewing the companies of the knights whenever it should be necessary. He appointed censors, an office which had long been discontinued. He increased the number of praetors."[77] Augustus also repaired Rome's buildings and even created Rome's first police and fire fighting forces.[78]

Augustus "showed generosity to all classes when occasion offered. For example, by bringing the royal treasures to Rome in his Alexandrian triumph he made ready money so abundant, that the rate of interest fell, and the value of real estate rose greatly; and after that, whenever there was an excess of funds from the property of those who had been condemned, he loaned it without interest for fixed periods to any who could give security for double the amount."[79] He also gave the people games and shows that "surpassed all his predecessors in the frequency, variety, and magnificence."[80] In other words, he gave the people "bread and circuses" to keep them satisfied and entertained.

Though cruel to his enemies and favoring government control over the economy, Augustus' reign was a good one. He used his wealth to help the Roman people, established peace with many of his enemies, and fortified the empire's borders. Thus began the two century long Pax Romana, Roman peace. Upon his death in 14 AD, after ruling Rome for over forty years, Augustus was deified and all subsequent emperors were given the names of Augustus and Caesar. The month of Sextilis was renamed August in his honor. It is said by many that Augustus was the best emperor Rome ever had. Most likely, Rome only became an empire because of Augustus' qualities. A lesser man may have taken the dictatorship, acted tyrannical, become unpopular, and been assassinated, just as happened to Julius Caesar. Augustus' successful reign established the imperial system, which led to the eventual decline and fall of Rome.

THE TYRANTS OF ROME

For the eighty years after Augustus, Rome had emperors known for their tyranny and incompetence. The Senate and people of Rome tried to restore the Republic more than once, but tyranny proved impossible to reverse once it took root. All countries go through periods of good and bad leadership. In a country where the central government is small, the people are not affected much by the nature and abilities of government officials. In contrast, the quality of absolute monarchs has a much greater effect on all citizens, for better or worse.

Tiberius

Augustus was succeeded by his step-son, Tiberius, in 14 AD. Tiberius played the demagogue, mostly out of fear that others would contest him for power or that some will try to assassinate him. Suetonius reports, "Though Tiberius did not hesitate at once to assume and to exercise the imperial authority, surrounding himself with a guard of soldiers, that is, with the actual power and the outward sign of sovereignty, yet he refused the title for a long time, with barefaced hypocrisy now upbraiding his friends who urged him to accept it, saying that they did not realise what a monster the empire was, and now by evasive answers and calculating hesitancy keeping the senators in suspense when they implored him to yield, and fell at his feet."[81]

Tiberius' reign began with high expectations and he ruled well for the first nine years. Suetonius writes, "He even introduced a semblance of free government by maintaining the ancient dignity and powers of the senate and the magistrates; for there was no matter of public or private business so small or so great that he did not lay it out before the senators, consulting them about revenues and monopolies, constructing and restoring public buildings, and even about levying and disbanding the soldiers, and the disposal of the legionaries and auxiliaries; finally about the extension of military commands and appointments to the conduct of wars, and the form and content of his replies to the letters of kings."[82] In keeping with his initial small government, he tried to keep taxes low: "To the governors who recommended burdensome taxes for his provinces, he wrote in answer that it was the part of a good shepherd to shear his flock, not skin it."[83] Suetonius summarizes the quality of Tiberius' initial reign: "he more often showed himself kindly and devoted to the public weal. His intervention was at first limited to the prevention of abuses. Thus he revoked some regulations of the senate and sometimes offered the magistrates his services as adviser, when they sat in judgment on the tribunal, taking his place beside them or opposite them at one end of the platform; and if it was rumoured that any of the accused were being acquitted through influence, he would suddenly appear, and either from the floor or from the judge's tribunal remind the jurors of the laws and of their oath, as well as of the nature of the crime on which they were sitting in judgment. Moreover, if the public morals were in any way affected by laziness or bad habits he undertook to reform them."[84]

However, Tiberius changed in 23 AD after the death of his son Drusus Julius Caesar at the hand of Sejanus, his advisor. Tacitus, the senator and historian (56-117), writes, "Suddenly fortune deranged everything; the emperor became a cruel tyrant, as well as an abettor of cruelty in others."[85] Tacitus continues "to present in succession the merciless biddings of a tyrant, incessant prosecutions, faithless friendships, the ruin of innocence."[86] Like all tyrants, Tiberius killed his political opponents and left the rest of the people in fear of him: "Executions were now a stimulus to his fury, and he ordered the death of all who were lying in prison under accusation of complicity with Sejanus. There lay, singly or in heaps, the unnumbered dead, of every age and sex, the illustrious with the obscure... The force of terror had utterly extinguished the sense of human fellowship, and, with the growth of cruelty, pity was thrust aside."[87] Yet, Tiberius tried to hide his tyranny. Montesquieu explains, "No tyranny is more cruel than the one practiced in the shadow of the laws and under color of justice — when, so to speak, one proceeds to drown the unfortunate on the very plank by which they had saved themselves. And since a tyrant never lacks instruments for his tyranny, Tiberius always found judges ready to condemn as many people as he might suspect."[88] Tacitus summarizes Tiberius' later rule as "a tyrant in peace, and ruinously unsuccessful in war."[89]

Suetonius writes that upon the death of Tiberius in 37 AD: "The people were so glad of his death, that at the first news of it some ran about shouting, "Tiberius to the Tiber," while others prayed to Mother Earth and the Manes to allow the dead man no abode except among the damned. Still others threatened his body with the hook and the Stairs of Mourning, especially embittered by a recent outrage, added to the memory of his former cruelty... When the funeral procession left Misenum, many cried out that the body ought rather to be carried to Atella, and half-burned in the amphitheatre."[90] Though Tiberius' death brought rejoicing as the people hoped that the next ruler would be more like Augustus than Tiberius, this sentiment would not last long when Tiberius was followed by another tyrant.

Caligula

Caligula was the nephew and adopted son of Tiberius. Rome was so excited by Caligula's ascension that, according to Suetonius, "he fulfilled the highest hopes of the Roman people, or I may say of all mankind, since he was the prince most earnestly desired by the great part of the provincials and soldiers, many of whom had known him in his infancy, as well as by the whole body of the city populace... When he entered the city, full and absolute power was at once put into his hands by the unanimous consent of the senate and of the mob, which forced its way into the House, and no attention was paid to the wish of Tiberius, who in his will had named his other grandson, still a boy, joint heir with Caligula."[91] The Romans were extremely disappointed when they discovered that Caligula was a "monster."[92] Caligula's evil began at home where he committed incest with his sisters[93] and killed his relatives.[94] Suetonius reports that Caligula treated all people equally; he killed senators, deposed consuls who forgot his birthday, flogged quaestors charged with conspiracy, forced gladiators to fight without equipment and one family to fight another, and would shut the granaries and make the people go hungry.[95] Caligula enjoyed torturing his victims and killing people for amusement.[96] He had affairs with married women and recounted "her charms or defects" in public[97] and spent extravagantly.[98]

As a result of his lavish spending and mismanagement of government, Suetonius writes, "Having thus impoverished himself, from very need he turned his attention to pillage through a complicated and cunningly devised system of false accusations, auction sales, and imposts."[99] Caligula "levied new and unheard of taxes...and there was no class of commodities or men on which he did not impose some form of tariff. On all eatables sold in any part of the city he levied a fixed and definite charge; on lawsuits and legal processes begun anywhere, a fortieth part of the sum involved, providing a penalty in case anyone was found guilty of compromising or abandoning a suit; on the daily wages of porters, an eighth; on the earnings of prostitutes, as much as each received for one embrace; and a clause was added to this chapter of the law, providing that those who had ever been prostitutes or acted as panders should be liable to this public tax, and that even matrimony should not be exempt. When taxes of this kind had been proclaimed, but not published in writing, inasmuch as many offences were committed through ignorance of the letter of the law, he at last, on the urgent demand of the people, had the law posted up, but in a very narrow place and in excessively small letters, to prevent the making of a copy."[100]

Caligula was quite unpopular and a number of conspiracies were formed against him. In 41 AD, the Praetorian commander Cassius Chaerea stabbed him to death. Caligula was just twenty-nine and accomplished all his tyranny in less than four years.

Claudius

With the assassination of Caligula in 41 AD, the conspirators sought to kill the entire imperial family to prevent another tyrant from taking the throne. The Senate attempted to restore the Republic but, according to Suetonius, "was dilatory in putting through its plans because of the tiresome bickering of those who held divergent views."[101] Meanwhile, Claudius, grandson of Mark Antony and

Actavia, sister of Emperor Augustus, managed to hide from the conspirators, added Caesar and Augustus to his name, and had himself proclaimed emperor by the Praetorian Guard, a task normally assigned to the Senate.

Claudius was in many ways a good emperor. Suetonius reports on how he always looked after his city and people: "He always gave scrupulous attention to the care of the city and the supply of grain. On the occasion of a stubborn fire in the Aemiliana he remained in the Diribitorium for two nights, and when a body of soldiers and of his own slaves could not give sufficient help, he summoned the commons from all parts of the city through the magistrates, and placing bags full of money before them, urged them to the rescue, paying each man on the spot a suitable reward for his services... He resorted to every possible means to bring grain to Rome, even in the winter season. To the merchants he held out the certainty of profit by assuming the expense of any loss that they might suffer from storms, and offered to those who would build merchant ships large bounties, adapted to the condition of each: to a citizen exemption from the lex Papia Poppaea; to a Latin the rights of Roman citizenship; to women the privileges allowed the mothers of four children."[102]

Claudius also completed much needed public works which "were great and essential rather than numerous... He brought to the city on stone arches the cool and abundant founts of the Claudian aqueduct... He constructed the harbour at Ostia by building curving breakwaters on the right and left... built upon it a very lofty tower after the model of the Pharos at Alexandria, to be lighted at night and guide the course of ships."[103]

Likewise, Claudius "very often distributed largess to the people. He also gave several splendid shows... He opened the games at the dedication of Pompey's theatre, which he had restored when it was damaged by a fire... The Great Circus he adorned with barriers of marble and gilded goals... In addition to the chariot races he exhibited the game called Troy and also panthers, which were hunted down by a squadron of the praetorian cavalry under the lead of the tribunes and the prefect himself; likewise Thessalian horsemen, who drive wild bulls all over the arena, leaping upon them when they are tired out and throwing them to the ground by the horns."[104]

Despite the good he did, regardless of whether his purpose was to help the people or to boost his popularity, Claudius and the Senate fought constantly during his thirteen year reign. A number of coups and rebellions were attempted during his rein. In turn, Claudius killed a number of those who conspired against him. Suetonius reports that Claudius "inflicted the death penalty on thirty-five senators and more than three hundred Roman knights with such easy indifference."[105] It is not clear which side is at fault, though blame can likely be given to both as Claudius was most assuredly wary of the senators after their attempt to restore the Republic following Caligula's assassination and the senators certainly still wished to overthrow Claudius and resurrect the Republic. Tacitus and Suetonius both had negative views of Claudius, favoring the side of the senate in the disputes. Suetonius writes, "That he was of a cruel and bloodthirsty disposition was shown in matters great and small. He always exacted examination by torture and the punishment of parricides at once and in his presence... At any gladiatorial show, either his own or another's, he gave orders that even those who fell accidentally should be slain, in particular the net-fighters, so that he could watch their faces as they died."[106] Tacitus also accuses Claudius of tyranny: "A temple also erected to the Divine Claudius was ever before their eyes, a citadel, as it seemed, of perpetual tyranny."[107]

Claudius was killed in 54 AD. Suetonius writes, "That Claudius was poisoned is the general belief, but when it was done and by whom is disputed... He was buried with regal pomp and enrolled among the gods."[108] Although Claudius was well liked by much of the public, thanks to his public works and for giving the people "bread and circuses," history does not remember him well. Claudius may not have been an outright tyrant like Caligula, but he too was a brutal emperor.

Nero

Claudius' reign was one of mixed results, but his successor was perhaps the worst emperor Rome ever had. Following the death of

Claudius, Nero, the seventeen year old nephew and adopted son of Claudius, assumed the throne.

Nero is most remembered for the Great Fire of Rome and his persecution of the Christians, which went hand-in-hand. Following the Great Fire in 64 AD, rumors began that Nero ordered the fire, so he quickly shifted the blame by accusing the Christians of arson. Tacitus writes, "But all human efforts, all the lavish gifts of the emperor, and the propitiations of the gods, did not banish the sinister belief that the conflagration was the result of an order. Consequently, to get rid of the report, Nero fastened the guilt and inflicted the most exquisite tortures on a class hated for their abominations, called Christians by the populace."[109] Nero found a scapegoat in the Christians and immediately began the persecutions. In tyrannical fashion, Nero brutally tortured innocents and made a public spectacle of it: "Accordingly, an arrest was first made of all who pleaded guilty; then, upon their information, an immense multitude was convicted, not so much of the crime of firing the city, as of hatred against mankind. Mockery of every sort was added to their deaths. Covered with the skins of beasts, they were torn by dogs and perished, or were nailed to torture-stakes, or were doomed to the flames and burnt, to serve as a nightly illumination, when daylight had expired. Nero offered his gardens for the spectacle, and was exhibiting a show in the circus, while he mingled with the people in the dress of a charioteer or stood aloft on a car. Hence, even for criminals who deserved extreme and exemplary punishment, there arose a feeling of compassion; for it was not, as it seemed, for the public good, but to glut one man's cruelty, that they were being destroyed."[110] The fire was most likely an accident, as Rome experienced great fires again in the years 69 AD and 80 AD, but the persecution of Christians would continue for over two hundred years. The emperors also disliked the Christians because they often refused to fight in the Roman military. As Christianity became more popular, this was hurting the Roman Empire's military strength. The Roman emperors had hoped that persecuting the Christians would weaken its appeal, but the people felt compassion for the Christians and were impressed by their morality compared to the tyrannical emperors.

This inspired many Romans to convert to Christianity, making the military's problem even more severe.

Although Nero did not fiddle while Rome burned, as the fiddle had not yet been invented, historians disagree about Nero's role in the fire. Suetonius writes that Nero "set fire to the city" and while "viewing the conflagration from the tower of Maecenas and exulting, as he said, in "the beauty of the flames," he sang the whole of the "Sack of Ilium," in his regular stage costume."[111] On the other hand, Tacitus writes, "Nero at this time was at Antium... However, to relieve the people, driven out homeless as they were, he threw open to them the Campus Martius and the public buildings of Agrippa, and even his own gardens, and raised temporary structures to receive the destitute multitude. Supplies of food were brought up from Ostia and the neighbouring towns, and the price of corn was reduced to three sesterces a peck. These acts, though popular, produced no effect, since a rumour had gone forth everywhere that, at the very time when the city was in flames, the emperor appeared on a private stage and sang of the destruction of Troy, comparing present misfortunes with the calamities of antiquity."[112] So Nero may or may not have started the fire. Likewise, he may have stood idly by while Rome burned or he may have helped the Romans in their time of need. What is known for certain is the brutality Nero dispensed upon the Christians as a result of this tragic event.

Even before the Great Fire and the subsequent persecution of the Christians, Nero was an unpopular tyrant. He seduced married women, abused young boys, spent money extravagantly, robbed stores, stabbed people on the street as they passed by, and executed those who disagreed with him, even his own mother.[113]

While Nero's self-absorption and tyranny grew, troubles increased overseas. Cassius Dio writes, "While Nero was still in Greece, the Jews revolted openly, and he sent Vespasian against them. Also the inhabitants of Britain and of Gaul, oppressed by the taxes, were becoming more vexed and inflamed than ever."[114] Nero's persecution of the Jews and Christians in Israel and high taxation were driving the territories against him. Nero sent his army to put down the rebellion in Gaul, but the Roman forces were defeated. Finally, the military abandoned Nero and declared Servius Sulpicius Galba the new emperor. In 68 AD, after "he had been pronounced a public enemy by the senate,"[115] Nero stabbed himself and died. Suetonius writes, "He met his death in the thirty-second year of his age, on the anniversary of the murder of Octavia, and such was the public rejoicing that the people put on liberty-caps and ran about all over the city."[116]

The Year of the Four Emperors

Nero was succeeded by Galba, the governor of Hispania Tarra-conensis. Just six months after becoming emperor, Galba was mur-dered by the Praetorian Guard, led by Otho, after Galba refused to reward the soldiers who fought against Nero's army. Otho took his place, but committed suicide just four months later after losing the First Battle of Bedriacum to Vitellius, who was leading a rebellion in Germany. Vitellius ruled for eight months, but the eastern provinces proclaimed Vespasian as emperor instead. The two went to war and Vespasian's army defeated Vitellius' at the Second Battle of Bedriacum. Vespasian's troops captured Rome, Vitellius was murdered, and Vespasian became the new emperor.

Being emperor was obviously a very dangerous job. These four emperors, who all ruled during the year 69 AD, were military com-manders fighting over control of the empire after the death of Nero. In the days of the Roman Republic, Cincinnatus had to be convinced to take on the role of temporary dictator, but now people literally killed to be emperor. A drawback of large government with control over people's lives is that it attracts ruthless men of ambition who wish to use the power of government for their own benefit.

Vespasian

Vespasian had gained fame by leading the Roman legions against the Jewish rebellion of 66 AD in Judaea. When Nero died, Vespasian used his control of Egypt and its grain supply to pressure Rome into naming him emperor. After his army defeated and killed Vitellius,

Vespasian sent much needed grain to Rome and Vespasian was declared emperor by the Senate in December of 69 AD.

While Vespasian was still in Egypt, Mucianus administered the empire and immediately raised taxes while skimming off part of the funds for himself. Cassius Dio writes, "Now Mucianus was gathering countless sums into the public treasury with the greatest eagerness from every possible quarter…and in accordance with this belief he not only constantly urged Vespasian to raise funds from every source, but also continued from the very first to collect money himself, thus providing large amounts for the empire and at the same time acquire large amounts for himself."[117] Though Vespasian was no tyrant, Mucianus was corrupt and attached himself to the emperor for his own personal gain.

Upon his return to Rome, Vespasian sought to help the people, by which he would also gain their support: "On reaching Rome he bestowed gifts upon both the soldiers and the populace. He also repaired the sacred precincts and the public works which had suffered injury and rebuilt such as had already fallen into ruin… He immediately began to construct the temple on the Capitoline… The property of his opponents who had fallen in the various conflicts he left to their children or other kinsmen of theirs; furthermore, he destroyed the notes that were long overdue belonging to the public treasury."[118]

To further ensure his popularity, he sponsored historians, poets, and artists so they would portray him favorably. Suetonius writes, "He was the first to establish a regular salary of a hundred thousand sesterces for Latin and Greek teachers of rhetoric, paid from the privy purse. He also presented eminent poets with princely largess and great rewards, and artists, too, such as the restorer of the Venus of Cos and of the Colossus."[119] At the same time, he persecuted those who dared disagree with him.[120]

Unfortunately, he was more interested in popularity than economics or saving money. Suetonius writes, "To a mechanical engineer, who promised to transport some heavy columns to the Capitol at small expense, he gave no mean reward for his invention, but refused to make use of it, saying: "You must let me feed my poor commons.""[121] Given to extravagance, Vespasian started a massive building project, which also acted as a jobs program for the poor. He built "the temple of Peace hard by the Forum and one to the Deified Claudius on the Caelian mount... also an amphitheatre in the heart of the city."[122] This massive amphitheatre would later be known as the Colosseum.

Vespasian was not an evil man. He was generous to the poor, but lacking wealth of his own, this money came from other taxpayers. Likewise, his building projects had to be paid for through higher taxes. He funded historians, poets, and artists, again from tax money, but disliked philosophers, killing one Helvidius Priscus.[123] Vespasian certainly tried to be good to his people and was no tyrant, however, the high taxes to pay for his generosity resulted in rebellions and "constant conspiracies were made against him."[124]

Titus

Vespasian died a natural death in 79 AD at the age of 70. His son Titus succeeded him. Titus had also gained renown in Judaea by besieging Jerusalem, destroying the Temple, and bringing its treasure back to Rome. Before assuming the throne, people feared that Titus would be another tyrant. Suetonius writes, "He also assumed the command of the praetorian guard, which before that time had never been held except by a Roman knight, and in this office conducted himself in a somewhat arrogant and tyrannical fashion. For whenever he himself regard[ed] anyone with suspicion, he would secretly send some of the Guard to the various theatres and camps, to demand their punishment as if by consent of all who were present; and then he would put them out of the way without delay... Besides cruelty, he was also suspected of riotous living, since he protracted his revels until the middle of the night with the most prodigal of his friends; likewise of unchastity because of his troops of catamites and eunuchs, and his notorious passion for queen Berenice, to whom it was even said that he promised marriage. He was suspected of greed as well; for it was well known that in cases which came before his father he put a price on his influence and accepted bribes. In short, people not only thought, but openly declared, that he would be a second Nero."[125]

In reality, Titus became one of Rome's better emperors. Suetonius writes, "His banquets were pleasant rather than extravagant... He took away nothing from any citizen. He respected others' property, if anyone ever did; in fact, he would not accept even proper and customary presents."[126] Unfortunately, Titus spent much tax money on games and shows, a fault apparently common to all Roman emperors: "And yet he was second to none of his predecessors in munificence. At the dedication of his amphitheatre and of the baths which were hastily built near it he gave a most magnificent and costly gladiatorial show. He presented a sham sea-fight too in the old naumachia, and in the same place a combat of gladiators, exhibiting five thousand wild beasts of every kind in a single day."[127]

A number of disasters occurred during his reign, in which Titus performed admirably. "There were some dreadful disasters during his reign, such as the eruption of Mount Vesuvius in Campania, a fire at Rome which continued three days and as many nights, and a plague the like of which had hardly ever been known before. In these many great calamities he showed not merely the concern of an emperor, but even a father's surpassing love, now offering consolation in edicts, and now lending aid so far as his means allowed."[128] Except for the wasteful spending on shows and games, Titus was a good ruler. He respected private property, gave freely to the people, and helped them during their time of need. But Titus' good rule lasted just two years before he was killed by plague.

Domitian

Titus' brother Domitian succeeded him, but Domitian did not continue in the path of his father and brother. Even before becoming emperor, Domitian "exercised all the tyranny of his high position so lawlessly, that it was even then apparent what sort of a man he was going to be."[129] After the death of Vespasian, Domitian believed that "he had been left a partner in the imperial power, but that the will had been tampered with. And from that time on he never ceased to plot against his brother secretly and openly, until Titus was seized with a dangerous illness, when Domitian ordered that he be left for dead, before he had actually drawn his last breath."[130]

Domitian's administration of government was just as poor and ruthless as his family affairs. Domitian sought popularity by spending extravagant sums of money on "grand costly entertainments, both in the amphitheatre and in the Circus," including chariot races, giant infantry, cavalry, and naval battles, wild beast hunts, and night time gladiator competitions.[131] He continued the giant public works programs of his predecessors, building "a new temple on the Capitoline hill in honour of Jupiter Custos and the forum which now bears the name of Nerva; likewise a temple to the Flavian family, a stadium, an Odeum, and a pool for sea-fights."[132]

The cost of these shows and building projects along with increased pay to the soldiers, put Domitian in serious financial straights. As a result, Suetonius writes he "had no hesitation in resorting to every sort of robbery. The property of the living and the dead was seized everywhere on any charge brought by any accuser. It was enough to allege any action or word derogatory to the majesty of the prince. Estates of those in no way connected with him were confiscated, if but one man came forward to declare that he had heard from the deceased during his lifetime that Caesar was his heir. Besides other taxes, that on the Jews* was levied with the utmost rigour, and those were prosecuted who without publicly acknowledging that faith yet lived as Jews, as well as those who concealed their origin and did not pay the tribute levied upon their people."[133]

Domitian executed his political opponents, killed many senators for plotting against him, slew those who made fun of him, and banished all philosophers from Rome and Italy. Suetonius writes, "After his victory in the civil war he became even more cruel, and to discover any conspirators who were in hiding, tortured many of the

---

* Jews most likely included Christians because the Romans at that time saw little difference between the two monotheistic beliefs.

opposite party by a new form of inquisition, inserting fire in their privates; and he cut off the hands of some of them."[134] Suetonius adds that "in this way he became an object of terror and hatred to all, but he was overthrown at last by a conspiracy of his friends and favourite freedmen, to which his wife was also privy."[135]

Domitian's murder in 96 AD was received with mixed reaction. Suetonius reports, "The people received the news of his death with indifference, but the soldiers were greatly grieved and at once attempted to call him the Deified Domitian; while they were prepared also to avenge him, had they not lacked leaders. This, however, they did accomplish a little later by most insistently demanding the execution of his murderers. The senators on the contrary were so overjoyed, that they raced to fill the House, where they did not refrain from assailing the dead emperor with the most insulting and stinging kind of outcries. They even had ladders brought and his shields and images torn down before their eyes and dashed upon the ground; finally they passed a decree that his inscriptions should everywhere be erased, and all record of him obliterated."[136] Cassius Dio adds, "His images, many of which were of silver and many of gold, were melted down; and from this source large amounts of money were obtained. The arches, too, of which a very great number were being erected to this one man, were torn down."[137]

Breeding Tyrants

After seeing the successful reign of Augustus, Rome suffered under the rule of his successors, most of whom are known for their brutal tyranny and incompetent governance. This is perhaps the biggest risk when a nation chooses a government with centralized control. When the initial leader of the imperial government is good and successful, as Augustus was, the people willingly give the government even more power. However, when his successors are evil and tyrannical, as most of the early Roman emperors turned out to be, the people have little choice but to suffer through this because they already gave the government much of their wealth and freedom. Even the assassination of the emperor only brings another tyrant to replace him.

Whereas so many of the emperors were tyrannical, few of the leaders of the Republic were so evil. During the Roman Republic, no man had so much power that his evil could do much damage. A small government gives the politicians little opportunity to enrich themselves at the people's expense or to further accumulate power. Occasionally, one would try to seize power, such as Spurius Cassius Vecellinus in 486 BC, but the Senate or people, still enjoying their freedom, would quickly stop him. However, once power is concentrated in one man or group, the potential damage that can be done is much greater. A large government gives a man of ambition the motivation to gather power for himself and wield it for his own benefit and agenda. It is best not to tempt these men of ambition because it often results in tyranny, as Rome experienced starting with Tiberius' turn for the worse in 23 AD after the murder of his son until the assassination of Domitian in 96 AD.

THE GLORY OF ROME

After the death of Domitian, the Senate proclaimed Nerva the new emperor. Nerva was a former consul and served as an advisor to Nero, Vespasian, Titus, and Domitian. Unlike his predecessors, Nerva did not seek popularity and fame. Instead he shrunk government, sold off government property, returned property that was taken by Domitian, put the Senate in charge of distributing public land to the poor, promised not to kill any senators, "forbade the making of gold or silver statues in his honour," and "abolished many sacrifices, many horse-races, and some other spectacles, in an attempt to reduce expenditures as far as possible."[138] Cassius Dio reckons that "Nerva ruled so well that he once remarked: "I have done nothing that would prevent my laying down the imperial office and returning to private life in safety.""[139] Unlike most emperors, he had no reason to fear conspiracies and assassination attempts.

Nerva ruled for just two years before dying of a stroke followed by a fever. Nerva's adopted son and heir, Trajan, succeeded him and continued in his adoptive father's good ways. This began a line of emperors who died of natural causes and were succeeded by adopted sons. Trajan ruled for nineteen years. Trajan's adopted son and heir, Hadrian, ruled for 21 years. Hadrian's adopted son and heir, Antoninus Pius, was emperor for 23 years. He was succeeded by his adopted son and heir, Marcus Aurelius, who ruled for 19 years. Marcus Aurelius also died of natural causes, but was succeeded by his natural born son, Commodus. Unlike his five predecessors, Commodus was not a good emperor and, as he became more unpopular, a conspiracy was formed against him and he was assassinated. Apparently, there was a benefit to choosing the next emperor, instead of going with the natural born heir, even if the choice was left to the emperor and not the people or their representatives.

The "Five Good Emperors," as they are known, marked the golden age of the Roman Empire, lasting 84 years. All five emperors were loved by their people and each died of natural causes, as few had reason to assassinate the good rulers. Contrast this to the period after Augustus, which had twice as many emperors, most of whom were tyrants, in a slightly shorter period of time.

Alexis de Tocqueville describes the hands off method of ruling that these Roman emperors employed: "When the Roman emperors were at the height of their power, the different nations of the empire still preserved usages and customs of great diversity; although they were subject to the same monarch, most of the provinces were separately administered; they abounded in powerful and active municipalities; and although the whole government of the empire was centered in the hands of the Emperor alone and he always remained, in case of need, the supreme arbiter in all matters, yet the details of social life and private occupations lay for the most part beyond his control. The emperors possessed, it is true, an immense and unchecked power, which allowed them to gratify all their whimsical tastes and to employ for that purpose the whole strength of the state. They frequently abused that power arbitrarily to deprive their subjects of property or of life; their tyranny was extremely onerous to the few, but it did not reach the many; it was confined to some few main objects and neglected the rest; it was violent, but its range was limited."[140]

In *The History of the Decline and Fall of the Roman Empire*, Edward Gibbon describes this period: "If a man were called to fix the period in the history of the world during which the condition of the human race was most happy and prosperous, he would, without hesitation, name that which elapsed from the death of Domitian to the accession of Commodus. The vast extent of the Roman empire was governed by absolute power, under the guidance of virtue and wisdom. The armies were restrained by the firm but gentle hand of four successive emperors, whose characters and authority commanded involuntary respect. The forms of the civil administration were carefully preserved by Nerva, Trajan, Hadrian, and the Antonines, who delighted in the image of liberty, and were pleased with considering themselves as the accountable ministers of the laws."[141]

Rome was extremely fortunate to have five good emperors in a row. It was not by some ingenious system or culture that enabled this success. It was just happenstance that the five selected emperors were good and moral men, uncorrupted by the power given to them. But this lucky streak only delayed the inevitable decline and fall of Rome as it suffered under the weight of its large bureaucracy and military obligations.

THE END OF THE EMPIRE

Marcus Aurelius died in 180 AD of natural causes, marking the end of the golden age of the Empire and Pax Romana, the Roman peace. His son Commodus succeeded him, but did not follow in the path of his five predecessors. Instead, he acted more like the tyrants of the first century AD.

After five good and successful emperors in a row, the Romans expected greatness from Commodus as well. Commodus was loved by the army, but the Senate hated him. Like most tyrants, Commodus was most interested in his own pleasure, taking up chariot racing, gladiator competitions, and combat with wild beasts. Cassius Dio writes, "For example, all alone with his own hands, he dispatched five hippopotami together with two elephants on two successive days; and he also killed rhinoceroses and a camelopard."[142]

Commodus returned to the old ways of killing his opponents, which only increased the conspiracies against him. Cassius Dio reports, "Commodus was guilty of many unseemly deeds, and killed a great many people. Many plots were formed by various people against Commodus, and he killed a great many, both men and women, some openly and some by means of poison, secretly, making away, in fact, with practically all those who had attained eminence during his father's reign and his own."[143]

Seeking fame and to soothe his big ego, Commodus "actually ordered that Rome itself should be called Commodiana, the legions Commodian, and the day on which these measures were voted Commodiana. Upon himself he bestowed, in addition to a great many other names, that of Hercules. Rome he styled the "Immortal, Fortunate Colony of the Whole Earth"; for he wished it to be regarded as a settlement of his own. In his honour a gold statue was erected of a thousand pounds weight, representing him together with a bull and a cow. Finally, all the months were named after him, so that they were enumerated as follows: Amazonius, Invictus, Felix, Pius, Lucius, Aelius, Aurelius, Commodus, Augustus, Herculeus, Romanus, Exsuperatorius. For he himself assumed these several titles at different times, but "Amazonius" and "Exsuperatorius" he applied constantly to himself, to indicate that in every respect he surpassed absolutely all mankind superlatively; so superlatively mad had the abandoned wretch become. And to the senate he would send messages couched in these terms: "The Emperor Caesar Lucius Aelius Aurelius Commodus Augustus Pius Felix Sarmaticus Germanicus Maximus Britannicus, Pacifier of the Whole Earth, Invincible, the Roman Hercules, Pontifex Maximus, Holder of the Tribunician Authority for the eighteenth time, Imperator for the eighth time, Consul for the seventh time, Father of his Country, to consuls, praetors, tribunes, and the fortunate Commodian senate, Greeting." Vast numbers of statues were erected representing him in the garb of Hercules. And it was voted that his age should be named the "Golden Age," and that this should be recorded in all the records without exception."[144]

In 192 AD, Commodus was killed and the declared a public enemy by the Senate. The statues of Commodus were torn down and the names of Rome, the legions, and the months were restored. Civil war broke out after Commodus' death. Five months and two other emperors later, Lucius Septimius Severus took power. Rome's finances worsened as Septimius Severus annexed even more land and increased the pay of the soldiers to keep them from rebelling.

Montesquieu explains, "A wise republic should hazard nothing that exposes it to either good or bad fortune. The only good to which it should aspire is the perpetuation of its condition... Rome was made for expansion, and its laws were admirable for this purpose... It lost its liberty because it completed the work it wrought too soon."[145] By this time, the Roman Empire's economy was based largely on plunder, but Rome had expanded to such a large size that there was little remaining to plunder. Rome was left with the massive expense of defending its borders with no real benefit to be derived from the empire.

In addition to the huge cost of defending the empire from external invasion, Rome spent heavily on "bread and circuses." The Roman emperors provided free food, gladiator competitions, and chariot races to the people. In addition, there was the cost of building the 50,000 seat Colosseum in the time of Vespasian and the expansion of the Circus Maximus under Trajan starting in 100 AD, increasing the seating capacity from an already large 150,000 to a huge 350,000. These expensive projects had to be paid for by higher taxes, plundering new territories, or cutbacks elsewhere. As Rome suffered economic decline, one would expect the emperors to reduce these frivolities. Instead, they were increased to keep the people happy and ignorant of the declining finances.

To pay for the growing extravagances, bureaucracy, and military, the Roman emperors resorted to raising taxes, plundering, and devaluing the currency. Nero was the first to debase the coinage, rather than commit the more obvious act of raising taxes. Claudius Gothicus (emperor from 268 to 270 AD) further devalued Roman coins, causing Diocletian (emperor from 284 to 305 AD) to institute strict price controls, under penalty of death, but they failed to stop the inflation.[146]

The Roman Empire relied heavily on price controls to keep grain prices low and prevent the poor from revolting. But with the debased coinage and price controls, producers could not profitably grow and sell their crops. The supply of food in the cities declined and the people moved out of Rome and on to farms to grow their own produce. The emperors tried restricting this exodus, but the starving people ignored the law.[147]

Rome employed another method to raise funds: selling state owned property. When the government ran out of sellable property, it confiscated the assets of wealthy citizens by falsely charging them with a crime. Montesquieu writes, "It is wearying, in the history of the emperors, to see the infinite number of men they put to death for the purpose of confiscating their wealth."[148] In the continued search for new ways of raising funds, the emperors reinvented the aurum coronarium. Originally, cities would voluntarily send crowns of gold to a victorious general. This was later changed to a monetary tribute and Julius Caesar decreed that such tributes should only be given if a triumph is declared. Under the emperors, the aurum coronarium was collected on many occasions, including minor military victories, for the sole purpose of generating revenue. The emperors also expanded Roman citizenship to ensnare more people within the tax system.[149]

The increasing tax burden, confiscation of wealth, devaluation of the currency, and price controls hurt Rome's economy with both the wealthy and poor suffering. The wealthy moved away from Rome to avoid the rising taxes, confiscation of wealth, and growing tyranny. Montesquieu explains, "Pursued by tax farmers, the citizens could do nothing but seek refuge among the barbarians or surrender their liberty to the first person who wanted to take it."[150]

Without the rich to pay the taxes, the burden fell upon the poor. The poor who had not already fled to work on their own farms also abandoned Rome and went to work on the estates of the wealthy, thus creating a feudal society. Gold and silver money disappeared from circulation as the people hoarded it. Rome was forced to collect taxes in kind. The produce collected was then shipped off to the armies on the front, which was a much more expensive undertaking than sending gold to purchase food locally. The Roman economy had completely fallen apart and, with everybody hoarding gold and silver money, trade within Rome and around the Mediterranean declined sharply.[151]

Rome had become a desolate city as the people moved away to escape the growing tax burden and confiscatory economic policy. Rome had already lost most of its power, wealth, and influence by the time of its sacking at the hands of the Visigoths in 410 and again by the Vandals in 455 and the deposition of the last emperor in 476. The government's increased intervention in the economy, including high taxes, price controls, and inflation, which were a direct result of the populace's demand for wealth redistribution and a central government to administer it, were the main causes of Rome's decline and ultimate destruction.

CHAPTER FOUR

ANCIENT ISRAEL

Judeo-Christian philosophy, values, and beliefs are a major basis for Western civilization's legal and moral code. The over 3000-year old story of the Israelites fleeing the tyranny of Egypt and entering the Promised Land as free people continues to inspire even today. It is no coincidence that the Pilgrims who came to America from England and the Founding Fathers of the United States saw themselves as modern days Israelites escaping the tyranny of Britain and establishing their own promised land. Western civilization has learned much about freedom from the Bible's account of ancient Israel and has used this story as inspiration in the fight for liberty, but has often neglected to heed the Bible's warnings about the problems of government power and its resulting tyranny.

THE SYSTEM OF CHECKS AND BALANCES

For the Israelites leaving Egypt and entering Canaan, freedom meant following the laws set forth by God in the Bible and creating a system of government, also detailed in the Bible, to administer those rules. In modern terminology, the ancient Israelites were a common people governing themselves with the Bible as their constitution.

The government of ancient Israel was composed of separate authorities with checks and balances on each other. Israel's first leader was the prophet Moses. Prophets delivered the word of God to the people and, therefore, the people listened to and obeyed them, most of the time. This was especially true for Moses, who spoke "face to face" with God,[1] and Joshua, whom God instructed Moses to choose in front of the people as his successor.[2] In total, three prophets stood out in that they created something new: Moses took the Israelites out of Egypt and gave them the Bible, Joshua conquered Canaan and distributed the land, and Samuel created the monarchy. As a result, these three prophets had nearly complete authority; whereas the people often ignored the other prophets, especially after the establishment of the monarchy when the people strayed toward idol worship.

After the death of Joshua, the period of the judges began. The main purpose of the judges, as the name implies, was to decide legal cases and religious questions, though they were often called to serve as military leaders, as was the case with Ehud,[3] Deborah and Barak,[4] Gideon,[5] Jephthah,[6] and Samson.[7] Nevertheless, without a large bureaucratic central authority, the people were mostly unbothered by matters of government. The last verse of the book of Judges succinctly describes the situation in that period of Israel's history: "In those days there was no king in Israel: a man would do whatever seemed proper in his eyes."[8] This was both a compliment and a criticism, implying that the Israelites voluntary followed God, but also that they strayed at times. Nevertheless, it shows the extent of Israelite freedom at that time.

The individuals made famous by the book of Judges were, in fact, part of a much larger legal system. While still in the Sinai desert, Jethro advised Moses to create a system of judges to try civil and criminal cases.[9] Later, God told Moses, "Gather to Me seventy men from the elders of Israel, whom you know to be the elders of the people and its officers; take them to the Tent of Meeting and have them stand there with you."[10] These seventy, plus the leader of the Jewish people, called the Nasi, became the Great Sanhedrin. This Great Sanhedrin heard cases regarding false prophets, decided on whether a battle is part of a war commanded by the Bible, and determined whether to enlarge Jerusalem or the Temple Courtyard. Smaller courts of twenty-three judges were established to try capital cases, while courts of three judges decided on civil cases, such as robbery and injuries.[11] With a well established legal system, the judges listed in the book of Judges are noted more for their military adventures than for their legal actions, though they were judges first and military leaders second, as the name of the book implies.

Throughout Jewish history, the priests who descended from Aaron have been granted additional respect and priority. In the times of the Tabernacle and the Temple, the high priest served as the ritual leader of the nation, led the ordinary priests in their sacrifices, and entered the Holy of Holies on the Jewish holiday of Yom Kippur to ask God to forgive the people.[12] Additionally, the high priest wore the "breastplate of judgment"[13] in which the Urim and Tumim* were placed, which would miraculously answer questions by lighting up different letters engraved on the twelve stones of the breastplate.[14] The Bible most often mentions the Urim and Tumim answering questions of a military nature, such as whether to engage in war with an enemy or who should lead the fighting,[15] though it could answer other important questions, as well.[16] Additionally, a special priest would go to war with the king to give encouragement to the troops.[17] By asking the Urim and Tumim military questions and bringing a special priest to offer encouragement to the troops, the king showed the people that he received consent from the priests and God. If the king had tried to go to war without consulting the Urim and Tumim or without the special priest, the people would likely abandon him until he consulted with the high priest and the breastplate of judgment. In fact, one time David asked the Urim and Tumim for advice and it told him to "strike the Philistines," but the people were still afraid. David asked again and was told, "I am delivering the Philistines into your hand." The troops were thus reassured and they defeated the Philistines.[18] Even a king or military general, as David was not yet king during this incident, needs the loyalty of his troops. In ancient Israel, even the king needed to consult with a higher power.

The Israelites had no king upon entering Canaan and lived for 400 years without one,[19] but once the kingship was established, the king

---

* There is some argument regarding what the Urim and Tumim were. One suggestion is that it was a piece of parchment with God's seventy letter name on it. (Scherman, *The Chumash: The Stone Edition* 470-471.)

became the most powerful leader of the ancient Israelites. Yet, despite the king's power base, checks and balances were maintained. Although the king was the military leader, the Sanhedrin was the primary legal institution, the priests were the ritual leaders, and the prophets were the moral leaders and delivered instructions from God. Maimonides writes that the king "should stand before the Sanhedrin and the Sages of Israel" in private, but in public "he should not stand before any-one… in order than the awe of him [will be implanted] in everyone's hearts."[20] Additionally, "A prophet must stand before the king and prostrate himself on the ground," but "the king stands before the High Priest…when he consults the Urim and Tumim."[21] Thus, there are times when the king demands more honor and times when the High Priest, Sanhedrin, and Sages do, showing the balance of power between them. Other restrictions are placed on the king. He may not confiscate land[22] nor amass great personal wealth.[23] In fact, his wealth is to be stored in the Temple treasury, thus giving the priests much power over the use of his wealth, which is intended "to be used for the needs of the community and their wars."[24] In total, the king is com-manded to "be lowly and empty at heart," "gracious and merciful to the small and the great," "protect the honor of even the humblest of men," "speak gently," and "conduct himself with great humility."[25] Yet, the king is given much power, including the right to levy taxes[26] and to take people to work for him, though he must pay them.[27] The king also has the right to wage a required war against one of the seven nations that occupied Canaan, against the nation of Amalek, or in defense of the country and people. He does, however, need approval from the Sanhedrin to wage a voluntary war, which is one to expand the borders or for glory.[28]

As a result of the division of power, the different leaders often fought against each other. By God's command, Samuel the prophet anointed Saul to be king, then took away his kingship and bestowed it on David. Thus, at this stage in ancient Israel, the prophet still held more power than the king. With the kingship of David and then Solomon, the king's power increased, but throughout the era of the kings, the prophets and priests sought to limit the powers of the monarchy to those granted by the Bible. For example, Elijah fiercely opposed King Ahab and Queen Jezebel, who had led the people away from God to idol worship.[29] On Mount Carmel, Elijah slaughtered Jezebel's prophets who served the idol Baal.[30] Seeking revenge, Jezebel threatened to kill Elijah who fled for his life.[31] Thus, the kings and the prophets fought for power and the loyalty of the people.

In addition to the four branches of government mentioned above, the ancient Israelites maintained a fierce tribal loyalty. Until the establishment of the kingdom and even for some time after, individuals identified more with their tribe than with the Israelite nation as a whole. This is evident when Ephraim complained that Gideon the judge did not summon them to fight against Midian.[32] The Ephraimites complained again years later against Jephthah for the same reason. This second time, it resulted in a civil war in which 42,000 members of Ephraim died.[33] Later still, eleven tribes rose up against the tribe of Benjamin after the rape of the concubine in Gibeah. Almost all of Benjamin was destroyed with tens of thousands killed on each side.[34] In a country with such tribal allegiances, consolidating power in the hands of a single ruler would be possible only under ideal conditions, which is why it was so difficult for David to consolidate his rule against Ish-bosheth.[35] This tribal loyalty would later be a major contributing factor to the splitting of Israel into two kingdoms.

MANIFESTATIONS OF FREEDOM

Ancient Israel had many of the same freedoms of modern man living in a free society. However, due to the laws of the Bible, those freedoms often manifested themselves in slightly different ways. In some respects, the ancient Israelites had their freedoms restricted by Biblical law, but they also had freedoms that society today lacks.

Free Speech

Excluding religious heresy and speaking God's name in vain,[36] the Israelites before the time of the evil kings were free to speak their mind to a nearly unlimited extent. The common people spoke freely throughout the Bible, though God often punished them for their complaints against Him and Moses in the desert,[37] only because these complaints showed a lack of belief in God. In contrast, when used constructively, the ancient Israelites were allowed to speak freely. When requesting a king, which was a Biblical commandment,[38] the Israelites criticized Samuel saying, "You are old, and your sons did not follow your ways."[39] Samuel was upset, both because they wanted a king to be "like all the nations"[40] and also because it appeared as if they were rejecting his leadership. God appeased Samuel's personal disappointment saying, "for it is not you whom they have rejected, but it is Me whom they have rejected from reigning over them."[41] Because this request for a king was a Biblical commandment, the Israelites had every right to do so. However, they were rebuked for requesting a king for the wrong reasons.

The true test of free speech involves political speech, which has been restricted or outlawed throughout history. Throughout the Bible, the prophets criticize both the rulers and the people. Initially, the prophets did so without fear of repercussion. Samuel condemned Saul after the battle with Amalek[42] and Nathan admonished David regarding the death of Uriah and David's marriage to Bathsheba[43] without repercussion. Yet later, when tyranny had taken over both the northern and southern kingdoms, the prophets could no longer speak freely. Micaiahu warned Ahab, king of Israel, and Jehoshaphat, king of Judah, not to listen to the false prophets and not to go to war with Aram, but was thrown in jail because of his criticism.[44] Jeremiah was put in prison many times because of his constant criticism of the ruling parties just prior to the destruction of the Temple.[45] In the early days of Israel, the prophets spoke freely; but during the tyrannies, they spoke only at great personal risk.

A stark contrast in the limits of free speech can be seen in the complaints of the tribe of Ephraim. After Gideon attacked and defeated Midian, Ephraim complained, "What is this thing you have done to us, not summoning us when you went to fight with Midian?"[46] Gideon replied soothingly and Ephraim's anger was mollified.[47] In contrast, after Jephthah attacked and defeated Ammon, Ephraim complained again, "Why did you cross over to make war against the Children of Ammon, and did not call on us to go with you? We shall burn down your house in fire upon you!"[48] Jephthah responded by assembling his army, a reasonable response to Ephraim's threats of violence, and killed forty-two thousand Ephraimites.[49] This is the contrast between using free speech to criticize the government and using it to incite violence. Even in free society, free speech must have limitations.

Private Property

After entering Canaan and conquering most of the land, the country was divided by lottery among the various tribes and families with the Levites receiving cities to dwell in, scattered among the people.[50] The land of Israel therefore became private property, except for some public roads, wells, altars to God, the Levite cities, and the cities of refuge, which were places of asylum for perpetrators of involuntary manslaughter.[51]

The major restriction on private property was that an Israelite could not permanently sell his land. All land returned to its original owner, or his heirs, upon the Jubilee, which occurred every fifty years.[52] In effect, land could only be leased, as the Bible says, "According to the greater number of years shall you increase its price, and according to the lesser number of years shall you decrease its price, for he is selling you the number of crops."[53] But this applied only to open land and houses in open towns.[54] Houses in a walled city could be sold.[55] As a result, the walled city had an advantage over the open towns and fields. With the ability to buy and sell property in walled cities, people were also able to buy and sell business establishments. In addition to providing protection against attack, walled cities, being larger than the open towns that were scattered throughout the countryside, became the centers of commerce.

After the construction of the Temple, Jerusalem became a major center of trade in ancient Israel. Even though many pilgrims brought their sacrifices, gifts to the priests and Levites, and first fruit with them to the Temple,[56] some purchased them in Jerusalem. Thus, Jerusalem's merchants must have been busy supplying the Temple and its worshippers, especially during the three pilgrimage holidays. Restaurants, hotels, and individuals renting out extra rooms must have also done quite well with the influx of tens of thousands of visitors during the holidays. Additionally, port cities such as Acre, Haifa, and Jaffa were vital centers of international trade. Because of the importance of these urban commercial centers, the ban on selling open land in Israel had a much smaller effect than initial appearances. The owner of the land could easily lease the land to somebody else, find a job in the city, freely save capital, and purchase a business of his own, if he so desired. His ancestral land would always be in his possession, but he need not be tied down by it.

The restriction on selling ancestral land also had a positive side effect: it was nearly impossible to take these lands from their owners because its ownership was clear and undisputed. Even much later, during the era of the evil kings, the kings could not grab another's land for themselves. In fact, if the owner did not want to sell, the king was legally powerless. Ahab wanted the vineyard of Naboth saying, "Give me your vineyard, so that I may have it as an herb garden, for it is close by my house; in its place I will give you a better vineyard, or if you prefer, I will give you its price in money."[57] Naboth responded, "Far be it from me before God that I give you my ancestors' heritage!"[58] Ahab became "sullen and angry... and would not eat any food."[59] However, evil Queen Jezebel had Naboth killed and Ahab inherited the property.* Only through deceit, conspiracy, and murder were Ahab and Jezebel able to take an Israelite's private property.

The Bible allowed free trade in movable property, including farm animals, capital equipment, and other items such as vessels, weapons, jewelry, and bullion. Excluding a ban on owning or benefiting from

---

* Ahab inherited the land either because he was the next of kin or because "Naboth was put to death for sedition against the king and such a person forfeits his property to the royal estate." (Scherman, *Tanach: The Stone Edition* 868-869.)

idolatry[60] and certain non-kosher items,[61] an Israelite could freely sell, rent, or lease any such movable property with no restriction. As a result of such freedom from government interference, ancient Israel developed an extensive legal system based on voluntary contracts.[62] Additionally, any profits derived from renting or leasing capital equipment or business ventures not involving agriculture were exempt from Biblical taxes, though it has become traditional and is considered meritorious for the average person to tithe and for the wealthy to give one-fifth of all such profits to charity.[63]

Another constraint on land which, at first, appears to be a major restriction on private property is the land sabbatical. Every seventh year, the Israelites were not allowed to sow, plant, prune, or harvest their fields and vineyards.[64] They could eat from the produce that grew on its own, but not sell it.[65] This would reduce production in the sabbatical year and the following year, but in return, God promised the Israelites, "I will ordain My blessing for you in the sixth year and it will yield a crop sufficient for the three-year period."[66]

Whether it was God's blessing, trading with other nations for food during the sabbatical year, or the consumption of stored food that enabled the Israelites to take a whole year off from farming, the Bible not once mentions a famine as a direct result of taking this year long break. The Bible mentions a number of other famines, including a famine during the time of Abraham,[67] another during the time of Isaac,[68] the famine predicted by Joseph in Egypt,[69] one during the time of the judges,[70] the famine during David's reign,[71] a famine after Elijah stopped the rain,[72] and twice during the time of Elisha the prophet.[73] But not once is there a mention of a food shortage caused by the land sabbatical. Droughts are common occurrences in the Middle-East and have caused many famines, but the land sabbatical appears to have had little bearing on when these famines occur.

It may seem extreme today to leave the land fallow for an entire year, but this was a common agricultural technique to replenish the nitrogen in the soil and reduce the level of weeds, pests, and diseases in the days before fertilizer and pesticides.[74] The only thing odd about the practice in ancient Israel is that all the land was left fallow at the same time, whereas most countries would leave only a portion of the land uncultivated each year.

Ancient Israelites employed a system of partible inheritance that promoted freedom and equality. When an Israelite died, the estate was split among all his sons, with the additional provision that the first-born received a double share[75] and further rules if there are no sons.[76] The Rabbis also proclaimed that the wife and unmarried daughters be provided for, including dowries, from the deceased's estate.[77] By dividing a man's estate among all his sons and further providing for other members of his family, the ancient Israelites dispersed "both property and power,"[78] thus promoting greater freedom and equality.

Interest

Another restriction on property in ancient Israel was the ban on collecting or paying interest.[79] In today's modern society, a world without interest seems impractical. However, the Israelites prospered despite this constraint. Like all ancient civilizations, the Israelite economy was based on gold, silver, and copper currency. As a result, monetary inflation was not an issue and interest rates primarily represented the risk of the debtor failing to pay back the loan. Ancient Israelites had no procedure for declaring bankruptcy and the Bible included methods for the creditor to get his money back from a defaulting debtor, including "slavery," thus minimizing default risk as well.

In a world with no interest income for the creditor, other methods of lending needed to be created to encourage lending to businesses needing capital. In the place of interest-bearing loans, the creditor could invest in the debtors business, receiving a percentage of the revenue or income. The creditor therefore becomes a business partner, with real risk if no goods are sold. This design was established so that the creditor would help the business achieve maximum profits as the creditor earns a profit along with the debtor. Conversely, in a loan situation, the creditor is only interested in getting his money back, even if the debtor loses money. By encouraging an investment instead of a loan, the interests of the two Israelites were aligned.

As a result of these business investments, interest-free loans were primarily made to the poor or to one's neighbors who have hit hard times. By not charging interest, these people would be able to borrow money without becoming ensnared in an ever-growing credit balance. Only a fool would lend to somebody who has a history of not paying back, but lending to a trustworthy individual hit by hard times is praiseworthy.

Even thousands of years ago, they knew that lending money, even to a trustworthy individual, involves risk. Instead of receiving interest to offset those losses, the Bible gives a method of recovering his loan. If an individual had debts that could not be paid off, he could be sold into "slavery" with the proceeds going to his creditors.[80] As a result, the creditor's risk of loss was minimal and the reward for helping the poor, both spiritually and macro-economically, outweighed the interest that was lost.

Slavery

Slavery in ancient Israel, at least concerning Hebrew slaves, was nothing like the present conception of slavery. In fact, calling these people slaves is questionable. The Hebrew word here for slave, *eved*, could also mean worker or servant, terms that seem much more appropriate. Slaves were often individuals who could not pay off their debts and had to sell themselves as a result. Some Israelite slaves were robbers who, unable to return the stolen good or pay back its value plus a penalty, were sold into slavery. But Israelites could never become slaves through the use of force against them by other Israelites. In fact, Israelite and even gentile slaves, to which different rules apply, are rarely mentioned in the Bible. Therefore, slavery was presumably uncommon and unimportant to the Israelite economy and way of life.

Slaves had to be treated well and could not be made to do overly strenuous work. The Bible says, "You shall not work him with slave labor. Like a laborer or a resident shall he be with you; until the Jubilee Year shall he work with you. Then he shall leave you, he and his children with him, he shall return to his family, and to his ancestral heritage shall he return. For they are My servants whom I have taken out of the land of Egypt; they shall not be sold in the manner of a slave. You shall not subjugate him through hard labor – you shall fear your God."[81] In many respects, the slave had to be treated like one of the family.[82] Furthermore, upon being freed during the sabbatical year,[83] the master "shall not send him away empty handed. Adorn him generously from your flocks, from your threshing floor, and from your wine cellar."[84] The maximum six years of service not only repaid the slave's debt, but he also received some extra compensation that would certainly help him rebuild his life. This form of slavery is more like a jobs training and welfare program than indentured servitude. The Talmud also insists that the slave receive similar food, drink, lodging, and bedding as his master, adding: "Whoever buys a Hebrew slave, buys a master for himself."[85]

Taxation

The ancient Israelites enjoyed a non-bureaucratic tax system that remained unchanged for hundreds of years. The tithes, donations, gifts, and offerings that made up the Biblical tax system were not really taxes in the modern sense of the word. Many of these tithes and offerings were produce or livestock that had to be consumed by the owner at the Temple. Many gifts, donations, and tithes were given by the owner to the poor person of his choice or collected by the local poor from the fields, making it charity and not a tax by today's definition. Only the portion given to the Levites and priests could be considered taxes, though these gifts were in exchange for the religious services they provided, as the Bible says, "To the sons of Levi, behold! I have given every tithe in Israel as a heritage in exchange for the service they perform, the service of the Tent of Meeting."[86] Even the payment of these taxes were done in the most free way possible, with the taxpayer voluntarily giving his tithe to the priest or Levite he selected.* In total, the owner gave "taxes" to the Levites and priests in exchange for the religious services they provided, to the poor as charity, or to himself to be consumed at the Temple in Jerusalem.

One of the biggest advantages to this system of taxation was its decentralized nature. Each individual was in charge of paying his own taxes and the priests, Levites, and poor were in charge of collecting their own charity. The lack of a large bureaucratic government administering the system saved on overhead and enabled a direct relationship between the taxpayer and collector, further uniting the nation. Furthermore, because the taxpayer chose to whom to give his charity and taxes, the priests, Levites, and poor must in some way work for their pay. The priests and Levites, who were the ritual leaders of the nation and served in the Temple, must do their duties or the people will deem them unworthy of their taxes. Similarly, a poor person who was capable of supporting himself, but was too lazy to do so, would receive little help from the public. The public gave their hard-earned taxes to those most worthy, creating an effective free-market tax and charity system.

One of the biggest disadvantages of modern tax systems is that its structure and rates constantly change. Income, sales, property, and estate taxes vary depending on economic conditions and the philosophy of the current administration. However, ancient Israel had the same tax system from the time they entered the land of Canaan until the kings initiated new taxes to build their palaces and the Temple. For more than four hundred years, taxes remained constant; a period of tax stability likely unmatched anywhere else in history.

In addition to the Bible's quasi-tax system, communities may have instituted taxes to build protective walls around the city, dig wells, provide general city services, and help the poor.[87] However, these additional taxes are not mentioned in the Bible until the time of the kings. Therefore, these taxes were likely low until Solomon "made our

---

* There was no infrastructure in ancient Israel to centrally calculate and enforce these "taxes."

yoke [of taxation] difficult."[88] Moreover, a city could have raised funds by charging a fee to trade in its market, in which farmers from around the region would assemble to sell their produce and buy needed food, clothing, and tools. Coastal cities could have generated additional revenue by charging fees to use their ports. Therefore, these additional taxes were likely not a significant aspect in the economic system of ancient Israel.

DESIRING A KING

Despite all the freedoms the ancient Israelites enjoyed during the era of the judges, life was far from ideal. As the Bible says, "The Children of Israel continued to do that which was evil in the eyes of God and they worshiped the Baalim, the Ashtaroth, the gods of Aram, the gods of Sidon, the gods of Moab, the gods of the Children of Ammon, and the gods of the Philistines; they forsook God and did not serve Him."[89] Twice it says, "In those days there was no king in Israel: a man would do whatever seemed proper in his eyes,"[90] referring, at least in part, to the Israelites forsaking God and worshiping idols.

During the time of the judges, the Philistines arrived in the area with superior weaponry made from iron. The Israelites and Philistines battled each other, but neither side could gain the upper hand. Samson, for example, sacrificed himself to defeat the Philistines,[91] but the victory was only temporary. The fighting continued and, after one victory, the Philistines even captured the Holy Ark, but it was returned after it afflicted the Philistines.[92] The Philistines attacked again, but this time the Israelites won and "The Philistines were humbled and no longer continued to enter the border of Israel."[93] Nevertheless, the Philistines continued to occupy land that God had promised to the Israelites. The Israelites hoped that a king would lead them to battle and victory over their arch-enemies. Furthermore, the Israelites hoped that the king would unite the tribes and end the fighting between them.

At that time, Samuel the prophet was the leader of the Israelites. "When Samuel became old, he appointed his sons judges over Israel...

But his sons did not follow his ways. They were swayed by profit; they took bribes and they perverted justice."[94] The commentaries say they did not actually take bribes, but they did take fees for acting as a judge, which Samuel never did.[95] Furthermore, they stationed themselves in Beer Sheva, which is far in the south, and made the Israelites come down to them[96] instead of traveling the land as Samuel did.[97] Disappointed with Samuel's sons and seeing Samuel age, the Israelites requested a king to judge them[98] and lead them to war against the Philistines.[99]

SAMUEL'S WARNING

After the Israelites requested a king "to judge us, like all the nations,"[100] Samuel was upset that they wanted to be like the other nations instead of wanting a king to lead and inspire them in the ways of God. In an attempt to scare the Israelites into reconsidering their desire for a king, or at least the reasons they wanted one, "Samuel told all the words of God to the people,"[101] including a list of all the evils that a king would do. God, through Samuel, produces one of the most succinct and accurate depictions of the evils of tyranny.[102] The Israelites obviously did not desire tyranny. They only wanted a king to lead them in battle against the Philistines, unite the various tribes, and represent them among other nations. The kingdom started in optimism, but God and Samuel predicted a very bitter end.

The first evil cited by Samuel is one that many countries continue to experience and the United States remembers not too fondly from its recent past. Samuel predicts, "He will take away your sons and place them in his chariots and cavalry, and they will run before his chariot."[103] This is the military draft, in which the nation's rulers force a citizen to kill and be killed for a cause he may not believe in.

The tyranny of the king extended well beyond the military: "He will appoint for himself captains of hundreds and captains of fifty, to plow his furrow and to reap his harvest, and to produce his implements of battle and the furnishings of his chariot. He will take your daughters to be perfumers, cooks, and bakers."[104] The argument for a military draft is that these people are needed for the worthy cause of national defense. Here, however, the king is drafting men and women for his own personal benefit, an inexcusable affront to freedom.

Samuel further warns the people that the king will tax them and confiscate their land to pay for his extravagant lifestyle: "He will take a tenth of your grain and vines"[105] and "He will take a tenth of your sheep."[106] Not a very high tax rate, but that is on top of the quasi-taxes already being paid to the Temple, priests, Levites, and the poor. Furthermore, the king "will confiscate your best fields, vineyards, and olive trees"[107] and "will take your servants and maidservants and your best young men and your donkeys and press them into his service."[108] Samuel was warning the people that the concept of private property, which had become so deeply entrenched over the past four hundred years as a result of the ban on selling one's ancestral land, will be destroyed by the new kings.

To maintain his power, a king has to have the solid support of his military leaders. A king would also like to thank his friends for their support. Therefore, Samuel predicts the king will take some of the confiscated property and "present them to his servants"[109] and take some of the taxes collected and "present them to his officers and servants."[110] Samuel is pointing out that the king will have the power to take property away from one group of people and give it to another.

Samuel's warning in the Bible follows a logical progression. He starts by predicting the king will impose a military draft, a reasonable decree when the people desired a king to defend the country and defeat the Philistines. But the situation worsens with time as the king soon drafts men to farm his land and then women to cook, bake, and make perfume. Then the king takes away the people's land followed by their servants and their livestock. Finally, "you will be his slave. On that day you will cry out because of your king whom you have chosen for yourselves – but God will not answer you on that day."[111]

Samuel's warning is a perfect example of how free society descends into tyranny. The people request a king to do good for them and at first he does. But the king begins encroaching on their freedoms and their property. Slowly but surely, the king assumes more power and the people lose their rights and freedoms. Finally, the people become slaves to the "king whom you have chosen for yourselves."[112]

The Israelites ignored Samuel's warning saying, "No! There shall be a king over us, and we will be like all other nations; our king will judge us, and go forth before us, and fight our wars!"[113] The Israelites saw only the good that the king will do and were blind to the bad. As surprising as this seems in hindsight, this is a common human weakness with two possible causes.

The Israelites may have been focusing on the short-term benefits and discounting the long-term effects. The Israelites saw their current problems and realized that a king could fix them. They were correct because King David unified the nation and defeated the Philistines and King Solomon judged the people. However, the price of centralized government was to be paid by later generations when the evil kings ruled.

A second possibility is that the Israelites believed that Samuel's warnings would not come true. Up until this time, the Israelites had just three king-like rulers: Moses, Joshua, and Samuel. With no experience of an evil ruler since leaving Egypt four hundred years earlier, they had little reason to believe that a tyrant would appear from among them. Frequently, when people are warned about an event they have never experienced, they pay no heed to the warning. This is similar to today in which many citizens of former socialist countries realize the evil and unfeasibility of that political-economic system, yet so many in free nations that have never experienced it continue to believe the promises of socialism.

THE GOOD KINGS

The first kings of ancient Israel were good, though not flawless. Foremost, they achieved their goals: uniting the people, defeating the Philistines, and judging the people wisely and fairly. Furthermore, they acted wisely by not attempting to conquer the whole world. Alexander the Great, Attila, Napoleon, Hitler, and so many others went on quests to dominate the world but were forced to stop because of a lack of funds, an insurrection back home, a military defeat, or death in battle or on the road. The kings of Israel expanded their territory, but did not seek the world. They stopped by choice when they had conquered the relatively small amount of land that God had promised them in the Bible. The amount of land conquered was more than enough for the population, so going farther made little economic, political, or military sense. Only pride, which has cursed so many generals and monarchs, would push a man any further than was necessary and wise.

Ancient Israel reached its pinnacle under King Solomon. At the same time, the size of government grew dramatically under Solomon. Solomon started large works projects, most notably the Temple in Jerusalem,[114] his palace,[115] the walls surrounding Jerusalem,[116] a number of new or rebuilt cities,[117] a palace for his wife,[118] two hundred ornamental gold shields,[119] a magnificent throne made of ivory and gold,[120] and the many gold and silver vessels of the Temple.[121] He also created a huge army of 1,400 chariots and 12,000 horsemen, importing the horses from Egypt and Keveh,[122] in addition to infantry troops and weapon manufacturers that must have numbered tens more thousands.

To produce such extravagant buildings, the many gold and silver ornaments and vessels, and the huge army, Solomon instituted a series of taxes and labor conscriptions. Thirty thousand men, "a levy from all of Israel," in shifts of ten thousand, were conscripted to go to Lebanon to cut down the cypress trees of Hiram, King of Tyre.[123] Solomon conscripted another seventy thousand to transport the materials and eighty thousand to hew stone from the mountains, in addition to 3,300 supervisors.[124] Later though, the Bible says that the conscripted labor was made up of the descendants of the people who lived in Canaan before Israel conquered it and that "Solomon did not enslave anyone of the Children of Israel."[125] It is not clear what percentage, if any, of these conscripted workers were Israelites. Some commentaries argue that the "levy" of thirty thousand means that Solomon literally conscripted thirty thousands Israelites whereas others claim that this was a tax on Israel to raise the funds to pay for the materials, food, and lodging for the conscripted non-Israelite workers.[126]

Additional taxes were imposed on the Israelites and on trade within Israel. These taxes were on top of the taxes that already existed: the tithes, donations, gifts, and offerings required by the Bible. Though the size of the taxes are not mentioned in the Bible, except perhaps the thirty thousand person "levy from all of Israel," taxes are mentioned at least four times during Solomon's construction frenzy.[127]

In contrast to Solomon's Temple, the Tabernacle built in the desert was funded fully by donations. In fact, the Israelites gave so much that Moses commanded the people to stop bringing gifts for the Tabernacle.[128] However, the Temple in Jerusalem was built through taxation, labor conscription, and gifts from foreign leaders. There is no mention in the Bible of donations given by the Israelites to build the Temple. It is possible that this difference between the two means of fundraising is why the Tabernacle was never destroyed but the Temple was. Beyond the spiritual argument that God may have favored the Tabernacle more than the Temple because it was built through generosity instead of obligation, there could also be a more practical reason. The Israelites gave donations to the Tabernacle, creating an emotional bond between them, even many generations later. In contrast, the Israelites were possibly less favorable toward the Temple built in Jerusalem because it was built with money forcibly taken from them. All of Israel helped erect the Tabernacle in Shilo,[129] where it would remain for 369 years before being moved.[130] On the other hand, after the death of Solomon and the division of Israel, Jeroboam actively prevented the citizens of his northern kingdom from traveling to Jerusalem and worshiping at the Temple of Solomon.[131]

Though David and Solomon were good kings, their actions paved the way for lesser men to commit evil using the government they created. By creating a large central government with a system of taxation and a large army, the monarch could do either great good or great evil. David and Solomon did great good: defeating their enemies, expanding the borders, building the Temple, creating economic prosperity, and uniting the people. However, the same apparatus used by David and Solomon for good was used for evil by their successors.

SECESSION AND RECESSION

After Solomon's death, Jeroboam "along with all the Congregation of Israel" told Rehoboam, Solomon's son and successor, "Your father made our yoke [of taxation] difficult; now, you alleviate your father's difficult workload and his heavy yoke that he placed upon us, and we will serve you."[132] The people tolerated the heavy taxes under Solomon due to his wisdom, righteousness, and the many worthwhile projects the money supported. However, under a new leader and with those projects completed, the people expected the taxes to be rolled back.[133] Rehoboam refused because the high taxes were the source of his wealth and power. Additionally, dictators need the people to obey them and cannot be seen as weak. When the Israelites complained about the high taxes, instead of lowering them, Rehoboam threatened to raise them even higher in a show of strength.[134] However, Rehoboam miscalculated and was not as powerful as he thought. The northern ten tribes stoned Rehoboam's tax collector[135] and seceded from the united kingdom.[136]

The southern kingdom of Judea declined economically, spiritually, and militarily. The people abandoned God and his Temple, just a few years after it had been built, and began worshiping idols.[137] In the fifth year of Rehoboam's reign, Egypt attacked Jerusalem and took the treasures of the Temple.[138] The two hundred ornamental gold shields made by Solomon were taken to Egypt and Rehoboam replaced them with copper shields. The economy of Judea had declined so much that they could not be replaced with gold or even silver substitutes.

For most of the next four hundred years, the kings of Judea were at odds with God, the Temple, and the prophets, each of which represented a limit on the king's power. Of the twenty kings of Judea, only Hezekiah and Josiah were loyal to God, the Temple, and the prophets.

In the north, Jeroboam, the leader of the tax protest, became king of the ten tribes. Unfortunately, Jeroboam was just another demagogue, fighting for the rights and freedoms of the people as a candidate, but then opposing them when elevated into power. He created two golden calves and told the people, "These are your gods, O Israel, who brought you up from the land of Egypt!"[139] To stop his people from traveling to Jerusalem, where they may attach themselves to God, the Temple, and King Rehoboam, Jeroboam created his own places of worship, holidays, priests, and altars.[140] Furthermore, the gifts that would have gone to the Temple, priests, and Levites, were instead given to priests appointed by Jeroboam,[141] creating a loyal constituency for his new kingship. Jeroboam was just the first in a long line of evil kings. The Bible comments that the kings "did what was evil in the eyes of God"[142] and "caused Israel to sin."[143]

In addition to the fights over taxation and religious practices, the two kingdoms conducted military campaigns against each other. Except for the occasional time when Israel and Judea allied to fight a common enemy,[144] the two kingdoms spent their time, if not actively battling each other, positioning against the other. Each would form alliances with foreign powers,[145] hoping that they would be able to defeat or at least defend against the other kingdom. The people were in constant fear that their ally would abandon them or turn against them in their time of need. Of course, the alliances were not free. Judea and Israel had to pay tribute to their foreign allies.[146] To pay the tributes, additional taxes had to be imposed on the people, further weakening their economies.[147] Additionally, by allying with a major foreign power, the kings deterred internal revolt because the people realized that any weakness would make their kingdom susceptible to military invasion by the opposing kingdom, their foreign ally, or another foreign power. The kingdoms of Israel and Judea slowly weakened as a result of their frequent wars, the tributes draining their treasuries, and the high taxes that were imposed to pay for the wars, tributes, and luxury of the kings.

DEFEAT AND EXILE

Ancient Israel controlled important trade routes connecting the Mediterranean with the eastern empires of Assyria, Babylonia, and Persia and connecting Egypt, the Red Sea, and Arabia in the south with Asia Minor, Phoenicia, and Mesopotamia in the north. During the time of the judges, when there was no powerful central government in Israel, Israel was not powerful enough to stop foreigners from traveling through the country nor was it interested in doing so as the Israelites profited greatly from selling the travelers food, drink, and lodging. As long as Israel allowed them to trade and travel freely through the area, the superpowers had little reason to desire control of the trade routes. The only battles Israel waged during this time were the border skirmishes with their neighbors, especially the Philistines. When David and Solomon united the kingdom, they actively promoted trade, with the Bible mentioning the strong trade relationship between Israel and Hiram, king of Tyre,[148] and many foreign rulers visiting Solomon bearing gifts and friendship.[149]

When the united kingdom split into the northern and southern kingdoms, trade between the two kingdoms was restricted as Jeroboam tried to prevent his people from traveling to the Temple in Jerusalem.[150] Additionally, the constant fighting between Israel and Judea made travel through the area extremely dangerous. The foreign powers had lost the benefit of free trade, and each wanted to restore and possibly control trade in the area. While Israel and Judea became weaker, Egypt and Assyria became stronger. Either could easily conquer Israel and Judea, but each feared provoking the other. It was only a matter of time until one of the foreign powers conquered Israel and Judea. After more than eight hundred years of self-rule, the northern ten tribes were exiled by Assyria[151] and then the southern tribes were exiled by Babylonia, Assyria's successor.[152] Ancient Israel was no longer, though the Israelites had lost most of their freedom and wealth many years earlier.

CHAPTER FIVE
COMMUNIST RUSSIA

S traddling the line between East and West, Russia is a conundrum. As Winston Churchill remarked, "It is a riddle wrapped in a mystery inside an enigma."[1] Russia was slow to join the industrial revolution and never fully embraced the liberal tradition that swept across much of the globe following the American and French Revolutions. Russia had numerous opportunities to create a truly free society, but mistakes by both the nobility and the people obstructed this advance.

While Russia lagged behind economically, politically, and socially, the Russian people were leaders in the use of revolutionary tactics, including union strikes, political assassinations, labor camps, and genocide. The Soviet Union that emerged out of the Russian Empire acted as an advocate for totalitarianism and Marxist socialism, also known as communism,* spreading them through the region and around the world. The Soviet Union's ultimate failure demonstrated to most of the world the impracticality of socialism; yet, to many, its appeal lives on.

LOST OPPORTUNITIES FOR LIBERTY

In the late nineteenth century, Russia was failing. It had fallen far behind Europe, the United States, and Japan in both economic and

---

* The un-capitalized *socialism*, *communism*, and *fascism* in the next three chapters refer to the ideologies or general movements, whereas the capitalized *Socialist*, *Communist*, and *Fascist* refer to the political party or the government controlled by said party.

military strength. Russia's defeat in the Crimean War revealed how its agricultural economy based on serfdom was no match for the industrialized economic giants of Europe.[2] Recognizing that Russia had fallen far behind its competitors, Czar Alexander II began a series of economic and political reforms. Prior to Alexander II's reign, the vast majority of Russians were extremely poor and had few if any rights. About eighty percent of the people were peasants, just under half of whom were serfs belonging to nobles.[3]

In 1861, Czar Alexander II freed the serfs, but they were given no land. The serfs could buy the land they had been working and living on from their former landlords, but most were too poor to do so. The government made loans available, but this just put the poor peasants deep in debt before they even started their new lives. Additionally, the land they could purchase would not be their own private property, but would be owned by their commune. This gave the people little incentive to improve their land because the improvements would belong to the communes and the communes would periodically reassign the land to different people.[4] Therefore, each peasant would use as much of the resources of the land as possible with no regard for its future users, a problem known as the tragedy of the commons. The Russian people were so obsessed with equality, making sure that nobody had more than his fellow, that they ignored the economic benefits of private ownership and the incentives to working hard, improving the land, making a profit, saving capital, and expanding production. Thus, a golden opportunity for Russia to create a free society was squandered by the fixation on equality. The new economic classes that would have resulted from such competition went against their egalitarian ideals. Therefore, the advantages of economic freedom and competition were disregarded and lost. As a result, the serfs were not much better off than they were before their emancipation.

Czar Alexander II made further reforms in the 1860s and 1870s. He established elected assemblies in rural local governments. Although they were primarily controlled by the land-owning nobility, it was still a step forward. He opened the school system to people from all classes. He made the Russian judiciary an independent branch of government and trials became public and by jury. Members of all classes would be subject to military conscription, not just peasants. Though Russia was still far from enjoying full freedom, the people were gaining more rights and liberty. As a result, the economy became more capitalist and the middle class expanded.[5] Russia was slowly becoming a free society.

Many Russians believed the reforms did not go far enough. They wanted a full-scale revolution, including the overthrow of the monarchy. Led by Nikolai Chernyshevsky, the revolutionaries believed that violent means, against both the oppressors and the oppressed, was justified to accomplish their goals.[6] In 1881, the revolutionaries assassinated Czar Alexander II, even though he had pushed through all the reforms and had even more planned.[7] The new Czar, Alexander III, was not like his father. He opposed increased freedom and rights for the people,[8] and immediately increased police powers, censored the press, reduced access to the school system, and weakened the judicial system's independence.[9] He decreased suffrage by raising the amount of land one had to own to vote. He was against the minorities, especially the Jews. A wave of pogroms was launched against the Jews, but Alexander III ordered his provincial governors to protect them because he feared the anarchy may cause an even more widespread revolution.[10] Afterwards, Jewish access to schools was limited, they were barred from holding government office, denied the right to vote, and restrictions were placed on where they could live.[11] While Alexander III's firm hand prevented further violence, the people lost rights they had gained under the Great Reforms of his father and the positive momentum disappeared.

Had the revolutionaries not assassinated Alexander II, the rights and liberties of the people would likely have expanded further. However, these revolutionaries were more interested in creating mayhem than increasing the rights of the people. Nikolai Chernyshevsky and the other revolutionary leaders were not peasants; they were educated elites supposedly working on behalf of the people.[12]

Chernyshevsky believed the peasants were "simply the raw material for diplomatic and political experiments."[13] These revolutionaries used the uneducated masses to gain power.

Alexander III died of kidney inflammation in 1894 and was succeeded by his inexperienced son, Nicholas II, who was not the least bit interested in politics or government.[14] Nicholas II was a firm believer in autocracy and called those who wanted more reforms "dreamers."[15] In response to the government's near total control of the economy[16] and the people's long work hours and dismal working conditions,[17] many Russians went on strike. They also formed political parties to reform or totally overthrow the government.

The Marxists formed the Russian Social Democratic Workers Party advocating a transition to capitalism and only later to socialism, as Karl Marx believed was necessary. However, the party split into two with the Mensheviks, Russian for minority, wanting widespread participation by the working class in the party, but the Bolsheviks, Russian for majority, favoring a centralized and elitist political party. The Mensheviks, therefore, adopted more popular and moderate tactics while the Bolsheviks favored radical tactics that required just a few revolutionaries to implement.

Whereas the Marxists believed that a period of capitalism must occur before socialism could be adopted, the Socialist Revolutionary Party wanted to go straight to socialism by immediately redistributing the land and socializing industry. While the Socialist Revolutionary Party used persuasion to gain adherents, they also used political assassination in their attempts to overthrow the government.

The liberals formed their own political parties, advocating civil rights, rule of law, and representational government. Most liberals were professionals, such as doctors, lawyers, and teachers. One would expect businessmen and factory owners to align themselves with this free-market group, but they had grown reliant on the government for most of their business[18] and they either did not wish to upset the government or believed that they would lose business, possibly to foreign competition, in a free-market environment.

Thus the Russian people had a number of choices. Some wanted to keep the monarchy, wherein the people had no political and economic freedom and were generally poor. Most of the people, though, wanted change, but they could not agree on which kind of change. Only the liberals promised economic and political freedom, but many were lured by the redistributionist policies of the socialists.

Even under the autocratic Czar Nicholas II, the economy continued to grow and the middle class expanded further.[19] Enjoying the fruits of the industrial economy, the growing middle class preferred moderate political reforms, including a constitutional monarchy, and opposed revolution, especially a violent one.[20] With time, the middle class gained more power, pushing Russia toward constitutional government with increased liberty and rights.

Karl Marx had argued that feudalism, or serfdom in Russia, would evolve into industrial capitalism and only after that would the working class rise up, destroy capitalism, and institute socialism.[21] Russia was definitely heading toward that capitalist stage. Whether or not socialism would result from it depended on the relative sizes of the working and middle classes. A large middle class would have been less likely to revolt, but a large working class would resort to revolution to obtain more rights and redistribute wealth. The radical revolutionaries recognized that the middle class was expanding, which would likely lead to permanent capitalism and not the socialism they desired. Their violent revolution had to begin as soon as possible, before the middle class became too large and socialism would become much less popular.

Though the economics of Russia under Czar Nicholas II were helping the liberals and their cause, political events were creating a demand for more rapid reforms. In the late 1800s, Japan and Russia competed for valuable land in Manchuria and Korea. After years of arguing about the land in northeast Asia, Japan attacked the Russian naval base at Port Arthur in January 1904. Japan had a big military advantage with better training and its military assets in closer proximity, whereas most of Russia's navy was over 4,000 miles away in the Baltic and its army was located near St. Petersburg and Moscow.

When the war began, the Russian government became more popular, as wars often increase the people's patriotism. But support waned when Japan defeated Russia in one battle after another.[22] Russia sent its navy from the Baltic to the Tsushima Straight between Japan and Korea, where they promptly suffered one of the worst naval defeats in history, with nearly the entire fleet destroyed or captured.[23]

The call for reforms grew louder as the government's incompetence in fighting the war became obvious. The liberals led a campaign for constitutional change in the fall and winter of 1904-1905. On Sunday, January 9, 1905, two hundred thousand workers marched on the Winter Palace, home of the Russian czars, asking for civil rights, a shorter working day, and a representational assembly. They did not call for socialism or the overthrow of the Czar. This assembly was peaceful until the government sent soldiers to disperse the crowd. The crowd refused to leave and the soldiers shot and killed 130 people. After "Bloody Sunday," the whole country protested as students went on strike, peasants attacked estates, soldiers mutinied, and people ignored the restrictions on public assembly

At this moment, Czar Nicholas should have compromised. In ancient Greece and Rome, the king or aristocrats granted the people more rights when they protested, thus spreading liberty to more people and preventing the total overthrow of those in power. The Czar could have done the same by giving in to their demands for an elected parliament, rule of law, and more rights including the right to form unions to demand better working conditions. This might have appeased the moderates and isolated the revolutionaries,[24] thus ending the protests and preventing further violence. But the Czar stubbornly refused any reforms, thus pushing the people toward revolution, which they now saw as their only way to obtain the rights and freedom they desired.

After a general strike shut down most of the country in October 1905, Nicholas II had no choice. He issued his October Manifesto, granting the people civil liberties and an elected legislature, called the Duma, without which the Czar could not enact any laws. The Duma functioned for eleven years and did much to improve the lives of the peasants, help the poor factory workers, and expand educational opportunities among the general population.[25] But Czar Nicholas II's response was too little, too late. If the Czar had issued his Manifesto back in January, before the violence grew out of hand, he might have saved the monarchy. But in the intervening nine months, rule of law had all but disappeared and anarchy prevailed.

Not everybody approved of Czar Nicholas' reforms. Just one day after the October Manifesto was issued, supporters of the monarchy attacked their opponents, most notably the Jews. In a two week period, 690 anti-Jewish pogroms occurred and 876 people were killed.[26] If the Czar was able to stop these pogroms, he saw little reason to do so. He never liked the Jews and, looking at the short term, was probably pleased to see his opponents killed off. He did not see that such lawlessness could cause his eventual overthrow; not realizing that a ruler with no power over his people was no longer a ruler at all. As a result, the lawlessness spread. The peasants attacked the estates of their landlords, took their grain, and burned down their houses.

In December 1905, the revolutionaries, led by the Bolsheviks, attempted their most daring act to date. They decided to seize control of the government in Moscow, hoping that their bold action would be imitated throughout the country and the government would be overthrown.[27] However, the governor-general of Moscow brought in light artillery and defeated the revolutionaries. The government then cracked down on revolutionaries across the entire country, using the soldiers who had just returned from the war with Japan.

Despite all the chaos and the rout of the revolutionaries, the elections promised by the October Manifesto took place and the liberal Constitutional Democrats won the most seats. But the Czar still held most of the power and he had little desire to work with the liberals in the Duma who wanted a constitutional monarchy and redistribution of land. The Czar and his cabinet largely ignored the Duma and, when the Duma refused to back down on its demands, the Czar had the Duma dissolved. After successfully stopping the revolutionaries, the Czar became arrogant and believed he would be able to suppress all threats against the government.[28] Therefore, he thought he could ignore the Duma and the people, which was a major miscalculation.

In ancient Rome, power and rights were slowly distributed to the people over hundreds of years. Here, the Russians wanted a complete overhaul, with land redistribution, done immediately. Not even Solon, "lawmaker of Athens," accomplished that much change in such a short period as he took a middle path and refused to redistribute the land. With the new Duma and the moderate liberals in power, the Russian people had yet another chance to achieve liberty. For years, it was always the Czar who refused to back down. This time, it was the Duma demanding too much, including the always contentious land redistribution. Another opportunity was wasted.

A new election was held in February 1907, but the Duma became even more radical as the Constitutional Democrats lost seats and the left-wing gained control. The Duma made the same demands and, in June, it too was dissolved. This time, the Czar changed the law and banned many of the peasants and minorities from voting in future elections. Just two years after winning the right to vote, the Russian people were already losing it.

The Revolution of 1905 had failed, largely because the various opponents of the autocracy did not work together. The liberals on one side and socialists on the other wanted two entirely different things, making it impossible for them to work together. Even the Socialist Revolutionaries and Marxists, who both wanted socialism but had different ideas of how it should be advanced, did not work well together. Friedrich Hayek explains, "It seems to be almost a law of human nature that it is easier for people to agree on a negative program - on the hatred of an enemy, on the envy of those better off - than on any positive task."[29] It is easy to attack the common enemy, but agreeing on a positive course of action is much more difficult.

When the people want change, they must present a solution, not just dissatisfaction with the current system. Even if the Czar had wanted to give up his powers and grant the people their liberty, Nicholas II had no way to satisfy all the political factions. Instead, he decided to satisfy none of them, which turned out to be a very bad decision. If he had worked with the least radical of the groups, such as the Constitutional Democrats when they controlled the Duma, Russia likely could have become a constitutional monarchy, in which the Czar would act as a kind of president or be a very wealthy royal figurehead. Instead, the Czars lost all their power as the most radical socialists took over in a surge of violence.

The Russians did manage to keep some of the newfound liberty as the czar still needed approval from the Duma for the enactment of most new laws. Though the lowest classes were disenfranchised, the upper and middle classes retained their right to vote, a right they lacked just three years earlier. Additionally, unions were no longer illegal and the press had more freedom.[30] There was still hope for liberty in Russia.

In 1906, Czar Nicholas II appointed Pyotr Stolypin as Prime Minister. Stolypin believed that further reforms were necessary to "renew" Russia and appease the population.[31] Stolypin initiated his "wager on the strong plan," which would enable peasants to achieve prosperity if they worked hard.[32] The centerpiece of his plan was making state-owned land available for sale to peasants, extending them civil and personal rights, and allowing peasants who belonged to a commune to claim the land they worked on as private property. Stolypin was trying to turn these peasants into property owners who would support the monarchy, favor more moderate reforms, and oppose revolution.[33] Stolypin expanded public education, another reform to help the peasants. He also tried to improve government efficiency, increase government tolerance of minorities, and lift restrictions on the Jews, but with little success.[34]

Stolypin was putting freedom ahead of equality. Stolypin was slowly distributing rights and liberty to the people, but too many people, especially the radicals, wanted quicker action. Additionally, their ideas of change did not match that of Stolypin. Stolypin was moving the country closer to capitalism, but the radicals wanted to move toward socialism. Stolypin could have been another Solon and, in fact, some newspapers were hailing him as a Russian Solon.[35] But Solon was supported by the people of Athens, at least initially, whereas Stolypin received little support from either side and had to deal with a large contingent of people advocating violent revolution.

Stolypin said his reforms needed twenty years of peace to transform the country,[36] but they only had ten before World War I broke out. By that time, only ten percent of peasants had broken away from the communes and started their own independent farms.[37] Stolypin's reforms were transforming Russia, but they were working too slowly. Many Russians enjoyed living in the commune and were reluctant to live on a farm far from any neighbors and with no support if they should happen to fail. Additionally, many men went to work in the city when there was no farm work to be done and the women enjoyed living with the other women in the commune while the men were away.[38] Many Russians were comfortable with the cooperative socialist philosophy and leery of the competitive capitalist system. Given time, Stolypin's system would have weaned the Russians off their communal system, but his assassination in 1911 by a supporter of the Socialist Revolutionaries,* World War I, and the Revolution of 1917 brought an abrupt halt to the liberalization of Russian government, economy, and society.

Although Russia had improved economically under Stolypin's reforms and it became a major industrial power, the standard of living of the average Russian citizen remained far behind Great Britain and Germany and even lagged behind poorer European countries such as Spain and Italy.[39] Despite the improvements Russia saw, Stolypin's successor did not continue the reforms and the Russian government returned to its old repressive ways. In 1912, the workers at the Lena gold mines in Siberia went on strike. The government sent in troops and killed 200 strikers. The people saw that the government was no longer on their side, as it had been under Stolypin, and they decided that further change can only succeed through violent uprisings.[40] The radical Bolsheviks defeated the more moderate Mensheviks in union elections and, as a result, the number of industrial strikes rose, just as Russia was going to war with Germany and the Ottoman Empire and needed maximum production.

---

* The Socialist Revolutionaries assassinated more than four thousand government officials between 1906 and 1910. (Kort, *A Brief History of Russia* 123.)

The outbreak of World War I initially brought a wave of patriotism, especially as the Russians beat the Austro-Hungarians. But when the Germans started beating the Russians, it became clear that Russia had a weak military due to the country's inefficient economy, social problems, and incompetent government.[41] Furthermore, the Russian people did not understand why Russia was fighting when they had no quarrel with Germany or Austria-Hungary. Czar Nicholas II only made matters worse by appointing his uncle as commander-in-chief, though he was unqualified for the position. After his uncle's lack of success, the Czar named himself commander-in-chief. Though Nicholas knew little about warfare, from now on, he would be held responsible for Russia's military success or failure.[42]

The economy suffered during the war as one-third of the working age population left the fields and factories to fight in the army. Production declined sharply as a result of the smaller workforce at a time when Russia needed even more production. For example, the number of working railway engines fell by half between 1914 and 1917 due to overuse and lack of people to repair them.[43] As food and consumer staples became scarce, the government began rationing in 1916, though it did little to alleviate the suffering.[44]

In total, 650,000 Russians were killed in the war and 2.5 million were injured. Even more staggering, more than 3.5 million were missing or taken prisoner as the Russian soldiers surrendered en masse.[45] The Russian people lost confidence in the Czar and his government regarding both economic and military matters. Not only were they suffering economically and from death and injury in war, they believed the government had no idea what it was doing and no means of improving the situation. The Russian people were ready to revolt and a few radical opportunists were there to steer the revolution toward Marxist socialism.

THE BOLSHEVIK REVOLUTION

When a new wave of protests led by the women textile workers of St. Petersburg began in February 1917, Czar Nicholas II ordered his military to break the strike with a shoot-to-kill order. Even the military had lost confidence in the government and the soldiers refused to shoot into the crowd with many switching sides and joining the protest.[46] With the population protesting and the military ignoring the Czarist government, the Duma pressured Nicholas II into abdicating. The Romanov dynasty ended after more than 300 years in power and the Duma formed a new Provisional Government.

The liberal Constitutional Democrats controlled the new government and they immediately pushed for decentralized government, increased freedom of speech and assembly, unionization, amnesty for political prisoners, universal suffrage, eliminating all social, national, and religious restrictions, and election of a new constituent assembly. But the Constitutional Democrats refused to redistribute land, fearing both a decline in agricultural output during the reorganization and soldiers deserting the army to return home to claim their share of the land redistribution.[47] The lack of land redistribution was unpopular among the peasants, as was the new government's decision to continue fighting in World War I.

The Conservative Democrats who ran the new government were primarily nobles, businessmen, and professionals.[48] The peasants and working classes, therefore, felt little allegiance to the new government.[49] The real power resided not with the Provisional Government, but with the workers' councils known as soviets, which were able to instruct the workers to strike and protest.[50] At the same time, the military was loyal to the Petersburg Soviet, leaving the Provisional Government with no means of stopping strikes, protests, or violence. Therefore, the Provisional Government only ruled with permission of the soviets, especially the one in St. Petersburg. If the soviets decided that its interests were different from the government's, it could withdraw its support, declare strikes and protests, and overthrow the government.

In June 1917, the Russians began a major offensive in the war, but it resulted in a rout of Russia's army by the Germans. Russian soldiers deserted and returned home while the soldiers still in Russia mutinied. Peasants seized land, workers took control of the factories, and regional minorities declared their independence. The military defeat, mutinies, opposition from the soviets, and lack of support from the workers and peasants left the Provisional Government extremely weak and vulnerable.

Vladimir Lenin had positioned his Bolshevik Party as the leading opponent of the Provisional Government. The Mensheviks and other socialist parties were working alongside the liberals and conservatives within the government, but the Bolsheviks kept their distance and benefited from the declining conditions. In September, the Bolsheviks gained a majority in the Petersburg Soviet for the first time and then did the same in the Moscow Soviet.[51] Though the Bolsheviks were not participating in the government, they controlled the more powerful soviets. With the support of the workers and control over the soviets, the Bolsheviks had positioned themselves to take over the government. Lenin predicted in late September 1917, "We will win absolutely and unquestionably."[52]

Just a month later, the Bolsheviks staged a military coup and overthrew the government. The Bolsheviks immediately declared an end to Russian participation in the war and began negotiations for peace with Germany, even though the other Allies continued fighting. The new Bolshevik government abolished private property, allowed the peasants to seize the land of the rich and nobles for themselves, eliminated military titles, and outlawed wage inequality.

Although the Bolsheviks took power through a military coup, it was only possible because the Russian people supported the overthrow of the Provisional Government, even if they did not fully support the Bolsheviks. Many people were understandably upset when they realized the Bolsheviks would suppress their political rights. But, as Ludwig von Mises writes, "The tyranny of a minority can never endure unless it succeeds in convincing the majority of the necessity or, at any rate, of the utility, of its rule."[53] The Bolsheviks did their convincing by giving the peasants the land redistribution they always wanted. By bribing the majority, the poor were appeased, the minority silenced, and the Bolsheviks gained control of the government.

THE SOVIET ECONOMY AND TERROR

Immediately after taking power, the Bolsheviks banned all opposition press, outlawed the Constitutional Democrats, and resurrected the Russian secret police. The Bolsheviks did allow the already planned November 1917 elections for a new Constituent Assembly to take place. The Socialist Revolutionaries garnered 41 percent of the vote versus just 24 percent for the Bolsheviks,[54] though the list of delegates was drawn up before the Bolsheviks seized power and likely did not fully reflect popular opinion.[55] Regardless of which party won the election, these two socialist parties combined received 65 percent of the vote, with other smaller socialist parties adding to that total. The Russian people obviously favored socialism, only disagreeing about which type of socialism to adopt and who would administer it.

The Bolsheviks allowed the new Assembly to meet for one day in January 1918 before shutting it down. Just months later, in June 1918, the Mensheviks and Socialist Revolutionaries were expelled from the soviets. Though there was little difference between the Socialist Revolutionaries, Mensheviks, and Bolsheviks, the Bolsheviks were not interested in sharing power, even with other like-minded socialists. The Bolsheviks had created a single party dictatorship.

Many members of the Socialist Revolutionaries, Mensheviks, Conservative Democrats, and other parties, known collectively as the Whites, began a civil war against the Bolsheviks, also known as the Reds. It is ironic that so many socialists who had tried to overthrow the aristocratic government of the Czar were now trying to overthrow a socialist government. The Whites were not unified and included factions from both ends of the political spectrum. Despite having more support than the Bolsheviks, the Whites' lack of cohesion gave the Reds a huge advantage.[56]

To help fight the civil war against the Whites, the Bolsheviks nationalized all industry, banned private trade, used forced labor for construction projects, took over the banks, and started inflating the money supply. By consolidating control of the economy, the Bolsheviks were able to direct production toward the food, weapons, and transportation they needed to defeat their enemy. This was called War Communism, stressing the emergency nature of these plans, but they were also Russia's first steps toward socialism, something the Bolsheviks certainly supported, whether waging war or not.[57]

Production, which had fallen sharply during the revolution, continued to fall under the new socialist regime. Industrial production fell 87 percent between 1913 and 1920[58] while food production fell in half.[59] In 1918, just before War Communism was implemented, 28 percent of wages were paid in kind, but that rose to 94 percent in 1921,[60] because nobody trusted the Russian currency after its peg to gold was dropped during World War I. It took just three years for Russia's experiment with socialism to reverse thousands of years of economic progress and turn Russia into a barter economy.

Rather than receive worthless paper money issued by the government, peasants simply reduced their output to the bare minimum. The resulting shortage led to the death of five million people from malnutrition during the civil war years of 1918 to 1920 and another five million in 1921 and 1922, after the fighting had already ended.[61] Faced with starvation, people fled the cities and went back to the farms where they could produce enough food for themselves and their families. Moscow and St. Petersburg lost half their population,[62] a rare achievement at a time when the industrial revolution and increased farm productivity were driving people all around the world off the farms and into the cities.

With the economy failing and the people facing poverty and starvation, the Russians started revolting against the Bolsheviks. The Bolsheviks responded by terrorizing the Russian people. Lenin instructed the public to kill the rich kulaks and collectivize their lands. The kulaks were just peasants who had worked hard, saved some money, and had slightly more wealth than the other peasants,[63] likely the very people who succeeded under Stolypin's "wager on the strong plan." The Red Terror also killed hundreds of thousands of Cossaks in 1919 and 1920[64] because they were perceived as a threat to the revolution and their land was very fertile and needed to be collectivized. In defense of the terrorism, The Red Sword, a Kiev newspaper, wrote, "To us, everything is permitted, for we are the first to raise the sword not to oppress races and reduce them to slavery, but to liberate humanity."[65] Though they claimed to be the first, many societies had already killed and terrorized to "liberate humanity." Unfortunately, more would do so in the future.

The revolt against the Bolsheviks and their failed policies hit its peak when, in March 1921, Russian sailors in Kronstadt, an island in the Gulf of Finland near St. Petersburg, rose up and demanded new elections for the soviets. In response, the Bolshevik government sent the army to attack Kronstadt, where they defeated the protestors and executed hundreds, if not thousands, without trials.[66]

Many foreign supporters of socialism were shocked by Lenin's cruelty.[67] But the brutality and immorality of this action should not have been surprising. The Red Sword already explained eighteen months earlier that "everything is permitted." In *The Road to Serfdom*, Friedrich Hayek explains how collectivism can act so brutally:

> "Where there is one common all-overriding end there is no room for any general morals or rules... Where a few specific ends dominate the whole of society, it is inevitable that occasionally cruelty may become a duty, that acts which revolt all our feeling, such as the shooting of hostages or the killing of the old or sick, should be treated as mere matters of expediency, that the compulsory uprooting and transportation of hundreds of thousands should become an instrument of policy approved by almost everybody except the victims, or that suggestions like that of a "conscription of woman for breeding purposes" can be seriously contemplated. There is always in the eyes of the collectivist a greater goal which these acts serve and which to him justifies them because the pursuit of the common end of society can know no limits in any rights or values of any individual."[68]

With the Whites defeated and all possible external opposition eliminated, Lenin's next step was to clean up his Communist Party.

The Bolsheviks rid themselves of internal dissent by banning all opposing factions and expelling those who did not subscribe to the party line, totaling about a third of the party members.[69]

Lenin was a brutal dictator, but he was also practical. He realized that War Communism was an economic failure and was prepared to make concessions. Lenin knew that the economy had to recover for him to maintain power, and it could not do so through the use of force.[70] With all opposition destroyed, Lenin could execute a "strategic retreat"[71] with no political risk.

The centerpiece of Lenin's "strategic retreat" was the New Economic Policy. The seizures of food by the government were replaced by taxes and the farmers were free to sell their produce on the open market, giving them an incentive to increase production. The new policy also allowed small businesses to operate privately, though the government maintained control of large businesses. Though Lenin and the Bolsheviks were forced to inject a certain amount of capitalism back into the economy, the economy remained mostly socialist. It is ironic, though, that Lenin used the free market to save Russia from the disaster of the country's first experiment with socialism.

As a result of the New Economic Policy, agricultural and industrial production rose along with wages, and the people's standard of living returned to their pre-war levels.[72] Russia was still far behind the rest of the industrialized world, but it had recovered from the depths of its despair under War Communism.

This limited return to capitalism was a mixed blessing for the Bolsheviks. While the economy improved under the New Economic Policy and the Bolsheviks were able to maintain power, it was because of the success of capitalism that conditions had improved. The socialist sectors of the economy, though, lagged behind.[73] Furthermore, the capitalist class was growing while the socialist class was shrinking.[74]

Just as the Russian economy was turning around, Lenin suffered a series of strokes in 1922 and 1923 that forced him to withdraw from politics. Taking account of his revolution, Lenin looked at the government he created. He noticed that many government officials were corrupt and used their positions to gain wealth and power. In fact, the communist officials acted just like those who worked for the Czar.[75] During the short history of the Soviet Union, government officials lived a life of luxury while the people lived in poverty. But this should not have been surprising because Aristotle wrote about this over two thousand years earlier: "As of oligarchy so of tyranny, the end is wealth; (for by wealth only can the tyrant maintain either his guard or his luxury)."[76] Lenin and his cronies used the wealth of Russia to raise an army, to put down revolts, and murder their enemies. Lenin also discovered that the wealth of Russia was being used to enrich the bureaucrats who so successfully administered his reign of terror.

With Lenin's absence from active politics, the leading Bolsheviks positioned themselves to take over control of the Communist Party and the Soviet Union. As general secretary of the Communist Party, Joseph Stalin was in charge of appointing party officials and, therefore, a very important bureaucrat. Stalin formed a triumvirate with G.E. Zinoviev and L.B. Kamenev, two other influential party members, to counter Leon Trotsky, who was probably the leading contender to replace Lenin. Once Trotsky was undermined by the trio, Stalin turned on his two accomplices and gained control of the party and the country.

Upon gaining power, Stalin launched his "revolution from above." He sought to abolish all private property, nationalize all industry and business, and turn the entire population into state employees. More important, Stalin wanted Russia to industrialize quickly. According to Stalin's Five Year Plan of 1928, industrial production was to rise 236 percent, including a doubling of coal output, tripling of iron production, and quadrupling of electrical output.[77] In setting these lofty goals, Stalin's motto was, "We are bound by no laws. There are no fortresses which Bolsheviks cannot storm."[78]

The rush to grow the Russian economy resulted in much waste. For example, the Soviet Union built a canal between the Baltic and White Sea that was too small to accommodate large ships.[79] More generally, Russia lacked the skilled workers needed to build and work in the factories and much machinery was damaged by incorrect usage.[80]

Despite all the waste, many of the lofty goals were met and, by the beginning of World War II, the Soviet Union had become the second largest industrial producer, behind the United States.[81] However, the increased industrial and military output was at the expense of consumer goods and agricultural production. While the Soviet Union could produce more industrial goods than nearly any other country, the Russian people were still very poor and their standard of living declined during the Five Year Plan.[82]

Stalin also decided to collectivize the farms, beginning in December 1929, believing it would increase production and free up resources for the industrialization. But the peasants were very much attached to their land and opposed Stalin's plan. Instead of giving up their land, grain, and equipment, the peasants often set their fields and buildings on fire and destroyed their equipment. Stalin sent in the army and secret police to remove about two million people.[83] Two-thirds of the peasants were forced onto collective farms within two years and ninety percent by 1936.[84]

Farm production declined as a result of the collectivization and removal of incentives. The resulting famine killed seven million people in 1932 and 1933.[85] Even more would have died if not for the small private plots of land the government allowed each peasant, where he grew fruits and vegetables or raised livestock for his own consumption.[86] Life for the average Russian was miserable. Food and other consumer staples were extremely hard to obtain and people lived in very cramped quarters. Crime was high, transportation was poor, and utilities such as electricity, sewage, and water were sub-standard.[87] Stalin and his cronies, though, did not share in the people's suffering. In fact, Stalin and other leading Communists lived in houses that had belonged to Russia's wealthiest families before the revolution.[88]

Amazingly, at a time of rapid industrialization and improved agricultural productivity nearly everywhere else in the world, grain production when Stalin died in 1953 was below that of 1913.[89] Stalin's reorganization of the agricultural industry could not match the success that Russia enjoyed under Stolypin's reforms, just before the revolution began.

But Stalin did not go down in history for his economic failure. He is best remembered for his tyrannical rule. Under his 24-year reign, the Soviet government directly killed ten to twenty million Soviet citizens and terrorized tens of millions more,[90] in addition to the tens of millions more who died from the famines and malnutrition caused by socialism.

Stalin's agricultural reorganization, which was meant to help the poor, resulted in social and economic reversals. The wealthy farmers, known as kulaks, were deemed enemies of the revolution and were stripped of their possessions and many were also sent to labor camps. Stalin also restricted the movements of the peasants, requiring them to have passports to leave their areas of habitation. Thus the peasants were treated just like the serfs who were tied to their landlord's land prior to the Great Reforms of 1861. All the rights and liberties the Russian people were granted under the Czars and Stolypin had disappeared. The Russians under socialism were worse off than they were under the Czars.

Conditions became even worse for the Russian people in 1934, after Sergei Kirov, the head of the Communist Party in Leningrad and possible successor to Stalin, was assassinated. Stalin began a wave of terror against the Russian people and against possible opponents within his own party. Both Zinoviev and Kamenev, Stalin's former partners, were expelled from the party, along with 800,000 others.[91] They were later tried and executed after confessing to plotting with Trotsky to kill Stalin and other leading Soviet officials. Trotsky, Stalin's major competitor for power, had already been deported in 1929 and was assassinated in Mexico in 1940. Trotsky's last words: "Stalin has finally accomplished the task he attempted unsuccessfully before."[92] In all, about one-half of army officers and seventy percent of the Central Committee were arrested.[93] Stalin thus eliminated all opposition to communism and to himself. Additionally, an estimated 900,000 innocent civilians were shot and another three million were sent to labor camps, where many of them died.[94] In total, up to 24 million people were forced into work camps know as Gulags or special settlements by the time of Stalin's death in 1953.[95] In fact, the security force administering the Gulags was the Soviet Union's largest employer.[96]

The Gulags were a giant waste of resources. They killed millions of people, who could have been productive members of society. Furthermore, the forced labor often went to build those wasteful projects, such as the White Sea Canal that was too small or railroads that went nowhere.[97] Furthermore, the slave labor they employed was very inefficient. One hundred years earlier, writing about the United States, Alexis de Tocqueville wrote about how free men were more productive than slaves. Tocqueville commented about how in Kentucky, "the population is sparse...the primeval forest grows back again everywhere; society seems to be asleep; man looks idle while nature looks active and alive."[98] In Ohio, "by contrast, a confused hum announces from a long way off the presence of industrial activity; the fields are covered by abundant harvests; elegant dwellings proclaim the taste and industry of the workers; in every direction there is the evidence of comfort; men appear wealthy and content; they are at work."[99] According to Tocqueville, "The two states differ in only one respect: Kentucky has accepted slaves but Ohio has rejected them from its lands."[100] Free people were simply more productive than slaves and, likewise, the Soviet Union's use of slave labor from the Gulag was grossly unproductive and a giant waste of resources, in addition to being a tremendous crime against humanity.

Hitler betrayed Stalin in 1941 by breaking the Treaty of Non-Aggression between the two countries. To win the support of the people and increase production for the war effort, Stalin granted the people more liberty, including more freedom to farm and sell their produce on the open market.[101] Nevertheless, the terror continued. The Gulags continued to operate at full capacity. One hundred fifty thousand Soviet soldiers were executed by their own military during World War II, compared to the United States executing just 125 of its own during the war.[102] The Soviet Union used Russian prisoners for suicide missions and to clear minefields by simply marching them through.[103] Even during this time of unity against a common enemy and relaxation of previous restrictions, the Communist government treated its own people with utter brutality.

When the war ended, the people had hoped Stalin would relax the government controls even further in recognition of the people's heroism and sacrifices.[104] Instead, Stalin did the exact opposite. He ordered all private land that was tolerated during wartime back into the collectives. Stalin exiled or killed intellectuals, artists, and musicians, banned jazz, and murdered Jewish leaders. Russians returning from foreign assignments or as prisoners of war were interrogated and often sent to the Gulag because Stalin feared they may have changed their minds about communism while overseas. Minority groups that may have given support to the Germans were also shipped off to the Gulags. Gulag labor hit its peak between 1950 and 1952.[105]

From the moment he took power and initiated the Red Terror until his final years as leader of the Soviet Union, Joseph Stalin terrorized the very Russian people he claimed to be working for. Lenin did much the same, but at least he recognized when his War Communism failed, admitted his error, and introduced a measure of capitalism back into Russian society. In contrast, when Stalin saw circumstances move against him, he placed further restrictions on the people and expelled or murdered his enemies. The main difference between Lenin and Stalin, besides the extent of Russia's suffering being much worse under Stalin, is that Lenin fought for what he believed in and listened to his people's suffering, whereas Stalin did not seem to care about his people and made conditions worse for them if they complained. Yet, it was Lenin who enabled Stalin's tyranny. It was Lenin who eliminated all competing political parties and it was Lenin who took over control of the entire economy. Stalin then used Lenin's foundation to terrorize the Russian people.

SUPPORTING INTERNATIONAL COMMUNISM

Terrorizing the Russian people was not enough for the Soviets. They were also determined to export communism and totalitarianism, spreading their own form of tyranny around the world. *The Commu-*

nist Manifesto by Marx and Engels ends with the call, "Workers of the world, Unite!" and the Soviet Union used it as their motto. Additionally, the coat of arms of the Soviet Union included a hammer and sickle that covered the visible side of a globe. The Soviet Union believed that it should help spread communism to the entire world and that "everything is permitted...to liberate humanity."[106]

The Soviet Union had other, more practical reasons to export communism around the world. After being attacked by Germany in World War II, Russia wanted to create a buffer to protect itself against future attacks. Furthermore, the Soviet Union, as the lone communist country prior to World War II, needed political and diplomatic support, especially within the newly created United Nations. The Soviet Union also wanted a league of communist countries spread across the world to help them in their defense against the United States and NATO.

Even as far back as 1920, the Russians attempted to spread its revolution. The Bolsheviks sent the Red Army into Poland in 1920, but the Poles drove them back. World War II provided the Soviet Union with an opportunity to create a buffer zone, export communism, and expand their territory. Between 1939 and 1942, Nazi Germany conquered Eastern Europe up to Leningrad, Moscow, and Stalingrad. But by 1945, the Germans had been pushed all the way back to Berlin. The Soviet Union suddenly found itself with Eastern Europe under its control and it established puppet communist regimes in Poland, Hungary, Czechoslovakia, Romania, Bulgaria, Albania, and East Germany. The communists rigged elections in Poland,[107] even though Stalin had promised at the Yalta Conference to allow free elections. The Russians saw these "republics" not as individual countries, but as part of the Soviet Union itself. Foreign Minister Vyacheslav Molotov said, "My task as minister of foreign affairs was to expand the borders of the fatherland as much as possible. And it seems that Stalin and I coped with this task quite well."[108]

But the Soviet satellites did not always cooperate and the Soviets ruthlessly blocked any moves toward democratic capitalism. In Hungary, the people overthrew the Soviet backed communist government in 1956. The Soviet Union sent in an army of 200,000 troops and 2,500 tanks, killed 27,000 Hungarians, and restored communist rule.[109] Two hundred thousand Hungarians managed to escape to the West before the communists closed the borders again.[110] Similarly, in response to a weak economy and discrimination against the Slovaks,[111] the people overthrew the communist government in Czechoslovakia in 1968 and began a series of reforms. Learning from the Soviet invasion of Hungary, the new Czech leadership tried to work within the system and not anger the Soviet Union. The reforms they instituted were called "socialism with a human face."[112] Nevertheless, the Soviet Union was not pleased with Czechoslovakia's move away from socialism and half a million soldiers and 6,000 tanks from the Warsaw Pact nations invaded Czechoslovakia,[113] occupied the capital, and restored pro-Soviet rule. Dozens were killed and hundreds wounded.[114] Soviet Premier Leonid Brezhnev defended the invasion, arguing that the Soviet Union had the right to intervene in any country that tried to replace socialism with capitalism.[115]

While the Eastern European satellites were the centerpiece of its fight against democratic capitalism, the Soviet Union also sought to create communist regimes and allies throughout the world. On August 9, 1945, the Soviet Union agreed to help fight the Japanese. On August 10, the Soviets occupied the northern portion of Korea down to the 38th parallel. The United States had already dropped the first atomic bomb on Hiroshima on August 6th and the second on Nagasaki on the 9th, making a U.S. victory inevitable. The Soviets were simply taking advantage of the situation to gain new territory. Even though U.S. President Franklin Roosevelt, British Prime Minster Winston Churchill, and Chiang Kai-shek, leader of the Republic of China, agreed at the Cairo Conference of 1943 to create a "free and independent" Korea, none of the three leaders were in power at the time the Japanese surrendered.* Stalin was not a party to the agreement and seized

---

* U.S. President Franklin Roosevelt died in office in April 1945. British Prime Minster Winston Churchill's Conservative Party was voted out of office in July 1945. Chiang Kai-shek was leading the Chinese Nationalists in a civil war against Mao Zedong's communist People's Liberation Army.

the opportunity, invading Korea at the last minute and bargaining for half the country. With the support of the communists in the Soviet Union and China, North Korea would go on to invade South Korea, hold their own against the United States military in the Korean War, and establish a ruthless regime that has most likely killed over a million of its own people in hard labor and concentration camps.[116] Additionally, socialism in North Korea has led to the death of millions due to starvation.[117]

Over in China, Stalin helped Mao Zedong and his Communist Party defeat the rival Nationalists and take control of the country.[118] Chairman Mao and the Communists set about changing the country, starting with a land redistribution plan in 1958, called the Great Leap Forward, and the elimination of all political opposition, called the Cultural Revolution, in 1966. To convert China into their utopia, the Communists borrowed Stalin's brutality, taking it to a whole new level, killing about 35 million fellow Chinese between 1949 and 1987.[119] According to the Chinese Minister of Public Security, the murdered included "landlords, rich peasants, counterrevolutionaries, bad elements, and rightists and their children, including babies."[120] Furthermore, Chairman Mao's Great Leap Forward, which created agricultural communes out of land taken from the peasants and shifted resources toward industry, resulted in a famine that killed about 27 million people.[121] In total, more than 60 million Chinese likely died as a direct result of their experiment with communism.

The Cold War between the United States and the Soviet Union reached its hottest point during the Cuban Missile Crisis of 1962. Though Castro seized power without any help from the Soviet Union, the two communist countries quickly became allies as the United States embargoed Cuba and, even more so, after the U.S.'s failed Bay of Pigs invasion of Cuba. In a very risky move, Soviet Premier Nikita Khrushchev secretly placed medium-range ballistic missiles in Cuba in 1962. United States spy planes discovered the missiles and, for thirteen days, the Cold War looked as if it might heat up. But the crisis ended when the Soviets agreed to remove the missiles and the U.S. promised not to invade Cuba. The U.S. was clearly the winner and Nikita Khrushchev fell from power just a couple of years later, partly due to the Soviet Union's humiliating defeat at the negotiating table.[122] Only years later did it become known that U.S. Attorney General Robert Kennedy told Soviet ambassador Anatoly Dobrynin that the U.S. would remove its Jupiter missiles from Turkey and Italy as part of the deal, something President John F. Kennedy had wanted to do before but could not because it was a NATO decision to place them there.[123] Because the removal of the missiles from Turkey and Italy was kept a secret, it looked like Nikita Khrushchev received nothing for withdrawing Soviet missiles from Cuba. Just as John F. Kennedy knew the power of the media and appearances when he ran for President in 1960, he knew that winning the propaganda war was more important than winning a military victory. Nevertheless, Fidel Castro remained dictator of Cuba and killed thousands of Cubans while tens of thousands more died at sea trying to reach the United States.[124]

In 1978, the communist People's Democratic Party staged a military coup and took over Afghanistan, but faced rebellion from the Islamic mujahideen backed by Pakistan. The new communist government requested help from the Soviet Union, which gave them weapons and sent in tens of thousands of troops, eventually rising to a peak of 115,000 men by the end of 1984.[125] At the same time, the United States, Great Britain, and Muslim countries gave money, weapons, and military training to the mujahideen. After nine years of battle and up to 25,000 Soviet dead,[126] the Soviets withdrew their troops. Three years later, the communist regime fell, but then the mujahideen fought among themselves until the Taliban finally captured Kabul and created a lasting government in 1996. In total, the war between the U.S., British, and Muslim supported mujahideen and the Afghani communists with Soviet support killed about 1.5 million Afghans, out of a population of just 16.4 million.[127] An additional 3 million Afghans were injured and 4 million fled to Pakistan.[128] Some place the blame on the United States and its allies for all the death and turmoil in Afghanistan. In reality though, the United States was defending Afghanistan's right to self-determination, whereas the Soviet Union was promoting communism.

These are just a few of the more obvious examples of the Soviet Union's attempts to spread communism around the world. In most cases though, the Soviets used hidden methods of supporting foreign communism, such as monetary support, selling or giving weapons, providing military training, extending favorable trade relationships, and subverting fragile governments in free countries. The Vietnam War is the most prominent case of Soviet support of communism without playing an official role. The Soviet Union provided the North Vietnamese with medical supplies, military training, and weapons to fight the South Vietnamese and the United States.[129] Though their direct involvement was kept secret at the time, it was later acknowledged that they had three thousand troops stationed in Vietnam during the war.[130] This supplying of weapons, training, and money was conducted around the world throughout the Cold War. The U.S., of course, also provided support to some of its allies, but such support was usually defensive. For example, the U.S. helped defend Japan, which was banned from possessing a military by its constitution after World War II. The U.S. also helped rebuild the infrastructure of many countries, including Western Europe by means of the Marshall Plan. Furthermore, such support was normally done in public, whereas the Soviet Union provided support in secret, hiding it from both its enemies and its own people.

THE FALL OF COMMUNISM

The United States defeated the Soviet Union in the 1980s without any large-scale military conflict. The Soviet Union lost a war of economics and ideas as capitalism and liberty bankrupted socialism and totalitarianism. The Soviet Union tried to keep up with the United States in military spending, but struggled to do so as its economy fell too far behind. As a result, the Soviet Union allocated a quarter of its economic output to the military, which was five times greater than what the U.S. had been spending on its military.[131] Thus, the Soviets produced less for consumer needs and had less capital available to increase production. The people living under communist rule were falling further behind the West and they knew it.

After World War II, the Iron Curtain was built between Eastern and Western Europe. This border fence was not built to keep enemies out, but to keep people in the prison of communism. The people in the Soviet Union, Eastern Europe, North Korea, Cuba, Afghanistan, China, and everywhere else there was socialism were desperate to escape and enjoy the wealth and freedom of the West.

Eventually, the Communists in the Soviet Union recognized the obvious: their economy was trailing behind the United States and this made it impossible for the Soviets to maintain the military balance between the two superpowers. In 1985, the Communist Party selected Mikhail Gorbachev to lead the Soviet Union. Gorbachev was in favor of economic restructuring, known as perestroika in Russian. He also favored restructuring other aspects of the Soviet Union. Glasnost reduced censorship and increased freedom of speech and the press. Demokratizatsiya called for more choices in elections. Though the Communists would still rule, the people would be allowed to choose which Communists would lead. Last, novoe myshlenie, new thinking, would open the Soviet Union to more interaction with foreign countries, including capitalist democracies.

A year after Mikhail Gorbachev took office, the Chernobyl nuclear power plant exploded. The news was first reported by the Western press as the Soviets tried to cover it up.[132] The Soviet Union even kept the news a secret from locals who should have been evacuated to avoid the deadly radiation. The explosion led the Soviets to question the quality of their infrastructure as they spent an overly large per-centage of their resources on the military. Foreign Minister Eduard Shevardnadze said the Chernobyl disaster "tore the blindfold from our eyes."[133] The Soviet Union could no longer ignore the country's disrepair, economic underperformance, and lack of freedom, each of which contributed to the disaster and its aftermath.

Gorbachev's reforms were meant to be limited, but once the people experienced increased freedom of speech and press, more choice in elections, and were able to travel more freely to foreign countries and purchase foreign goods, they demanded even more liberty. For most Russians, this was the first time they had tasted real freedom and choice and they preferred it over the Soviet Union's closed society, repressive government, and the long lines to purchase simple consumer staples. Gorbachev opened the door to freedom and 300 million Soviet citizens were all clamoring to get through at the same time.

After living under communism for so many years, it was difficult to imagine something different, especially for bureaucrats like Mikhail Gorbachev. Even Gorbachev, who realized the Soviet economy was far behind the West and was leading the reform movement, did not consider abandoning socialism. Gorbachev and the other Communists thought the system could be reformed into an improved socialism, without realizing that it was socialism itself that caused the Soviet Union to fall so far behind.

With the Soviet Union struggling at home, it could no longer financially and militarily support communism around the world. In 1988, Mikhail Gorbachev addressed the United Nations in New York and announced plans to reduce the size of its military and withdraw troops from Eastern Europe.[134] The Soviet Union was loosening its grip on its satellite states and, after years of living under the Soviet Union's repressive rule and with weak economies,[135] the Eastern European countries decided it was time to grab their freedom and independence. Starting in 1989, each Eastern European government was forced by their people to adopt democratic and capitalist reforms. All of Eastern Europe, except for one country, peacefully transitioned to democratic capitalism. Only in Romania, did the people overthrow and execute its leader, President Nicolae Ceausescu, after he refused to reform the communist government.

In June 1991, the Russian Republic, the largest part of the Soviet Union, held its first popular election in its 1,100 year history.[136] The

Russian people chose Boris Yeltsin as their president. Yeltsin had been kicked out of the Communist Party in 1987 for arguing against the slow pace of reforms. Therefore, Yeltsin was considered a true reformer and held blameless for the recent economic decline. When the Soviet Union fell apart in the latter half of 1991, Boris Yeltsin became President of the Russian Federation, which was the successor to the Russian Republic and recipient of the Soviet Union's important seat in the United Nations. In June 1992, Boris Yeltsin told the United States Congress, "The world can sigh in relief. The idol of communism, which spread everywhere social strife, animosity and unparalleled brutality, which instilled fear in humanity, has collapsed."[137]

While those living under communism certainly desired liberty and representative government, they also wanted the consumer products that the West had enjoyed for years. They envied the West's wealth and abundance. Socialism had promised them wealth and equality, but delivered only equality of suffering. Not that students of history were surprised. Alexis de Tocqueville said in 1848, "Democracy and socialism have nothing in common but one word, equality. But notice the difference: while democracy seeks equality in liberty, socialism seeks equality in restraint and servitude."[138] Winston Churchill expressed a similar sentiment in 1945, at the height of the Soviet Union's power and when socialism seemed most promising, when he said, "The inherent vice of capitalism is the unequal sharing of blessings. The inherent virtue of socialism is the equal sharing of miseries."[139]

In 1988, just prior to the collapse of communism, per capita economic production in the Soviet Union, as defined by Gross Domestic Product (GDP), was just one-quarter of that of the United States. Similarly, per capita GDP in Eastern Europe was one-quarter of Western Europe's.[140] Perhaps the best comparison would be between East and West Germany. Except for the prior forty years, the people in these two countries had the same history, culture, and beliefs. The only thing that divided them was an imaginary line that became a real one as East Germany erected a wall to keep its citizens from fleeing to

West Germany. Yet, capitalist West Germany flourished while communist East Germany failed. In 1991, communist East Germany had per capita GDP that was just 31 percent of West Germany's.[141] Clearly, capitalism was outperforming communism. Those living under communism heard about these discrepancies and wanted the freedom and wealth of the West.

The former communist countries had a bumpy transition to capitalism. Per capita GDP dropped an astounding 74 percent in Russia and 57 percent in Eastern Europe between 1988 and 1999. At the same time, Western Europe saw its per capita GDP rise 46 percent while it rose 62 percent in the U.S.[142] Clearly, the turmoil caused by communism's collapse wreaked havoc on the average Russian and Eastern European. But those countries experienced a remarkable recovery as they developed their market systems and many established themselves as low tax nations. Between 1999 and 2007, per capita GDP grew 584 percent in Russia and 339 percent in Eastern Europe, compared to growth of just 62 percent in Western Europe and 38 percent in the United States.[143] Despite the initial chaos and economic collapse, the former communist countries are catching up to the West. Nevertheless, they still have a way to go as Russia's per capita GDP is now just 20 percent of the United States' and Eastern Europe's is just 20 percent of Western Europe's.[144] Clearly, the former communist countries have not yet approached the economic success of Western Europe or the United States, but their economies are now growing faster than those of the West.

Even with the mixed results in Russia and Eastern Europe, the situation there is certainly preferable to the economic disaster of the Soviet Union and the millions of people it killed in foreign wars and at home as it forced communism upon the Russians and neighboring nations. Furthermore, the formerly communist countries no longer suffer from mass starvation, though communist North Korea still does. Additionally, in 1989, about a quarter of the Soviet Union's GDP went to military spending. Today, Russia spends just 4 percent of GDP on the military, leaving much more money for consumer goods.[145]

Throughout the history of the Soviet Union, the government directed the economy toward heavy industry and military spending, ignoring consumers. Now, Russians and Eastern Europeans have become consumers and savers like the rest of the free world. Thus, the GDP statistics tell only part of the story. It may take decades to catch up to the West, if the former communist countries ever do, but the Russians and Eastern Europeans are already enjoying their freedom and improved standards of living.

THE REBIRTH OF SOCIALISM

Even after the fall of the Soviet Union and its Eastern European satellites, many people continue to believe the promises of socialism. Friedrich Hayek was correct when he wrote in 1956, "Though hot socialism is probably a thing of the past, some of its conceptions have penetrated far too deeply in the whole structure of current thought to justify complacency."[146] Today, ideologues use these utopian beliefs to reshape society, while demagogues use the socialist promises of wealth and equality to gain power for themselves. The rise of Hugo Chavez in Venezuela is perhaps the best example of the continued belief in socialism.

Even prior to his election in 1998, Hugo Chavez lusted for power. Chavez attempted a military coup against President Carlos Andres Perez in 1992. When his coup failed, Chavez called for his followers to lay down their arms, but added "for the moment" to his admission that "the objectives that we had set for ourselves have not been achieved."[147] Chavez was imprisoned, but President Perez was replaced by Rafael Caldera and Chavez was pardoned after just two years in prison. While in prison, Chavez remained determined to become president[148] and, upon gaining his freedom, he formed a socialist political party, the Fifth Republic Movement, with a plan to use the political process, instead of military coups, in his quest for power.

Hugo Chavez promised to bring a new form of socialism to Venezuela based on the progressive ideals of Simon Bolivar, which included democracy, independence, land reform, and universal education.[149] Chavez adopted this new Bolivarianism because socialism in Russia had failed so badly and would be difficult to sell to the people. Chavez noted in 2005:

> "We have to re-invent socialism. It can't be the kind of socialism that we saw in the Soviet Union, but it will emerge as we develop new systems that are built on co-operation, not competition... It is impossible, within the framework of the capitalist system to solve the grave problems of poverty of the majority of the world's population. We must transcend capitalism. But we cannot re-sort to state capitalism, which would be the same perversion of the Soviet Union. We must reclaim social-ism as a thesis, a project and a path, but a new type of so-cialism, a humanist one, which puts humans and not machines or the state ahead of everything."[150]

Nevertheless, this reinvented socialism is fundamentally the same as all other forms of socialism, with the prohibition of private property as its ultimate goal. Hugo Chavez said in March 2009, "The land is not private, it's social property. If you put up a fence, or farm it, or have some barns, well these things are private, but the land belongs to nobody in particular, it's everybody's."[151]

Hugo Chavez combined his socialist agenda with calls of national-ism. For the 1998 election, Chavez positioned his party as the "patri-otic pole," labeled the old political parties as the "pole of national destruction," claimed Venezuela's new fifth republic would have "a national and popular character," and spoke often about the "national community" and the "fatherland."[152] More recently, at his 2007 inauguration, Chavez declared, "Toward victory always! Fatherland, socialism or death! We shall prevail!"[153] Speaking about socialism, he added, "I don't have the slightest doubt that is the only path to the redemption of our peoples, the salvation of our fatherland."[154] Chavez even adds a religious foundation to his socialism. At his 2007 inauguration, Chavez commented, "I swear by Christ — the greatest socialist in history."[155] In a 2005 interview, Chavez claimed, "I am a socialist and I follow the teachings of Jesus Christ, who was the first socialist, just as Judas was the first capitalist."[156]

Chavez's calls for socialism and nationalism, along with his evangelical eloquence,[157] enabled him to take power in Venezuela quite easily. In December, 1998, just four and a half years after leaving prison, the Venezuelan people elected Hugo Chavez president with 56.2 percent of the vote. He subsequently won reelection in 2000 with 59.8 percent of the vote and again in 2006 with 62.8 percent. Both Chavez and his agenda are hugely popular in Venezuela. Three weeks prior to the 2006 election, an Associated Press-Ipsos poll found that 62 percent of Venezuelans supported further nationalization of private companies.[158] Hugo Chavez and socialism are equally popular in Venezuela, with one reinforcing the other.

Hugo Chavez pushed for a new constitution during his campaign for president in 1998. In 1999, with 71.8 percent of the vote, Venezuela adopted a new constitution that extended the president's term from five to six years but limited the president to two terms. It also expanded the powers of the president and converted the bicameral legislature to a single body, thus reducing the checks and balances in the government. The new constitution had given President Hugo Chavez more power than his predecessors. After his 2006 reelection, Chavez called for yet more constitutional reforms that would have centralized even more power within the government and the presidency. These changes were defeated with 51 percent voting against it. At his 2007 inauguration, Chavez started calling for the end of the term limit rule that was established in 1999 and would bar him from running again. In February 2009, 54.3 percent voted to eliminate term limits for the president. These constant changes to the constitution have given Hugo Chavez and the government immense power over the economy and people of Venezuela.

As promised, Hugo Chavez has used the presidency to promote socialism. Chavez used windfall profits from rising oil prices to nationalize large portions of the economy, including the oil, power, telecommunications, steel, and cement industries. Chavez has instituted price controls on hundreds of food items and imposed production quotas on corporations to keep supply up despite the price caps. Chavez has also confiscated land from large farms and given it to smaller farmers.[159] In his ten years as president, Chavez has confiscated over six million acres of private farmland.[160] As a result, Venezuela has experienced food shortages. In 2006, Venezuela experienced a severe food shortage and even coffee, a staple crop in the area, was hard to obtain as the government capped prices and farmers refused to produce and sell it at a loss.[161] The government intervention has also created shortages in products such as milk and chicken.[162] According to the Association of Venezuelan Cattlemen, Venezuelan agricultural production now meets only 30 percent of the country's needs, down from 70 percent.[163]

Venezuela has also experienced water shortages because of its socialist policies. Shortly after taking office, Chavez took over five water companies. In 2003, he set prices 20 percent below the cost of delivering the water to consumers.[164] Caracas residents now live without water for up to 48 hours per week.[165] To alleviate the problem, Hugo Chavez is calling for three-minute showers, announcing on television, "Some people sing in the shower, in the shower half an hour. No, kids. Three minutes is more than enough. I've counted, three minutes and I don't stink."[166] In typical socialist fashion, Chavez blamed the rich capitalists. "What will the rich fill their swimming pools with? With the water that is denied inhabitants in the poor neighborhoods."[167] Chavez also nationalized an electricity company in 2007 and Venezuela suffered at least five major blackouts in 2009.[168]

Oil is the lifeblood of the Venezuelan economy, yet Chavez has mismanaged this vital industry, as well. Oil comprises one-third of GDP, half of government revenue, and 80 percent of exports.[169] Yet, oil production has declined 26 percent, according to the International Energy Agency, since Chavez took office,[170] because he failed to reinvest in the Venezuelan oil industry. Furthermore, foreign oil companies left Venezuela after PDVSA, the state-owned petroleum company, seized approximately sixty oil service companies and Venezuela imposed an 85 percent windfall tax.[171]

Just as the Soviet Union created a league of communist countries, Hugo Chavez is trying to create an alliance of far left countries. Chavez makes friends with tyrants and turns allies into enemies. Chavez denounces the United States and its allies, but praises modern day tyrants President Mugabe of Zimbabwe and Fidel Castro of Cuba. He has established close ties with Cuba, Bolivia, Ecuador, and Nicaragua, calling the group the "axis of good," while labeling the United States and its allies the "axis of evil."[172]

It remains to be seen if Venezuela is turning into a tyranny, but the people have definitely lost many of their rights and the economy is in decline. The only thing that has saved Venezuela from total economic disaster, so far, is high oil prices. As of today, the Venezuelan republic is still alive and the people maintain the right to vote. The people voted for Chavez three times and he rules with the consent of the people. This demonstrates that socialism, especially when combined with nationalism and a charismatic leader, remains attractive to vast numbers of people, despite the failure of socialism in Russia and Eastern Europe.

CHAPTER SIX

FASCIST ITALY

Woodrow Wilson took the United States into World War I claiming, "The world must be made safe for democracy."[1] Instead, after the turmoil of the war and the social unrest that followed, communists and socialists on the left fought for radical social and economic change while the conservatives on the right tried to maintain their republican governments. Amid the political chaos, a new movement appeared proposing a middle path that promised to incorporate the best of capitalism and socialism. If granted control of the country, these fascists promised economic recovery, social unity, and national rebirth.

Employing violence, political assassination, and paramilitary organizations, the fascists seized power or pressured the ruling government to relinquish it to them, thus abolishing the freedom of the people in a number of countries. These fascist takeovers were not merely military coups against popular governments; they were supported by large portions of the population and overthrew governments that had already lost the favor of most of their people.

Because fascism was never defined by its creators, historians disagree regarding which characteristics make up fascism's necessary elements and the list of fascist movements and regimes vary based on these definitions. The term *fascism* comes from the word *fascio*, figuratively meaning *league* or *union*, coming from the Latin word for the bundle of rods that was carried ahead of the consuls in ancient Rome. Unlike *socialism*, *communism*, *democracy*, *republic*, and *capitalism*, whose definitions are self-explanatory, the term *fascism* leaves its true nature hidden. Therefore, historians analyze the policies and actions of Mussolini and his Fascist Party to determine the true composition of fascism.

Today, very few people claim to be fascists. Instead, the term is used to denigrate political opponents; equivalent to calling the person a tyrant or a Nazi. It is certainly praiseworthy that fascists, Nazis, and tyrants are now vilified, especially considering that, in the past, they generated much enthusiasm for their causes. Despite today's nearly universal condemnation of fascism, it is still necessary to study its causes and effects in Fascist Italy, Nazi Germany, and elsewhere, to avoid repeating the mistakes of the past.

UNIFICATION, REPUBLIC, AND WAR

After the fall of Rome in the fifth century, Italy ceased to be a united country. For one thousand four hundred years, the Italian political landscape was composed of different kingdoms, duchies, principalities, marquisates, states, republics, and territories. During this time, Italy was often the subject of inter-state battles for territory and foreign invasions. Disunited, Italy was weak compared to the stronger Spanish, French, British, and Austro-Hungarian Empires. Italy longed to be united and powerful once again.

Following Napoleon's defeat and the division of Italy into eight parts at the Congress of Vienna in 1815, the Italians began an active pursuit of unification. In 1870, King Victor Emmanuel II of Sardinia finally unified the country and became the first king of Italy. Italy adopted the constitution of Sardinia, the Statuto Albertino, which King Charles Albert I granted to his Kingdom of Sardinia in 1848. Under the Statuto Albertino, Italy would have a king, a parliament made up of a Senate appointed by the king and an elected Chamber of Deputies, and a judiciary chosen by the king.[2]

Italy's ministers were responsible to parliament, not the king, and the Prime Minister became the unofficial leader of the legislature and government by creating a majority coalition within the parliament. The political parties represented different geographic areas and, therefore, the coalition governments were based on regional similarities instead of political ideologies.[3] This system made it more difficult for a single ideological party, such as the socialists or republicans, to gain power. However, as the economic growth in the North exceeded that of the South, two distinct economic classes emerged and the regional parties became ideological.[4]

Although the Italian people had representational government under the Statuto Albertino, the vast majority of Italians were not initially given the right to vote and only the landed elite had a real say in the selection of government officials.[5] Suffrage was expanded in 1881 to small business owners and skilled workers,[6] but universal suffrage was not granted until 1912.[7] Just as in ancient Rome, rights gradually descended from the upper classes to the entire population.

The republican, socialist, and radical parties gained strength following the 1881 expansion of the election rolls.[8] Political scandals and economic depression in the 1890s led to labor unrest and the formation of the Italian Socialist Party.[9] The conservative Italian government tried repressing the protests and banning the socialist parties, but their measures failed and the government realized that they had to grant the people even more rights to stay in power.[10]

With the country unified for the first time since the end of the Roman Empire, the monarchy and upper classes wanted Italy to be an international power, as it had once been. The newly opened Suez Canal provided Italy with access to the East and the opportunity to establish a colony on Africa's east coast. In 1869, Italy conquered Assab in Eritrea. Italy further expanded its territory in 1885 when it seized Massawa in Sudan, taking advantage of a conflict between Egypt and Great Britain and the fall of Egyptian rule in Khartoum. In 1895, Italy invaded Ethiopia, but failed to conquer it, and was forced to retreat to Eritrea. In 1911, trying to remove its status as the weakest major power in Europe,[11] Italy invaded Libya and won it from the Ottoman Empire. Italy had its overseas empire, pushing it into the ranks of global powers and satisfying its desire for international respect.

In 1912, Italians acquired universal suffrage, increasing the voter rolls from 3 million to 9 million. With the availability of new voters, the socialists moved toward more radical positions and appealed to the working class' aversion toward the military and empire-building.[12] Instead of supporting the reform process that had already given them more rights, including universal suffrage and better economic conditions, the new lower-class voters believed the utopian promises of the socialists. On the other side of the political spectrum, the successful war against Libya energized the growing nationalist movement, which was gaining support from the anti-socialists. The growing economic disparity between the North and South also contributed to the creation of a bi-polar political system with a very weak center.

As World War I began in 1914, Italy was officially an ally of Germany and Austria-Hungary. Nevertheless, Italy remained neutral in the early stages of the war, claiming that the Triple Alliance was for defensive purposes only and that Austria-Hungary was the aggressor. In reality, Italy stalled to see which side was winning the war and which would offer it a better deal. The Triple Entente of Great Britain, France, and Russia knew that Italy and Austria-Hungary were traditional enemies, despite their official alliance, and that Italy, surrounded by water on three sides, must fear Britain's naval supremacy. Therefore, the Triple Entente actively sought Italy's support. In 1915, Italy signed the Treaty of London with the Entente. This opened a new front against Austria-Hungary. In exchange, Italy would receive new territory when the war was won.

The decision whether to support the war effort caused a split among the socialists. The hard-line socialists maintained their anti-militarist positions, but the revolutionary socialists wished to use the war to create a more centralized government and overturn the republican system.[13] Benito Mussolini, a socialist revolutionary, was tossed out of the Socialist Party and removed as editor of the Socialist newspaper Avanti! for supporting the war.[14] Mussolini and most of the early fascists were ex-socialists alienated from the Socialist Party over the issues of nationalism, World War I, and revolutionary tactics.[15]

In the first few months of battle against Austria-Hungary, Italy made four offensives in the mountainous terrain along the Isonzo

River. Italy gained little ground but suffered 235,000 casualties, including 54,000 killed, 160,000 wounded, and 21,000 taken prisoner.[16] For the next two years, Italy and Austria-Hungary fought along their border, with neither side gaining much of an advantage, but each losing tens of thousands of troops. When Russia exited World War I in 1917, Austria-Hungary and Germany moved their troops from the Eastern Front to the Isonzo front. Austria-Hungary finally broke through the line, routed the Italians in the Battle of Caporetto, and advanced toward Venice. The French sent six infantry divisions and the British sent five to help the beleaguered Italians. With these reinforcements, the Italians defeated the Austro-Hungarian army at the Battle of the Piave River and the Battle of Vittorio Veneto.

In many respects, despite their poor record in battle, with few victories and at least 460,000 killed in battle,[17] Italy was a big winner in the end. Italy gained new territory, thanks to help from Britain and France. Additionally, Austria-Hungary, Italy's traditional enemy, was broken up into smaller countries. However, Italy did not gain as much territory as it had hoped and Italy was largely ignored at the peace conference in Paris. The Italians viewed this as a "mutilated victory," as Italian poet, journalist, novelist, and war hero Gabriele D'Annunzio called it.

At the peace negotiations in Paris, the Italian delegation tried to improve upon the Treaty of London by claiming Fiume and Monte Nevoso. When U.S. President Woodrow Wilson sided with the Slavs instead of the Italians and claimed the Treaty of London violated his Fourteen Points, the Italian delegation left the peace conference in protest. While the delegates in Paris argued over how to divide the disputed territories, Gabriele D'Annunzio seized the disputed state of Fiume and held it for fifteen months, against the wishes of all the disputants, including his own government. Italy finally forced D'Annunzio out of Fiume when Italy and Yugoslavia signed a treaty in 1920, recognizing Fiume as a free state. Fiume returned to Italian control in 1924 after Italy and Yugoslavia signed a second treaty giving it to Italy while its eastern suburb of Susak went to Yugoslavia. Italy's behavior at the Paris Peace Conference and D'Annunzio's military actions in Fiume further damaged Italy's reputation.[18]

D'Annunzio's capture and rule of Fiume in 1919 gathered widespread support from both the right and the left, who hoped he would overthrow the parliamentary government and restore Italy to its former glory. Even though Italy ended D'Annunzio's fifteen-month occupation of Fiume in December 1920 and D'Annunzio did not accomplish what his followers had hoped, his regime in Fiume was a precursor to fascism in Italy, with the same groups that supported D'Annunzio later backing Mussolini.[19] Mussolini and his Fascist Party copied D'Annunzio's style and his attempt to meld the ideas of both the right and left.[20] D'Annunzio invented the straight-arm salute of the Fascists and the Nazis. D'Annunzio's troops wore black shirts, which Mussolini copied. D'Annunzio even created a civil religion with its own ceremonies and rituals, as Mussolini and Hitler would later do. D'Annunzio and Alceste De Ambris, a leader of revolutionary syndicalism, created a constitution guaranteeing personal liberty and tolerance, but also establishing a corporatist state to consolidate business and labor into government-regulated corporations.[21] This corporatism became the essential economic characteristic of fascism.

The economic situation in Italy after World War I was bleak. Unemployment rose as the army disbanded and soldiers returned to civilian life. At the same time, the cost of living increased substantially during the war due to disrupted international trade and the loss of capital consumed by the war effort.[22] Italy also suffered from political turmoil and growing conflict between labor and business as the number of strikes increased appreciably in 1919 and 1920, with millions of industrial and agricultural workers protesting each year.[23] The people blamed the government for the weak economy, the growing social unrest, the military weakness during the war, and the humiliation at the peace conference in Paris.[24]

The government sided with the workers and pressured employers to make concessions.[25] As a result, many centrists and conservatives abandoned the liberal coalition that was running the government.

Whereas the working people joined the Socialist parties who were helping organize the strikes, the business owners and middle class joined the right wing parties, including the Fascist Party.

In the November 1919 parliamentary election, the people voted for change. The Italian Socialist Party jumped from 52 to 156 seats, becoming the single largest party, though the liberal coalition still had a larger total share despite dropping from 400 seats to 220. The Catholic anti-socialist Italian People's Party won 100 seats, up from 28.[26] Despite being the single largest party and tripling its popularity, the Socialists were disunited as one wing of the party argued for cooperation with other parties to promote reform while the other wanted to copy Lenin's Bolshevik revolution. Therefore, the Socialists were unable to use their strength to defeat their enemies and change the political system.[27] With the growing popularity of the socialists on the left and the nationalists on the right, the coalition of republicans, liberals, conservatives, and centrists was losing power. Italy wanted change, but first had to decide whether to adopt the change of the socialists or the nationalists.

THE FASCIST AGENDA

Though the Italians blamed their government for the country's military and economic weakness, the Italian people were even more afraid of a violent Bolshevik style revolution. Fascism presented itself as the solution to the socialist revolution of the left and the political ineffectiveness of the right. Fascism promised stability, order, and effective government—everything the people wanted.[28]

The two major political beliefs of the early twentieth-century were liberalism, which supported democratic republics and free-market capitalism, and socialism, which supported a move to a collectivized economy. The fascists proposed a "third way," as they called it, that would be neither capitalist nor socialist, but instead advocated personal liberty with national goals.[29] The Fascists promised to end the threat of violent revolution by eliminating the socialists. They also

vowed to protect Italy from external threats, an important considera-
tion after the devastation of World War I, through a strong central
government and overseas expansion.[30]

The fascists believed in government control of the economy, directing it for the well-being of the entire nation, but also believed in
maintaining private property.[31] To create this mix of capitalism and
socialism, the fascists proposed a corporatist system in which the
government would organize large-scale industries into heavily
regulated syndicates or corporations, but leave small businesses and
individuals alone.[32] As a result, the fascists were neither capitalist nor
socialist. Instead, they tried to find some balance between the two
systems. In this way fascism pretended to be populist by promising the
people the best that both capitalism and socialism could offer, but the
fascists actually held the people in contempt and manipulated them to
gain power.[33]

Because the fascists most often competed with the socialists for
power, fascism is often mistakenly called a right-wing political
movement and even pro-capitalist.[34] The fascists created alliances with
the right to oppose the socialists primarily because violent socialism
was a significant threat as workers went on strike, attacked businesses,
and threatened to overthrow governments throughout Europe. The
fascists thus portrayed themselves as right-wing pro-capitalists to
gather allies and fight the socialists. The fascists even sent in strike-
breakers to stop the socialist activities, thus winning the support of
many businessmen.[35] Fascism though was not pro-capitalist. At best,
the fascists were for highly regulated capitalism and, at worst, they
were in favor of restricting the creation of new businesses, limiting the
profits of entrepreneurs, and nationalizing privately owned companies. The corporatist state relies on centralized control of the economy
to organize the different sectors into corporations and to restrict
competition from startups. This government control over the economy is closer to socialism than to free-market capitalism.

Proposing a "third way" economic system certainly would not be
enough to excite the masses of people, but economics was never the

primary attraction of fascism. In many respects, fascism stressed style more than detailed programs.[36] Both to gain support and to lead the country, the fascists believed that they needed a bold and charismatic leader, one of society's elites. Friedrich Nietzsche, the nineteenth century German philosopher, argued that, at times, an Ubermensch, or superman, would rise above ordinary men.[37] Mussolini was an admirer of Nietzsche[38] and the fascists believed that this Ubermensch should run the government and lead the nation.

With a single leader heading up their movement, the fascists created a cult around their "infallible" leader and the fascist movement became their new religion. The fascists believed that a secular religion was needed to restore morals and values to the people,[39] with the government replacing God and the party boss becoming a Messiah, leading the people to a utopian society. The fascists furthered their secular religion by creating their own iconography, including symbols, flags, uniforms, and salutes.

The fascists believed in a militarist state and operated their movement in similar martial fashion, not surprising considering that many of fascism's leaders, including both Mussolini and Hitler, were military men, not politicians or bureaucrats. The fascists even created party militias to fight their socialist opponents. However, they generally did not use their militias to stage coups. Instead, the fascists aligned themselves with the conservatives and compromised with them to gain power. Both the Fascists in Italy and the Nazis in Germany took power by working within the system, not by overthrowing it. Because of their militarist position, many unemployed veterans, who made up a large portion of the population during the recession after World War I, became a natural source of supporters for the fascist parties.[40]

Once the fascists gained power, they used this militarism in their governments as well. The fascists established governments with top-down bureaucracies headed by a single authoritarian commander while demanding unquestioned obedience from the people. A large army was a centerpiece of fascism, to be used to defend the nation, attack weaker countries, expand the borders, and display the might of the nation to its people and the world. Even domestically, the country was to act like a giant military force attacking its enemies, whether that enemy be a foreign country, capitalism, communism, or a weak economy. This unity against a common enemy, concrete or abstract, was another central characteristic of fascism. Whereas socialists try to pit the poorer classes against the richer ones, fascism's goal was always to unify the country through promises of social, cultural, and economic rebirth.[41]

Italy, recently humiliated in World War I and at the peace conference in Paris, longed to restore the glory of ancient Rome. Instead of admitting that Italy was weaker than many of its neighbors, Italians blamed the structure of government and those who administered it, believing that a better system with better management would make Italy a superpower once again. Fascism sold itself as that better system and Mussolini sold himself as the Ubermensch who would lead Italy to glory.

Most of the early Italian Fascists, including Benito Mussolini, were ex-socialists. In 1919, the Fascist Party promised political freedom and increased government control of the economy. Specifically, the Fascists promised abolition of the monarchy, establishment of a constitutional republic, extension of the right to vote to women, decentralization of the government, elimination of the non-elected Senate, disarmament, ending compulsory military service, an eight-hour workday, labor rights, a minimum wage, regulation of corporations, confiscation of war profits, unproductive capital, and church property, creation of collectivized farms for the peasants, and employee management of industry.[42] Thus, the Fascist agenda at that time was very similar to that of the socialists. However, because the Fascists had to appeal to the right for support, fascism became a mix of left-wing and right-wing ideas.[43] Mussolini believed in the welfare style economic proposals of the left but also the authoritarian nature of the right.[44] He also believed that war would enable a nationalist authoritarian party to transcend normal class divisions, appeal to the masses, and advance a working class revolution.[45] Thus, Mussolini and the Fascists offered both nationalism and partial socialism.

In an environment where the socialists promised total redistribution of wealth and the fascists promised national rebirth and greater economic equality, the liberals could only offer the people a chance to succeed if they worked hard. As long as the people were willing to fool themselves into thinking they could "depend for their livelihood on the property of others,"[46] the liberals had no chance of winning over the masses. Therefore, the real battle for the hearts and minds of Italy was between the fascists and the socialists.

THE RISE OF FASCISM

After World War I and the Bolshevik Revolution, Italy was ready for revolution. In 1919 and 1920, the socialists aggressively advanced their agenda. The socialists organized strikes, occupied factories, and committed acts of violence against management. Whereas the government could not maintain order, the Fascists fought back. Fascists would gather from the surrounding area, besiege a town, burn down the Socialist Party headquarters, and beat the socialist leaders. In the first six months of 1920, the Fascists destroyed about 300 labor chambers, cooperatives, and peasant league offices.[47] With their success against the socialists, the Fascist Party rapidly gained members, mostly students, small business owners, and young professionals who hated the socialists and their support of the peasants and laborers.[48] Additionally, the militaristic tactics of the Fascists appealed to war veterans who comprised half of the Fascist membership in November 1921.[49]

At the same time, the Fascist Party began its political campaign. The Fascists proposed an alternative to socialism: a corporatist, authoritarian, and nationalist government led by society's elites to advance the causes of the entire nation.[50] The Fascists implied that socialism only advances the interests of the poor while capitalism only advances the interests of the rich. By moving away from their socialist roots, Mussolini and the Fascists compromised on their original ideology to gather additional support. The Fascists scaled back their socialist policies by dropping their calls for collective farms, and began espousing imperialism as the Fascists became more nationalistic.[51] In their quest for power, Mussolini and the Fascists altered their political platform to attract voters.

The Fascists biggest selling point was that they were not socialists. Those in power and in business feared Bolshevik style revolution, as did most of the population. Mussolini was an adept politician and sought the support of different groups. Not surprisingly, the Fascists already had the support of the military.[52] D'Annunzio endorsed fascism in 1922, which helped Mussolini gain further support among nationalists.[53] The Fascists announced they favored supporting Catholic private schools, thus winning the support of the important Catholic Church.[54] In a speech on September 29, 1922, Mussolini assured the monarchy that it would not radically alter the economic system, a promise it had been making to those in power for some time.[55]

Now that the Fascists had the support of the monarchy, nationalists, military, Catholics, and many other anti-socialists, Mussolini gambled big and won. In October 1922, Mussolini and the Fascists marched on the major cities, including the famed March on Rome, with the goal of capturing public buildings and major railway stations. Although the Fascists were a large, highly trained, and militaristic party, they were still no match for the Italian army.[56] However, Mussolini gambled that the government would relent rather than fight a civil war.[57] When the king refused to sign a proclamation of martial law, which would have allowed the government to use troops against the Fascists, the powerless government resigned and Mussolini was named the new Prime Minister.

Because Mussolini was invited into the government and the Fascists received less than fifteen percent of the vote in 1921,[58] Mussolini led a coalition government, not a one-party majority. The people who put Mussolini in charge of the government wanted to prevent the socialists from staging a violent revolution. They wanted Mussolini to create a temporary calm in which to rebuild the political system.[59] In fact, their plan succeeded, at first, as the Fascists worked within the system for a while. But pressure from within the Fascist party and opposition from the socialists and liberals forced Mussolini to move toward a more totalitarian government.[60]

The ruling elite that handed power to the Fascists did not realize the extent of fascism's tyranny.[61] Or they believed they could stop it before it got out of control. They never suspected the Fascists would create a totalitarian regime. Italy got its first taste of fascism's tyranny in 1923, when the Fascist coalition passed the Acerbo Law, which gave two-thirds of the seats in parliament to the party or coalition that received 25 percent of the vote. Because the Fascists were virtually assured of winning a quarter of the vote, with no other party likely to come close, the Fascists would control the government after the following election, even if they fell far short of a popular majority.

The Fascists left nothing to chance. They formed a National List with other fascist and conservative parties. The National List won 66 percent of the vote and 70 percent of the parliamentary seats in the 1924 election, though they used violence and intimidation to achieve such a high total.[62] The Italian people could have voted for any of the Catholic, socialist, or liberal parties, yet the Fascist Party won 42 percent of all seats in parliament,[63] with another 28 percent going to their National List allies. Thus, there is little doubt that the Fascists had widespread support among the people, even if they failed to win an outright majority.

The Fascists faced one more challenge before gaining complete control of Italy. Just two months after the 1924 election, Giacomo Matteotti, a popular Socialist deputy who criticized the violence of the recent election, was murdered and two Fascists were accused of the crime. Mussolini was also blamed for his role in creating the military squads that physically attacked the opposition.[64] Opposition parties increased their political attacks on the Fascists and morale within the ruling coalition sank. A number of liberals, socialists, and Catholics withdrew from the government and Mussolini's regime nearly fell, but the right wing continued to support Mussolini, still fearing socialist revolution more than the corrupt and brutal Fascists. With majority

support in parliament and the army on his side, Mussolini consolidated power. The Fascists passed a law making the Prime Minister
responsible only to the king, greatly reducing parliament's power
within the government. Opposing political parties were banned and
political appointments replaced elected officials in local governments.
By 1927, Italy was a single-party state with Mussolini acting as
dictator.

FASCIST GOVERNMENT

The Italian economy improved in the first few years under the
Fascists as the new government restored order and international trade
resumed following the end of World War I. Mussolini drastically
reduced the size of the military, allowing government spending to fall
sharply and the budget to be balanced for the first time since the war.[65]
Although liberal economist Alberto De Stefani deserves much credit
for liberalizing the Italian economy with lower taxes, reduced regulation, and privatization of major industries,[66] he was also active in the
economy, propping up banks and industries hard hit by the recent
economic crisis.[67] As a result, there is some debate about whether the
Fascists, in general, and Stefani, specifically, adopted a free-market
economic policy upon taking power in 1922.[68] Most likely, Italy's
economic rebound was the result of the concurrent worldwide
economic recovery more than the product of its own policies.

After gaining full control of the government following the 1924
election and the Matteotti scandal, Mussolini fired Stefani. The
Fascists abandoned the economic liberalization and consolidated
industry into cartels. By 1932, 144 corporations, less than one percent
of the total, would control 51.7 percent of all corporate capital.[69] The
government expanded dramatically and "cooperation" between
government and private business increased.[70] The government
replaced banks as the provider of credit to industry and promoted
heavy industry at the expense of agriculture and consumer production. It also revalued the currency, increased tariffs, and began a series

of public works programs. The government restricted the opening of new industrial businesses by requiring licenses for new operations employing over one hundred workers in urban areas.[71] By restricting new businesses from forming, the Fascists also curtailed innovation. In addition, because small businesses are a major source of new jobs, the restrictions on new businesses pushed up the unemployment rate.[72]

Instead of allowing consumers to decide the allocation of economic production, the government did so by cartelizing the economy, keeping wages low, and controlling the workforce, who no longer had unions or socialists to defend them.[73] With the Fascist government actively interfering in the economy and helping one sector over all others, this certainly was not free-market capitalism. Through their corporatist system, the Fascists over-allocated resources toward heavy industry and under-allocated them to agriculture and consumer production. Although this is exactly what the Fascists wanted, the result was a lower standard of living for the Italian people.[74]

As the agricultural industry suffered from neglect and the diversion of resources toward heavy industry, the Fascists realized they had to appease the farmers. To help Italian agriculture, the government increased tariffs on grain imports, which resulted in higher prices for consumers. Furthermore, prices of other food products went up as farmers redirected resources away from fruits, vegetables, olives, and livestock to the more profitable grain business. Though designed to help agricultural workers, it hurt everybody else through higher prices, a decrease in total food production, and falling consumption.[75]

Government intervention like this often backfires. The government helps one industry only to realize the unintended consequence of hurting another industry. The government then provides assistance to this industry, as well, which hurts yet another industry. By the end of the cycle, the government is supporting every industry and the people are paying higher prices, either at the store or through higher taxes. By this time, the people have grown dependent on the government and removing the system of supports would create massive economic dislocation. As a result, the people prefer keeping the inefficient and expensive big government rather than lose the "gifts" their government is providing them.

The Great Depression that struck the world economy in 1929 caused less damage in Italy than elsewhere. The Italian stock market fell just 39 percent compared to 89 percent in the United States. Exports dropped 25 percent, much less than the 49 percent in Germany, 51 percent in France, and 64 percent in the United States. However, because Italy's economy did not perform as well as others in the 1920s, its decline was from a much lower base.[76] The Italian government tried to support the economy by increasing spending and expanding public works programs, but this resulted in a dramatic increase in the budget deficit. This state intervention in the economy had the same lack of success in Italy as it did in the other nations that tried much of the same, including the United States under Presidents Herbert Hoover and Franklin Roosevelt. At least in the United States, the government concentrated on public works projects that lifted employment, wages, and consumption. With its emphasis on public ownership and control of large corporations, Italy did the opposite as it tried to keep wages low and consumption down as it again focused on the production of heavy industry.[77] Whereas the United States did not seize control of private business, only affecting them indirectly through higher taxes, minimum wage laws, increased regulation, and trade policy, Italy took over corporations and organized industries into cartels. Thus, the Italian economy became more centralized and the people's standard of living fell further.[78]

The Italian financial system was not prepared for the stock market crash and Great Depression. In Italy, the banks often held large equity interests in industrial corporations. When the market crashed and industrial companies were on the verge of bankruptcy, the banks saw their capital disappear and were also nearing bankruptcy. Instead of allowing the industrial companies and banks to go bankrupt, the Fascist government seized the stock holdings of the banks and took control of the nearly bankrupt corporations. As a result, the Italian government owned controlling interests in many industries, including iron production, naval construction, and shipping, and large positions in many others sectors.[79] In fact, of the European governments, only the Soviet Union owned a larger proportion of the country's industrial sector.[80]

Yet again, the Italian government was promoting heavy industry by nationalizing it instead of letting the companies go bankrupt. The reason these companies became "too big to fail" in the first place was that the Fascists emphasized heavy industry and organized production into large corporations. If the Fascists had not interfered with the economy in the 1920s, less intervention would have been needed in the 1930s. In contrast, the United States did not promote large corporations. In fact, the United States government actively promoted smaller companies through its use of antitrust laws, including the division of the country's largest company, Standard Oil, into 34 smaller companies in 1911. Because of its freer and less concentrated economy, the United States did not need to bail out large companies during the Depression, even though the stock market and exports declined more in the U.S. than in Italy.

Italy invaded Ethiopia in 1935, accompanied by a massive propaganda campaign using radio, film, newspapers, and even schools designed to boost support for the war and, consequently, increase the popularity of Mussolini and the Fascists.[81] The people supported this "poor people's imperialism," believing Italy had a right to foreign colonies.[82] The war had two side effects: the domestic policies of the Fascists took a back seat to the war and propaganda campaigns, and the Fascists became racial elitists, believing that contact between Italians and Africans should be regulated.[83] This racism brought Italy closer to Germany, even before World War II began. This led Italy to adopt anti-Semitic policies, though the country previously had good relationships with the Jews, with the Italian Fascist Party including a proportionally large share of Jewish members.[84] In September 1938, Italy revoked citizenship for recently-arrived foreign-born Jews, banned Jews from attending or teaching in regular schools, banned mixed marriages, kicked Jews out of all associations, and restricted them from owning land or a business employing more than one hundred people. However, Italy likely enacted these new laws only to appease Germany, on whom they were growing more dependent, and did little to enforce them.[85]

Italy and Germany grew even closer as both countries expanded their empires. Germany's remilitarization of the Rhineland in 1936 upset the League of Nations, as did Italy's war in Ethiopia. Mussolini refused to support any actions against Germany regarding the Rhineland and, in 1936, agreed to recognize Austria as a German state in exchange for German recognition of Italy's claim to Ethiopia, thus ending the League of Nations' attempts to isolate Italy for its act of war.[86] This "Axis," as Mussolini called it, also supported General Francisco Franco's Nationalists in Spain against the republicans and became the foundation of World War II's Axis Powers.

The war with Ethiopia, troop and equipment support to Spain, and World War II helped alleviate Italy's unemployment problem as men left the workforce and went to the front. It also helped Italy's industrial companies, who benefited from the war contracts. However, the focus once again was on heavy industry at the expense of consumer goods. While a select few benefited from the war, the vast majority suffered.

Mussolini, like many tyrants before him, used war to increase patriotism and boost his popularity. It also kept the people occupied as soldiers went to the front and those at home produced munitions and equipment for their friends and family in harm's way. He further used the war to grant large contracts to his supporters in heavy industry, just as tyrants use their position to accrue wealth for themselves and pay off their supporters. Though Mussolini's tyranny did not kill tens of millions as did the tyranny of Stalin, Hitler, and Chairman Mao, death and destruction are not necessary conditions for tyranny. Aristotle defined tyranny as "a kind of monarchy which has in view the interest of the monarch only."[87] Although socialists, communists, fascists, and other ideologists supposedly act for the benefit of the people, other considerations are even more important to them. In fascism, the nation and military take precedence over the individual. Instead of trying to benefit all the people, the fascists in Italy promoted Italian nationalism, the military, and heavy industry while neglecting or even oppressing other groups, such as women, consumer goods producers, and small businesses. The tyranny of Mussolini and the Fascists is not measured by the number of people killed, but by the enslavement of the Italian people to the government, which controlled prices, wages, and the availability of jobs, consumer goods, and food. Furthermore, Mussolini was never able to convert the Italian government into a fully fascist totalitarian state, as he wanted.[88] Just as the fascism in Italy was incomplete, so too was its tyranny. More important, perhaps, than Mussolini's achieved and attempted tyranny was the trend toward authoritarianism, militarism, nationalism, and corporatism that became popular around the world after the Fascists took power in Italy.

As Italy approached war with Ethiopia, the government set prices, established production quotas, and stockpiled "important commodities."[89] Although agricultural land was privately owned, the agricultural sector was controlled by the state through these mechanisms. Because of Mussolini's economic policies, including his price controls, quotas, and tariffs, Italy suffered a large trade deficit. Trying to stem the outflow of gold, the Fascists further restricted imports, tightened foreign exchange controls, and regulated the distribution of raw materials.[90] After the war with Ethiopia ended, these restrictions remained as Italy moved closer to a state of perpetual war readiness.[91] Tyrants are loath to give up temporary powers, even after the reasons for taking those powers are no longer valid.

The state of permanent war had a deleterious effect on the Italian economy, even before the outbreak of World War II. Government spending rose and the budget deficit increased sevenfold between 1934 and 1937.[92] Because of the deficit spending and misallocation of resources by government bureaucrats, prices rose and the value of the lira collapsed. This was an unwanted change from the early 1930s. Like most of the industrialized world, Italy experienced deflation in the early 1930s, which helped the Italian people recover some of the lost wages and asset values caused by the market crash and Great Depression. However, Italy experienced high rates of inflation in the latter half of the 1930s, which resulted in worsening economic conditions at a time when the United States, Germany, and other countries began recovering from the Great Depression.

The weak economy forced the Fascists to neglect many of its earlier promises. The Fascists failed to support women's suffrage, as they had promised, and left professional restrictions against them in place.[93] Women were given the right to vote in 1926 but, at that time, the Fascists suspended democratic elections.[94] The Fascists even began supporting discrimination against women in the workforce, not surprising considering the women were taking the jobs of men, many of whom were war veterans.[95] Under new Fascist rules, women were not allowed to teach in schools of higher education, men received preferential treatment in hiring, and females were limited to ten percent of the workforce in any private or public organization, except for certain jobs such as telephone operator and typist.[96]

As Germany strengthened its military, annexed Austria and the Sudetenland, and prepared to invade Poland, Italy stayed neutral in the growing European conflict as long as possible, too weak and ill-prepared to be a major factor in the geopolitics of the late 1930s.[97] Italy waited for the opportune time and declared war on France and Great Britain a month after Germany invaded France, when the German side looked superior. Looking to contribute to the war, but afraid of the mighty British navy, Italy opted to attack the relatively weak and nearby countries of Greece and Yugoslavia. Italy had little success in the Balkans on its own, but German assistance finally helped Italy defeat Greece and conquer parts of Slovenia, Montenegro, and the Dalmatian coast. However, Britain took East Africa away from Italy, leaving Italy with mixed results.

Despite all the Fascist promises of an efficient economy, strong military, and national glory, Italy performed poorly in World War II. At this point, the Fascists had been in power for nearly twenty years, yet Italy was still a laggard among the major powers. Italy's corporatist economy did not produce the best of capitalism and socialism as the fascists promised. Italy's economy lagged far behind those of the capitalist countries, such as the United States and Great Britain, but also lacked the organizational capabilities of socialist Soviet Union and the more centrally controlled Germany. Italy's "third way" corporatism was a complete economic failure and, as a result, Italy was less prepared for World War II than it was for World War I, even though it had more time to get ready.[98]

THE FALL OF FASCISM

Italy's poor performance in World War II produced cracks in Mussolini's fragile political coalition. Even though Mussolini was a dictator and Italy was a single-party Fascist state, the King and Church continued to hold much symbolic power and influence over the people. The people, under pressure from a losing war, weak economy, inflation, and low wages, protested against the government. When the Fascist government could not subdue strikes in March 1943, conservatives realized that Mussolini and the Fascist government had failed, in both economics and war, and a new government was needed. In a meeting of the Grand Council of Fascism in July 1943, the first such meeting in four years, the Council voted nineteen to seven to replace Mussolini as head of the Fascists, after which the King of Italy had Mussolini arrested. If the vote to overthrow him had been close, maybe Mussolini would have fought to maintain power. But Mussolini realized he was finished when his own party voted overwhelmingly against him. Lacking its leader and the support of the people, the Fascist Party, an organization with three million members, disappeared virtually overnight and was banned by the new government just two days after Mussolini was deposed.[99]

The conservatives did not fundamentally disagree with Mussolini and the Fascists over how government should be run, at least no more so than back in 1922 when they made Mussolini Italy's Prime Minister. The alliance was one of convenience against a common enemy, the socialists. With the reappearance of worker strikes, the war a failure, and the economy suffering, the conservatives' interests were no longer aligned with the Fascists. The Fascist promises of nationalism, militarism, and authoritarianism did not interest the industrialists. They wanted suppression of socialism and a stable social and political environment. When the Fascists could no longer provide it, the conservatives, including the Church and King, abandoned the party and government.

The combination of the misguided Fascist policies and World War II devastated the Italian economy. By 1945, real wages were just half of their pre-war levels, half of Italian households lacked a kitchen, and three-quarters had no private bathroom.[100] After the war ended and the Italians regained their political and economic rights,* Italy experienced an "economic miracle" as it transformed itself from a weak agricultural economy into a leading industrial nation. While Italy certainly benefited from the Marshall Plan, it also promoted trade by joining NATO in 1949 and the European Economic Community as a founding member in 1957. Whereas the Fascists tried to help Italian producers by increasing tariffs and protecting the home market from competition, the new Italian Republic promoted free trade. The Fascists' protectionism failed, but the Republic's free trade policies contributed greatly to Italy's recovery.

The Fascists had restricted the movement of rural Italians, fearing masses of unemployed people in the major Italian cities, where they could join the socialists, form unions, and attack businesses. The Italian Republic loosened these restrictions on its labor markets, enabling rural Italians to move to the urban centers and pursue work in Italy's industrial sector. Approximately 200,000 southerners per year moved to the northern industrial region in the late 1950s and early 1960s.[101] Additionally, the elimination of government planning and establishment of liberal free-market principles encouraged businesses to innovate once again. The combination of entrepreneurship and availability of cheap labor enabled industry to grow dramatically.

The Fascists tried so hard to industrialize Italy using government controls, but once those controls were lifted, Italy rapidly industrialized through the invisible hand of capitalism. The Fascists directed

---

* In 1946, a popular referendum abolished Italy's monarchy. A new constitution was adopted in 1948.

their industrial production to heavy industry and war manufacturing, but ignored consumers. With the freedom to respond to market demands, Italian industry began producing what Italian and foreign consumers wanted and the economy boomed as a result.

LITTLE MUSSOLINIS

Possibly the most important and long-lasting result of Italian fascism was the spread of the fascist ideology around the world. Though historians argue about which countries were truly fascist, a number of countries imitated fascism's main elements of authoritarianism, nationalism, militarism, and "third way" methods of managing the economy through government organization of industry, often labeled corporatism or national-syndicalism. Although the proposals these imitators put forward and the systems they developed were not always fully fascist, the leaders of these fascistic movements copied the style of Mussolini and borrowed many, if not all, of the elements from the fascist ideology.[102] Some of these countries even received support from Mussolini and Hitler.

The common goal of all fascists was the renewal of the nation, society, and culture.[103] Thus, fascism was always nationalist, which is a major reason fascism is so hard to define. To employ nationalist patriotism in gaining followers and renewing its society and culture, each country's fascist party had to adapt its platform to fit the country's unique history and traditions. As a result, fascism in one country differed from fascism in another, whereas communism in one country was nearly identical to that in another.[104] For example, a large portion of German society believed in Aryan supremacy and glorified nature and, therefore, they persecuted the Jews, who they viewed as racially impure and urban industrialists.[105] In contrast, Italy longed for a return to Roman glory, which was not based on race or religion and, therefore, they did not persecute Jews or other minorities, at least not until the war with Ethiopia and alliance with Germany pushed Italy toward more racist practices.

Perhaps the most fully fascist regime after those of Italy and Germany was that of Spain. In 1876, Spain adopted a new constitution, which established a popularly elected lower House and an upper House whose members the King selected. The King also had the power to revoke laws and was commander-in-chief of the army. This system provided Spain with political stability for about fifty years.

In 1921, the Moorish population in Morocco rose up against Spain and defeated the Spanish military in the Battle of Annual. The Spanish parliament called for an investigation into the military and King Alfonso XIII. To forestall the investigation, the military overthrew the parliamentary government in 1923 and installed Captain General Miguel Primo de Rivera as dictator. In support of the coup, King Alfonso named de Rivera prime minister. De Rivera claimed his dictatorship would only be temporary and that Spain would soon return to a constitutional republic. Although de Rivera denied imitating fascism in his administration, he expressed admiration for Italy's regime and sent his labor minister to Rome in 1926 to observe their development of corporatism, with the idea of copying it in Spain.[106] However, de Rivera never seriously advanced corporatism[107] and never created a political base to maintain his rule.[108] Nevertheless, Mussolini approved of de Rivera's nationalist authoritarian government and was disappointed by the collapse of de Rivera's regime in 1930.[109]

The people grew tired of de Rivera's dictatorship, which was supposed to be temporary. Furthermore, the worldwide economic depression that began in 1929 dragged down de Rivera's popularity. In 1930, de Rivera finally stepped down after the military told him that he no longer had their support. The people also blamed King Alfonso for supporting de Rivera's dictatorship and he abdicated in 1931 after the military told him that he no longer had the army's loyalty. After de Rivera's government fell, Spain enjoyed its Second Republic, the only European government to move away from fascism and authoritarianism in the 1930s.[110] The first governments were all center left, but in 1933, the Spanish Confederation of the Autonomous Right (CEDA), a union of various conservative, fascist, and Catholic groups, won the most seats in parliament. CEDA favored a corporative and authoritarian Catholic republic,[111] but it was a non-violent movement and tried to reform Spain's constitutional system instead of overthrow it.

In 1933, José Antonio Primo de Rivera, son of the late dictator Miguel Primo de Rivera, founded the Falange movement, which was much more comparable to Italian fascism than was CEDA. Falange is Spanish for phalanx, symbolizing the militarist nature of the party. José Antonio combined right-wing nationalism with left-wing revolutionary tactics.[112] The Falange adopted Twenty-Seven Points as their official program, which, according to Stanley Payne, "exhibited all the main points of fascistic doctrine."[113] To support this fascist movement, Italy gave financial aid to the Falange in 1935 and 1936.[114]

In 1936, the left-wing Popular Front coalition beat CEDA's National Front coalition in new elections. The new government arrested José Antonio, pushing the Falange to join other right-wing nationalist parties in an attempt to overthrow the Republic. General Francisco Franco led 30,000 troops from the Spanish Army of Africa into Spain, with air support from Nazi Germany and Fascist Italy, while the Soviet Union supported the communists and Popular Front government. In 1937, Franco took over the Falange movement and began building a broader base of support by merging it with other right-wing parties. By 1939, after 365,000 died in the Spanish Civil War,[115] Franco had conquered Spain. In his 39-year tyranny, Franco would execute an additional 100,000 to 200,000 political opponents.[116]

During World War II, Spain allied with the Axis powers, but did not involve themselves in the fighting. After the war, Spain was isolated because of its fascist regime and former alliance with the Axis. As tensions between the United States and Soviet Union increased, the U.S. befriended anti-communist Spain and gave it economic assistance in return for hosting U.S. military bases. Because of the new alliance with the United States and Spain's reintegration into Europe and the world, Franco relaxed many of his fascist programs, especially on the economic front. In 1957, Franco created a new cabinet whose job was to reduce the government's control and regulation of the economy. In 1958, Franco dropped the fascist Twenty-Seven Points. The liberalization of the economy and resumption of foreign trade led to the Spanish Miracle, an economic boom that lasted from 1959 to 1973.

Franco looked for a successor and turned to the monarchy for a candidate. He passed over Juan de Borbón, who was heir to the throne as son of former King Alfonso XIII, because Franco saw him as too liberal. Instead Franco named Juan Carlos, son of Juan de Borbón, as his successor, but only after Franco made Juan Carlos swear loyalty to him. Much to the disappointment of Franco's supporters, upon assuming power after Franco's death, King Juan Carlos instituted reforms, legalized political parties, held new elections, created a new constitution, and relinquished the absolute power that Franco had transferred to him.[117]

Austria also moved toward fascism in the 1930s, but a strong anti-Nazi sentiment among a large portion of the population prevented the fascists from fully implementing their agenda. In the 1920s, the Heimwehr, "home guard," was organized to defend the borders and prevent Marxism from taking hold.[118] Mussolini provided the Heimwehr with financial support. In 1930, the leaders of the Heimwehr took the Korneuburg Oath, endorsing the main elements of fascism, including nationalism, authoritarianism, and corporatism, further cementing the alliance between the Italian Fascists and the Austrian right-wing.

When Austria's National Socialist (Nazi) Party scored big wins in the 1932 election, the ruling right-wing Christian Social Party, led by Engelbert Dollfuss, turned to the Heimwehr and Fascist Italy for support rather than form a parliamentary coalition with the Nazis or the left-wing Social Democrats.[119] The Christian Social's majority had fallen to just one seat in parliament and, as a result, legislative business came to a standstill. In March 1933, the speaker and two deputy speakers resigned, freeing themselves to vote on a matter that was currently deadlocked in parliament. With no speaker, Engelbert Dollfuss claimed that parliament could no longer function properly, dissolved it under the War Economy Emergency Powers Act of 1917, and announced plans to create a Christian corporative state with himself as dictator, supported by the army, Catholic Church, and Fascist Italy. He also dissolved the Constitutional Court, created the Fatherland's Front Party, banned opposing political parties, restricted the press, and halted all federal, state, and local elections. Austria's National Socialist (Nazi) Party assassinated Dollfuss in July 1934, but the Fatherland Front continued their "Austrofascist" rule. The new government under new Chancellor Kurt von Schuschnigg was less ideological than its predecessor and guaranteed equality to all citizens, including Jews, but continued its ban on opposing political parties. Mussolini continued to support the Austrian fascists, including the Fatherland Front, until he formed the Axis with Germany in 1936, at which time, Italy officially recognized Austria as a German state and ended its support of the Austrian government, thus paving the way for Germany's invasion and annexation of Austria in 1938.[120]

Historians often point out that the fascists in Italy, Germany, Spain, and elsewhere never garnered a majority of the vote. This is often cited as proof that the Fascists, Nazis, Nationalists, and para-fascists ruled against the will of the people and never really had their support. It is true that the fascists in Europe never received a majority of the vote, but they did convince a very large portion of the voting public to support them and formed coalitions with other similarly minded parties that, together, represented a majority of the public. Nevertheless, there is an example of a para-fascist regime, one that was largely fascist but had some differences, taking power by twice winning an outright majority in popular elections. Juan Peron's nine-year presidency over Argentina had most of the fascist characteristics, though it only had limited authoritarianism.[121]

In 1939 and 1940, Juan Peron served as military attaché in Fascist Italy, where he certainly learned about fascism. Peron believed in fascism and admired Mussolini, but also admitted his errors. Peron said, "Mussolini was the greatest man of our century, but he committed certain disastrous errors. I, who have the advantage of his prece-

dent before me, shall follow in his footsteps but also avoid his errors."[122] Peron also admired the government of Franco's Spain[123] and
settled there after he was overthrown in 1955.[124]

In 1946, Peron won Argentina's presidential election with 53.6
percent of the vote.[125] Recognizing the errors of his fascist predecessors and the unique history and culture of Argentina, Peron adapted
fascism for Latin American and Argentine conditions.[126] He kept the
"third way" economics of European fascists, subsidized industry to
appease the right-wing, and redistributed income to satisfy the left-
wing.[127] Though he verbally attacked rich businessmen, he did so
merely as a demagogue and never seized their property outright and
never imprisoned, exiled, or killed them.[128] He did, however, purchase
and nationalize foreign owned companies.[129]

As the economy deteriorated, the result of his verbal attacks on
capital, poor investments, and redistributionist policies, Peron
demagogued for votes from the working classes by promising further
redistribution of wealth, but this only further alienated foreign
investment and further weakened the Argentine economy.[130]

Although Peron only had limited authority, he used the power he
did have to commit acts of tyranny. He had his opponents fired from
their jobs, imprisoned, and tortured. Although opposing political
parties were allowed, Peron closed down or took over control of the
media, thus silencing his opponents. His attacks on opposition press
helped him win reelection in 1951[131] with 63.5 percent of the vote.[132]

The economy suffered under the Peron government, growing just
16 percent from 1943 to 1955, a low 1.2 percent annual growth rate.[133]
He had also upset the Church by taking away privileges that had
previously been granted to it. In 1955, President Juan Peron was
overthrown by the upper class who had grown upset with the high
inflation, corruption, weak economy, and redistribution of wealth.[134]
Peron proved that a tyrant need not take power subversively. A tyrant
can assume and maintain power by making promises to the people
and winning elections. However, in the end, the people suffered under
Peron's redistributionist policies and the tyrant increased his oppression of the people in an attempt to maintain his hold on power.[135]

CHAPTER SEVEN

NAZI GERMANY

T he National Socialist, or Nazi, regime of Germany was a most extreme example of what may occur when a country's citizens hand over complete control to the government. But the Nazis did not magically appear out of nowhere to take over Germany, as many would like to believe. In three consecutive elections, the Nazis, under the leadership of Adolf Hitler, convinced the German people to give them large pluralities of the vote. With 44 percent of the vote in the 1933 election, 26 points more than the second largest party,[1] the Nazis controlled the German parliament and used that power, with help from Nazi paramilitary groups, to oppress their political opponents and install Hitler as dictator.

The Nazis took the fascist ideas of Italy and combined them with racial ideology and social Darwinism[2] to create a most brutal, murderous, and imperialistic regime. The Nazis brought war to the world; impoverishment, servitude, and destruction to their own people; and death to Jews, Poles, Russians, Gypsies, and countless other "undesirables." The Nazi regime was possibly the most tyrannical in history but, like the Fascists in Italy and Peron in Argentina, they took power primarily through legal means. That the tyrannical Nazis convinced large portions of the population to vote for them and power was given to them according to the constitution, demonstrates the fragility of freedom and the ease at which tyranny can emerge.

THE WEIMAR REPUBLIC

World War I was a historic turning point for Germany. The war resulted in a tremendous loss of life and caused severe economic problems. Britain and its powerful navy blockaded Germany, cutting off its supply of food, oil, and equipment. Germany also faced a labor shortage when many of its men left the fields and factories to join the fighting. The democratically elected Reichstag gave control of the economy to the military, thus directing all of the nation's resources toward the war. Therefore, long before the socialists or fascists were able to take over, Germany was already experiencing centralized control of the economy. This government control failed as the economy declined and Germany lost the war. Furthermore, the government kept German military defeats a secret from the people.[3] The German people should have learned then that an authoritarian central government is unable to effectively manage an entire economy and will lie to the people to maintain its power.

Even before World War I, Germany grew fascinated with socialism and its promises of prosperity and equality. In the 1880s, German Chancellor Otto von Bismarck tried to stop the growing appeal of socialism in Germany, partly by adopting some of its policies, including universal health insurance, accident insurance, and pensions. Many people saw this as an endorsement of the socialist agenda and its appeal continued to grow. By 1912, the socialist Social Democratic Party became the largest party in Germany.

The political disputes between the right and left intensified during World War I. The right largely supported the war, but many socialists and others on the left protested it. The Reichstag was evenly divided and, as a result, it passed a peace resolution in July 1917 but also voted to continue funding the war.[4] In response to the Reichstag's contradictory votes, the right-wing denigrated their parliamentary democracy as "hypocritical" and "English."[5] The right-wing also blamed the Jews and their profiteering[6] for the military failures. The right reshaped the war, which presumably began as a defensive war against Russia, into a battle between Germany's militarism and Britain's materialism.[7] Thus the right, disappointed with the free democratic system, began favoring a more authoritarian government combined with a "third way" economic system.

The right-wing authoritarian government, led by Kaiser Wilhelm II, was dealt a stinging defeat with Germany's loss in World War I. Adding to the pressure on the government, German Admiral Reinhard Scheer launched an attack on the British Royal Navy, without approval from the government, after the war had ended and armistice negotiations were in progress. Mutinies and revolution spread from one city to another, socialists and anarchists seized power in Munich and declared a "Free State of Bavaria,"[8] and the people called for the Kaiser to step down, which he did days later. Germany held new elections in January 1919 and the Social Democratic Party received 37.9 percent of the vote.[9] The Communist Party of Germany won just 7.6 percent,[10] forcing the Social Democrats to form a coalition with centrist parties. Nevertheless, the right-wing authoritarian government had lost its power after decades of control due to its ineffective management of the war and economy.

Not wanting the violence of the Bolshevik revolution and forced to work with the centrist parties, the Social Democrats opted for a path of reform instead of revolution.[11] With the center-left in control and the Kaiser in exile, the Reichstag created a new constitutional government. The new constitution granted universal suffrage to all Germans aged twenty and up with proportional representation in the Reichstag and direct election of the president. In *The Rise and Fall of the Third Reich*, William L. Shirer describes the new constitution as "the most liberal and democratic document of its kind the twentieth century had seen, mechanically well-nigh perfect, full of ingenious and admirable devices which seemed to guarantee the working of an almost flawless democracy."[12] The Germans had their civil rights, but it remained to be seen what kind of government they would vote for.

The new government had to face some serious issues. Britain's naval blockade, the shifting of resources to military production, and the loss of much labor as men went to fight in the war had created a weak German economy and forced the government to fund the war effort by issuing debt. This expansion of credit, along with promises of higher wages to appease the working class, drove up inflation. The new government tried to reduce inflation by raising taxes, thinking it would reduce the money in circulation. Instead, companies raised prices to offset the higher taxes, thus pushing up inflation even further.[13] The finance minister who instituted the failed taxation policy and had been involved in the increasingly unpopular peace resolution of 1917 and armistice ending World War I was forced out of office.

The higher taxes and inflation drove the right-wing away from the centrist government[14] and hurt the ruling Social Democratic Party in the June 1920 election. The Social Democratic Party dropped 16 points to 21.6 percent of the vote, though other left wing parties picked up the lost Social Democratic votes, leaving the left-wing socialists with the same 40 percent.[15] The increasing division among the left, though, made forming a stable coalition increasingly difficult and the government went through a number of failed center-left coalitions over the following years.

France invaded part of Germany in January 1923 in an attempt to recover reparations they were owed. The German government called for passive resistance and, in a wave of patriotism, the German people went on strike, thus blocking France from receiving the reparations from the invaded areas. The German government continued to pay the striking workers and gave credits to the shut businesses, which the Reichsbank paid for by printing money. Inflation turned into hyperinflation and the exchange rate rose from 21,000 marks to the dollar in April 1923, to 110,000 in June, and 4,200,000,000,000 marks per dollar by November.[16]

The people revolted against the inept government. The various political parties vied for power, with many proposing socialism and some calling for national dictatorship.[17] The radical right and left attempted coups throughout Germany, including Hitler's failed Beer Hall Putsch in Munich, but most were stopped and the centrist government retained power.

In 1924, Hans Luther, minister of finance, and Hjalmar Schacht, a prominent banker acting as currency commissioner, restored the stability of the German Mark by instituting new economic policies, acting fiscally responsible, and backing the currency with mortgaged land. The new financial stability restored some of Germany's international standing and the Allies agreed to reduce the reparations, provide Germany with a sizable loan, and invest in Germany. This greatly helped the German economy, though the reparations continued to weigh on it.

Nevertheless, this economic revival was not enough to save the centrist parties, who were blamed for the financial and political chaos of 1923. As a result, the centrists lost seats in the 1924 election to both the radical right and left.[18] Over the next few years, the center would continue to lose power. In 1925, Field Marshal Paul von Hindenburg won the presidential election by running on the right.[19] At the same time, the Social Democratic Party moved further left by supporting redistribution of land owned by the German princes.[20] One government after another fell because no coalition of the right, left, or center was able to garner a majority of seats. Despite the dramatic recovery in the German economy,[21] the growing political divide showed that, even though Germany had a republican government, there were too few republicans to form a majority coalition.[22]

The Great Depression, which began in 1929, hit Germany hard. Industrial production fell 42 percent between 1928 and 1932.[23] Agricultural prices dropped 40 percent between 1927 and 1933.[24] Unemployment rose from three million to eight million, wages dropped by a third, and 40 percent of the workforce depended on government support.[25]

The radical right and left immediately went on the offensive, blaming the center and the democratic republican system of government for Germany's problems. Though the left and right disagreed on most issues, they both favored more government control and the two opposing sides worked together to drive out the centrist republican liberals from Germany. Friedrich Hayek explains, "It was the union of the anticapitalist forces of the Right and of the Left, the fusion of radical and conservative socialism, which drove out from Germany everything that was liberal."[26] It was just a matter of time before the right or the left gained a majority in parliament or, if the two were equally balanced, the two sides would fight for power in the streets instead of at the voting booth.

The German government already had enormous control of the people's lives, even before the socialists on the left or the fascists on the right took over. Friedrich Hayek writes, "In Germany as early as 1928, the central and local authorities directly control the use of more than half the national income (according to an official German estimate then, 53 percent), they control indirectly almost the whole economic life of the nation. There is, then, scarcely an individual end which is not dependent for its achievement on the action of the state, and the "social scale of values" which guides the state's action must embrace practically all individual ends."[27] The central government's control of the economy would make it easy for the left or the right to implement their socialist or fascist plans once one side managed to gain power.

NAZI PROMISES

Throughout the 1920s, the Nazis were a non-entity in German politics. In the May 1928 federal election, the National Socialist German Workers Party received just 2.6 percent of the vote.[28] Within four years, the Nazis would become Germany's largest political party. After another year, Adolf Hitler would become dictator of Germany and all other political parties would be banned. This remarkable rise to power came about through the skilled use of populist rhetoric, including promises of wealth, equality, and national rebirth. The German people, disillusioned with the failures of the center-left coalitions of the 1920s, were swayed by this new party that promised the benefits of both left-wing socialism and right-wing authoritarianism and nationalism.

As the name implies, the National Socialist German Workers Party was founded primarily to promote socialism in Germany. National Socialism originally stood for partial collectivism aimed primarily at large industrial corporations, leading financial institutions, and wealthy landowners, as detailed in the party's Twenty-Five Points of

1920.[29] The Twenty-Five Points included the following socialist demands:[30]

- "Every citizen shall have the possibility of living decently and earning a livelihood."
- "All unearned income, and all income that does not arise from work, be abolished."
- "Total confiscation of all war profits."
- "Nationalization of all trusts."
- "Profit-sharing in large industries."
- "Increase in old-age pensions."
- "Communalization of large stores which will be rented cheaply to small tradespeople."
- "A law to expropriate the owners without compensation of any land needed for the common purpose."
- "The abolition of ground rents, and the prohibition of all speculation in land."
- "Usurers, profiteers, etc., are to be punished with death, regardless of creed or race."
- "The State must assume the responsibility of organizing thoroughly the entire cultural system of the people."
- "Specially talented children of poor parents, whatever their station or occupation, be educated at the expense of the State."
- "COMMON GOOD BEFORE INDIVIDUAL GOOD."

Many today believe that the Nazis were capitalists, despite the evidence of Nazism's socialist roots and agenda. Jacques Ellul, a leader of the French Resistance in World War II, philosopher, and law professor, writes, "The dogmatic and elementary interpretation of Nazism as having been conceived by capitalists to counter communism, and a bourgeois tool in the class struggle, has gained incredibly broad acceptance as a self-evident fact, despite its contradiction of fact. Even after his alliance with certain capitalists, Hitler controlled them as much as they did him."[31] In 1927, Hitler said, "We are socialists, we are enemies of today's capitalistic economic system for the exploitation of the economically weak, with its unfair salaries, with its unseemly evaluation of a human being according to wealth and property instead of responsibility and performance, and we are determined to destroy this system under all conditions."[32]

The Nazis failed to draw left-wing support away from the Social Democratic Party and the Communist Party, so they toned down their socialist economic propaganda beginning in 1927, though they continued to believe in government control of the economy.[33] The Nazis adopted the "third way" style of the Italian Fascists by supporting partial socialism with some government ownership of business and heavy regulation of large businesses, but limited regulation of small businesses and individuals.[34] In 1931, Hitler said, "I want everyone to keep the property he has acquired for himself according to the principle: common good takes precedence over self-interest. But the state must retain control and each property owner should consider himself an agent of the state... The Third Reich will always retain its right to control the owners of property."[35] Hitler claimed that property could be privately owned but, in reality, the individual would not retain control over it. By controlling "the owners of property," the state obviously controls the property as well. Stanley Payne, the eminent authority on fascism, writes that Hitler "boasted that there was no need to nationalize the economy since he had nationalized the entire population."[36] As late as 1941, Hitler declared, "basically National Socialism and Marxism are the same."[37]

Though Hitler and the Nazis remained committed to socialism throughout, in theory and in practice, their new toned-down "third way" socialism found support among the middle class,[38] who feared the radical left but were still enchanted by the utopian promises of socialism. The new Nazi economic platform also found support among the land-owning farmers. Whereas the Twenty-Five Points vowed to take land away from its owners without compensation "for the common purpose,"[39] by 1930 the Nazis had dropped that proposal[40] and were offering aid to the land owning peasant farmers and praising the peasants as the defenders of German morality and tradition.[41] The Nazis also promised high prices and ready markets for the farmer's agricultural products and extolled the virtues of "blood and soil" and the "agricultural estate."[42]

Considering the working class was already aligned with the Marxist parties, Hitler and the Nazis focused their campaign on the middle class, who were also suffering under the weak economy.[43] The new strategy resulted in gains in state elections and increased campaign donations.[44] The Nazis also sought the support of the industrialists, a natural ally when they started presenting themselves as the alternative to the communists and other radical left-wing socialists. Many industrialists were wary of the new, unstable, violent, and radical Nazis, yet some industrialists still gave the Nazis much needed financial support in the 1920s, though they also supported the much larger and less radical conservative German National People's Party.[45] As the Nazis attracted larger shares of the vote in elections and especially after Hitler became Chancellor, the industrialists gave much more money to the Nazis,[46] partly to help the Nazis defeat the communists, but also to win their favor after their inevitable political victory.

The Nazi agenda went well beyond promises of economic prosperity. The Nazis also promoted German nationalism and Aryan superiority, which helped lift the spirits of many native Germans after the humiliating defeat in World War I, the disastrous hyperinflation of the early 1920s, and the economic depression that began in 1929. Point four of the Twenty-Five Points detailed the Nazis' German exclusivity: "Only those who are our fellow countrymen can become citizens. Only those who have German blood, regardless of creed, can be our countrymen. Hence no Jew can be a countryman."[47] Although this anti-Semitism became a centerpiece of the Nazi agenda once in power, it was not instrumental in the Nazis' rise to power because they toned down their anti-Semitic propaganda during their election campaigns.[48] Thus, the rising fortune of the Nazis had little to do with any anti-Semitic rhetoric, though everybody voting for the Nazis understood their hatred of the Jews, given that it was part of the Twenty-Five Points and was a centerpiece of Hitler's *Mein Kampf*. Nevertheless, by promoting Aryan superiority and blaming the Jews, capitalists, republicans, and other liberals for Germany's problems, German nationalism became the centerpiece of the Nazi agenda and enabled the Nazis to attract members from all economic and social classes.[49]

Like their fascist cousins in Italy, the Nazis also took a pro-military position. After World War I, the Weimar republic did not support the military, even refusing to build a monument to the war dead or issue a commemorative medal.[50] Of course, this upset many veterans and families of the war dead, and the Nazis pursued these disaffected Germans by favoring a strong military, reoccupation of territory lost in the war, and expansion of Germany to include all German-speaking people. The Nazis claimed "National Socialism means peace," arguing that only a strong Germany can defend against an invasion by France or the Soviet Union.[51] Like the Fascists in Italy, the Nazis were always seen in their military uniform. When Hitler met Mussolini for the first time in 1934, Hitler wore civilian clothing at the insistence of his advisors, whereas Mussolini was dressed in his military uniform. Hitler appeared weak next to Mussolini and he vowed never to make that mistake again. From then on, Hitler was always in uniform when making public appearances.[52]

The Nazis managed to exceed the Italian Fascists in their develop-ment of a myth culture, with their ever-present swastika and promo-tion of the old German folk traditions and rituals. The Nazis also exalted Hitler, well beyond what the Italians did with Mussolini. Many Nazis saw Hitler as a Christ or a Messiah[53] who will save Germany from Jews, foreigners, capitalists, and communists. For example, in 1941, the Nazi newspaper Volkischer Beobachter announced, "The Fuhrer is the highest synthesis of his race… He embodies the univers-alism of Goethe, the depth of Kant, the dynamism of Hegel, the patriotism of Fichte, the genius of Frederick II, the realism of Bis-marck as well as the tumultuous inspiration of Wagner, the perspicac-ity of Spengler."[54] Thus, their youth organization was not called the German Youth or even the Nazi Youth, but the Hitler Youth. Hitler became the infallible god of the Nazis and of Germany.

By adapting their agenda to meet the desires of the people and courting unaffiliated groups, the Nazis drew support from various geographic areas and several economic and social classes.[55] Their focus on nationalism, a strong military, authoritarian leadership, and "third way" socialism, with promises of economic prosperity and equality, enabled the Nazis to win over industrialists on the right, peasants on the left, and many in the center, especially World War I veterans. By organizing this coalition of disparate interests, the National Socialists quickly grew from a political non-entity into Germany's dominant political party.

THE RISE OF THE NAZIS

The Great Depression hit in 1929 and the radical parties used it as an opportunity to blame the republican form of government and the ruling centrist parties. The Communist Party jumped from 10.6 percent of the vote in the 1928 election to 13.1 percent in the 1930 election. At the same time, the Nazis surged from a mere 2.6 percent to 18.3 percent, suddenly making them the second largest party. Meanwhile, the conservative German National People's Party fell from 14.2 percent to just 7 percent.[56] Though the Social Democratic Party remained the largest party by a decent margin, they now had even more difficulty building a coalition. With the radical right and radical left stealing votes from the conservative right and centrist parties, historian Martin Kitchen writes, "The elections of September 1930 mark the end of German liberalism."[57]

The country's economic problems worsened and the government approached bankruptcy. To reduce the budget deficit, the government raised unemployment insurance premiums, increased duties on wheat and barley, reduced pension and unemployment benefits, and cut the salaries of civil servants. The Social Democratic Party's popularity declined even more when these measures pushed up unemployment even further and weakened the already fragile banking system.[58] The government was trapped in a no-win situation. It cut back on spending to avoid bankruptcy, but this increased hardship on the people and reduced the government's popularity. On the other hand, the government could have continued providing welfare to the people, but this would likely have forced Germany to default on its debt, which would have resulted in massive inflation and a flight of capital out of the country. The German government's large deficits, which were the result of the economic depression combined with Germany's already semi-socialist economy, forced Germany to decide between two equally bad choices. The resulting economic and political crisis was inevitable, regardless of what the government chose to do.

Eighty-four-year-old Paul von Hindenburg announced he would stand for reelection as president in the 1932 election. Hitler also announced he would run for president, but first the Austrian had to become a German citizen, which he did by securing a low-level civil servant appointment. The first round of voting in March 1932 resulted in no majority winner, but Hindenburg won with 53 percent of the vote in the second round in April with the support of the Social Democrats. Hitler received 37 percent of the vote.[59] Hitler and the Nazis were clearly gaining in popularity.

A new parliamentary election was called for July 1932. The Communists and Nazis used violence against the centrists and the ruling government did nothing to stop it.[60] The Social Democratic Party dropped another 2.9 percentage points in the election to 21.6 percent while the Nazis' popularity rose even further as they garnered 37.3 percent of the vote, up 19 points from the 1930 parliamentary election.[61] The Nazis were now, by far, the largest party and Hitler demanded to be named chancellor. The Nazis and Communists, combined, controlled a majority in the new Reichstag and, because both parties wished to end parliamentary democracy in Germany, the constitutional republic's days were limited.[62] The people of Germany never gave the Nazis a complete majority, but they most certainly did vote to end the republic and establish a new authoritarian regime, though they disagreed on who would lead it.

Disappointed in the election results, Hindenburg called for new elections in November 1932. The Communists and Nazis marched together in support of a transportation strike just prior to the election, demonstrating yet again that both wanted to overthrow Germany's parliamentary democracy and were working together to do so.[63] The conservative parties did a little better in this election, thanks to fears of the radical Nazis and a slight improvement in the economy.[64] The Nazis fell 4.2 points to 33.1 percent,[65] while the Communists gained. Nevertheless, the Nazis remained, by far, the largest party and no government could be made without the Nazis or the Communists. Business and political leaders, realizing that a coalition must be formed with one of these two parties, decided that the Nazis were preferable.[66] This realization came at an opportune time for the Nazis because they were low on funds, which hurt their propaganda efforts in the election campaign and was a major reason their share of the vote declined.[67]

Wishing to maintain the government's centrist coalition, President Hindenburg had the military issue a report warning that a civil war between the Nazis and Communists would lead to an invasion of Germany by Poland. At the same time, Hindenburg appointed General Kurt von Schleicher chancellor. Schleicher then tried to divide the Nazis by offering Gregor Strasser, head of the Nazis in Berlin, the post of vice-chancellor. This scheme had a good chance of working as the Nazis were out of money and their support had declined in the most recent election.[68] However, while Strasser contemplated Chancellor Schleicher's offer, Hitler called a meeting of the Nazis' Reichstag deputies and won their support. Strasser declined Schleicher's offer, resigned his positions within the Nazi party, and the plans of Hindenburg and Schleicher failed.

As the Reichstag was set to reconvene, it was obvious that the Schleicher government would not survive a vote of confidence.[69] Thus, on January 30, 1933, Hindenburg had no choice but to appoint Hitler as chancellor. The following day, Hitler requested new elections, which were called for March 5. To secure the support he needed to become chancellor, Hitler agreed to a number of cabinet selections by Hindenburg and the conservatives. As a result, the cabinet contained just two Nazis and the conservatives thought Hitler was working for them.[70]

Hitler campaigned vigorously over the next month, and did little to hide his hatred for Germany's parliamentary democracy and vowed to impose authoritarian rule. When requesting the new election, Hitler even told the cabinet that this would be the last Reichstag election and Germany would never return to a parliamentary system.[71] He told the same thing to a group of leading industrialists on February 20, 1933, who were delighted with the news and gave monetary support to the financially starved Nazi Party.[72] In speeches, Hitler blamed the republicans for the economic distress, social discord, and national decline since World War I.[73] Though he gave no concrete solutions to these problems, he spoke with such passion in his promise to unite the nation that the people reacted with similar positive support. Martin Kitchen writes, "In this highly-charged emotional atmosphere what mattered was not a carefully crafted program but a spontaneous and passionate reaction."[74] Hitler spoke with such eloquence and passion, making promises the German people wanted to hear, that the people were ready to give the Nazis an overwhelming victory at the ballot box.

NAZI TYRANNY

The Nazi tyranny began even before the March 1933 election. The Communists, who in the previous election marched side-by-side with the Nazis, found themselves abandoned by their former allies. The Communists called for a general strike but, with unemployment so high, few heeded the call.[75] To stop the strikes, Hitler gave himself the power to restrict freedom of the press and assembly. In the midst of the election campaign, these powers enabled Hitler to silence his political opposition.[76]

On February 27, 1933, the Reichstag was set on fire. The Communists blamed the Nazis and the Nazis blamed the Communists, though an anarchist named Marinus van der Lubbe likely acted alone in setting the parliament ablaze.[77] In response, President Hindenburg issued the "Decree for the Protection of the People and the State." Treason and arson became punishable by execution and Nazi opponents could be arrested or placed in protective custody and often ended up in a concentration camp. The Nazis violently attacked the

Communists and other opponents during the election campaign, breaking up democratic meetings, beating opposing politicians, and burning down opposition newspaper offices. The Nazi Sturmabteilung, the SA stormtroopers, murdered about 600 and arrested 100,000 during the election campaign.[78]

In the face of all this violence, the Nazis won 43.9 percent of the vote,[79] 6.5 points better than its prior high and ten points better than its tally in the previous parliamentary election. The Social Democratic Party received just 18.2 percent of the vote and the Communist Party just 12.2 percent.[80] With an 88.8 percent turnout,[81] the Nazis had a clear plurality and received many more votes than any other party for the fourth election in a row. Clearly, the Nazis were the most popular party in Germany, as they were even before the recent violence and oppression, and earned the right to form a government. Though the Nazis lacked a majority and did not win the right to violate or abolish the constitution, the Nazis and Communists combined, both of whom wished to destroy the republic and establish authoritarian rule, received over 56 percent of the vote. The German people voted to abolish the republic and establish authoritarian rule, though some would have preferred a Communist regime instead of a Nazi one. Nevertheless, a Communist regime may have been just as tyrannical, as the Communists in Russia demonstrated.

After the election, the SA overran local government offices, raised the Nazi flag, and chased away government officials. New commissars were appointed in each state and police chiefs were replaced by Nazi officials.[82] Meeting in the Kroll Opera House in Berlin, the new parliament passed the Enabling Act, easily achieving the two-thirds majority required to pass it because all 81 Communist members were banned and 26 Social Democrats were arrested prior to the vote.[83] The Enabling Act gave the cabinet the authority to enact laws without the approval of the Reichstag. The Reichstag was thus stripped of almost all power and Hitler, as prime minister of the cabinet, became dictator. The Enabling Act was for only four years, but was extended twice, making Hitler the legal dictator of Germany for 12 years. Hitler

further centralized power by making state governors political appointments instead of elected officials, thus killing local democracy in
Germany.[84]

The Nazis banned unions and arrested union leaders. Opposing
political parties were outlawed and the leaders of the Social Democratic Party, those who had not yet fled Germany, were arrested. Over
half of the Communist Party's 300,000 members were either imprisoned or sent to concentration camps while 30,000 were murdered.[85]
By July 1933, Germany had become a single party state. Nevertheless,
the government promised plebiscites to approve or disapprove of the
government, thus giving the people the fiction of freedom and rights
when the only party to vote for was the Nazis.

The Nazis paid particular attention to the media as they purchased
media companies, censored those that promoted opposing viewpoints,
and subsidized pro-Nazi films. With the media supporting them, the
Nazis subsidized the purchase of radios and, by 1939, Germany had
the highest ownership of radios in the world with over seventy percent
of homes owning one.[86]

The Nazis created a program of "Coordination," whereby the government took over control of all associations, clubs, and societies. For
example, Walter Darré took control of the farmers' associations and
was then made minister of agriculture, thus giving him complete
control over Germany's agricultural industry. The Nazis also took over
medical, legal, and engineering associations. Even unimportant
groups like the beekeepers' associations and cycle clubs were brought
under party control.[87] Thus, the Nazis coordinated the actions of
industry, without officially nationalizing private property. Nevertheless, by controlling the whole of industry, they were little different
from communists and other socialists.

Just as in Fascist Italy, women were driven out of the workforce in
Nazi Germany.[88] Women competed with men for jobs and, with
unemployment high, the Nazis pushed women out to help the men.
Furthermore, the Nazis wanted women to stay home and procreate to
enlarge the Aryan race.[89] Women in Germany were forced out of
professional jobs and most who worked did so at unskilled positions.[90]

As a result, college enrollment of women declined.[91] Nevertheless, a higher percentage of women worked in Germany than in Britain or the United States,[92] probably due to a shortage of husbands and male workers as men joined the military and went off to fight in the war. This labor shortage and increase in the number of single women would explain why the number of women working outside the home rose 50 percent between 1933 and 1939, though most were at low-paying menial jobs.[93]

In April 1933, the "Law for the Restoration of a Professional Civil Service" barred Jews and other undesirables from serving in the civil service, including as university professors, and was later expanded to ban them from other professions, including lawyers, doctors, dentists, and accountants. Jewish, communist, and other anti-Nazi authors, professors, and artists were forced to resign their positions and their works were banned. The list of banned authors included world renowned Germans such as Karl Marx, Albert Einstein, and Sigmund Freud. In May 1933, the Nazi German Students Association organized book burnings throughout the country.

Immediately after taking power, the Nazi SA stormtroopers beat and murdered Jews and vandalized their property. Tens of thousands fled the country. Hitler disapproved of this public oppression, not wishing to upset the German people and lose their support, instead preferring to continue his oppression, torture, and murder of political opponents and undesirables behind closed doors.[94] Hitler weakened the unruly SA and gave greater power to the more disciplined Schutzstaffel, better known as the SS. Hitler also transferred the SA concentration camps to the SS. The SS was much better organized, already having divisions charged with combating communism, liberalism, homosexuality, Free Masons, abortion, political churches, sects, Jews, and foreigners.[95]

In 1934, the conservatives who had helped Hitler rise to power realized that he could not be tamed, as they had hoped, and that Hitler had to be removed. The conservatives argued that they supported conservative authoritarianism, which was designed to maintain order, but did not approve of Hitler's totalitarian aspirations, which was creating the violence they had hoped to avoid by opposing the communists.[96] In response, Hitler cracked down on his enemies. On June 30, 1934, the Night of the Long Knives, Hitler arrested and executed the leaders of the SA as well as the Bavarian minister-president, a prominent Catholic leader, former Nazi leader Gregor Strasser, and former chancellor Kurt von Schleicher. Hitler murdered at least 85 victims in this purge.[97]

On July 3, the cabinet passed a law retroactively legalizing these actions against "treasonable attacks."[98] Thus, every immoral, illegal, brutal, and murderous act of Hitler and the Nazis could be legalized after the fact. Furthermore, Hitler and the Nazis could ban any activity it deemed objectionable. Therefore, under the "law," Hitler and Nazis could do no wrong while any individual or group can be arrested or executed for acts that were legal when committed. As Nazi supporter Carl Schmitt remarked, "The will of the Fuhrer is the highest law."[99]

When President Paul von Hindenburg died in 1934, Adolf Hitler, with the approval of his cabinet, combined the offices of president and chancellor, despite this being unconstitutional. Furthermore, the German army was to swear allegiance to Hitler, instead of to the constitution. Hitler was now complete dictator. A vote was held and 89.9 percent of the people approved of Hitler's appointment as supreme leader.[100] Though Hitler's tally was likely inflated due to coercion, fear of reprisal for voting against him, and ballot rigging, Hitler probably would have done quite well as his popularity was even higher than that of the Nazi Party.[101] In a separate free election in 1935, 90.9 percent of people in the Saar region voted to rejoin Germany.[102]

Germany appeared tranquil for the next few years as it recovered economically, prepared its military for war, and created a "third way" welfare state. The German people were willing to bear the reduction in freedom in exchange for the reborn Germany.[103] The economy improved and unemployment dropped sharply, partly the result of mandatory volunteerism and military conscription.[104] Nevertheless, wages did not rise much despite the labor shortage[105] due to pressure from the involuntary labor of both Germans and non-Germans.

All the while, Hitler consolidated his power. The cabinet, which according to the Enabling Act was the official source of power, met 72 times in 1933. However, with the 1934 referendum confirming Hitler as dictator, the cabinet met only infrequently after 1934 and stopped meeting altogether by 1938.[106]

The Nazis passed numerous laws to manage every aspect of people's lives and to criminalize every day behavior that may be against the state in some way. One such law was even named "Acts Contrary to the Healthy Feelings of the Volk."[107] With this, even the promotion of negative feelings was made illegal. For example, the Nazis executed sixteen thousand for minor treasonous offenses such as listening to BBC or Radio Moscow.[108] To administer all these new laws, the Nazis created new courts whose decisions could not be appealed. The Nazis also created their secret police, the Gestapo, which could act as lawmaker, judge, jury, and executioner. Even the court system had no jurisdiction over Gestapo activities.[109] In fact, the Gestapo could arrest a judge it disliked and place him in a concentration camp.[110] The people had no rights or freedom and lived in constant fear.

In 1935, Germany enacted the Nuremberg Laws that made marriage or sexual intercourse between Jew and non-Jew illegal and granted civil rights only to those with "German or similar blood."[111] Thus, even Jews whose families had lived in Germany for hundreds of years had their civil rights revoked. Jews were kicked out of public schools, banned from public parks, theaters, and cinemas, and their property was confiscated. Nevertheless, the Jews were not yet put in concentration camps and the Nazis encouraged them to leave, with 40 percent doing so.[112] On the Night of Broken Glass, Kristallnacht, in November 1938, about one hundred Jews were murdered, synagogues were burned down, Jewish property was vandalized, and thirty-thousand Jews were sent off to concentration camps. The German people did not support this violence in the street, so the Nazi government quickly blamed the Jewish victims, saying the transgressors were provoked by the murder of a German diplomat in Paris by a Polish-German Jew. To help pay for the damage caused on Kristallnacht, the remaining 250,000 Jews were fined a billion marks, insurance claims were confiscated by the government, and Jewish stores were seized and sold off to Aryan Germans.[113]

Kristallnacht is often used to mark the beginning of the Holocaust. Although Jews were certainly the largest and most important target of Nazi tyranny, they were not the only "enemies" of the German people. The Nazis also targeted the Gypsies, homosexuals, and the mentally and physically handicapped.[114] When not murdering them, the Nazis sterilized less threatening undesirables, including repeat criminals, prostitutes, alcoholics, and those will low intelligence, schizophrenia, epilepsy, or manic-depression.[115]

When Hitler assumed power, Germany's weak military and suffering economy prevented any military action. Hitler bided his time as he put Germany's economic house in order and slowly revitalized the military. Like his predecessors in the Weimar Republic, Hitler continued pushing for revocation or alteration of the Treaty of Versailles, trying to recover lost territory and pride. Hitler signed peace agreements with Poland and the Soviet Union, but supported the Austrian Nazis, which forced the closing of the border between Germany and Austria.[116] In 1936, Germany violated the disarmament clauses of the Treaty of Versailles by creating an air force and remilitarizing the Rhineland. The League of Nations did nothing because Italy supported Germany's move in exchange for German support of Italy's claim to Ethiopia. As Hitler signed peace agreements, outmaneuvered the League of Nations, and won 98.8 percent of the vote in a 1936 referendum, Hitler started believing his own propaganda and added messianic references to himself in his speeches.[117]

After spending five years remilitarizing Germany, Hitler was finally ready to begin his campaign for Europe. In March 1938, Germany invaded Austria and annexed the country. Virtually overnight, Austria became a province of Germany with the German mark replacing the Austrian schilling and Austrians suddenly forced to drive on the right side of the road.[118] The SS followed right behind the invading army and the persecution of Jews began immediately.

After his Austrian success, Hitler eyed Czechoslovakia. Hitler made demands that he knew could not be met and incited violence in the much-desired Sudetenland. Britain and France were willing to give Hitler parts of the Sudetenland, but Hitler demanded even more than they offered. Hitler was itching to go to war over this disagreement, but the majority of Germans were against it.[119] With encouragement from Mussolini, Hitler met with British Prime Minister Neville Chamberlain and French Prime Minister Edouard Daladier, who gave Hitler the German parts of the Sudetenland without even consulting the Czechs. Hitler had won a second easy international victory, yet he saw it as a defeat. He wished to go to war with Czechoslovakia, a war Germany would have easily won. The German people, though, were against war at this time and they saw Chamberlain and Daladier as heroes,[120] temporarily frustrating Hitler's desires.

The easy diplomatic victories combined with greater desires for war drove Hitler to tyrannical extremes. It was at this time that Hitler started speaking of conquering all of Europe and killing all the European Jews.[121] In March 1939, just five months after receiving the German parts of the Sudetenland, Germany invaded the Czech part of Czechoslovakia while the Slavic portion declared its independence as an ally of the Nazis. Shifting his attention from one country to the next as the world did little to stop him, Hitler set his eyes on Poland. In April 1939, Hitler rescinded the peace treaty with Poland and sent Foreign Minister Joachim von Ribbentrop to negotiate a peace treaty with the Soviet Union that would enable Germany to invade Poland. The two sides agreed to the Treaty of Non-Aggression, pledging that neither country would attack the other and agreeing to split Poland between them. On September 1, 1939, Germany attacked Poland. Britain and France finally had enough and they declared war against Germany on September 3, but they were too late to help Poland. Within weeks, Germany and the Soviet Union had conquered their portions of Poland and the fighting ended just a month after the first shots were fired.

At last, the world realized that appeasing Hitler had been a terrible mistake and that they had to prepare for war. On September 2, Neville Chamberlain admitted, "Everything that I have worked for, everything that I have hoped for, everything that I have believed in during my public life has crashed into ruins. There is only one thing left for me to do: that is devote what strength and power I have to forwarding the victory of the cause for which we have sacrificed so much."[122] On September 3, 1939, after years of political exile, partly because of his warnings about the Nazi threat, Winston Churchill was made a member of the War Cabinet and appointed First Lord of the Admiralty. Over in France, Edouard Daladier declared in a nationwide broadcast, "We took up arms against aggression. We shall not put them down until we have guarantees for a real peace and security, a security which is not threatened every six months."[123] Both countries were finally preparing for war, but they were far behind Germany, which had been planning and preparing for years.

With German troops moving east, the Nazis were concerned about the absorption of Poland's three million Jews and the possible addition of the Soviet Union's six million Jews. Previously, the Nazis persecuted the Jews and encouraged them to leave, but that policy only worked with Germany's relatively small number of Jews who were also generally well off. With millions of new Jews, most of whom were poor and could not afford the passage to other countries, if any countries were willing to take them, the Nazis looked for a new way to deal with the Jews. The Nazis herded the Polish Jews into ghettos, threw potential enemies into concentration camps, and killed anybody who actively opposed Germany. Germany annexed about half of its portion of Poland, taking the property of and deporting 325,000 Poles.[124] Germany built death camps to execute communists, Poles, the sick, and Jews.

A number of leading Nazis proposed shipping the Jews to Madagascar, but shipping restrictions due to the war scuttled that idea.[125] With the Jews herded into the overcrowded ghettos, unable to grow their own food, and barred from finding work among the gentiles, the Nazis had trouble feeding and guarding the Jews. Their "final solution to the Jewish problem" was to exterminate them. At first, the Nazis shot the Jews or poisoned them with carbon monoxide, but the Nazis found those methods too cumbersome. Additionally, shooting them put too great a psychological strain on the soldiers.[126] The Nazis needed a less personal and more efficient method of murdering their victims. Nazi scientists developed new methods of mass murder, including gas chambers, such as those at Auschwitz-Birkenau that killed ten thousand Jews per day using Zyklon B poison gas.[127] By the end of the Holocaust, the Nazis killed six million Jews, about half in concentration camps with the remaining divided between shootings and starvation in the ghettos. Areas of Europe that once had vibrant Jewish communities had become devoid of all Jews, with the lucky minority fleeing to Britain, the United States, or British-controlled Palestine. The Nazis killed 72 percent of Jews in German controlled areas, including 90 percent of Jews in Lithuania and Latvia and 85 percent of those in Poland.[128] The Nazis used these same methods to kill three million Poles, three million Soviet civilians, 3.3 million Soviet prisoners of war, half a million Gypsies, and countless others. All told, the Nazis murdered about 15 million people, not including those who died in battle, and they already had plans to kill thirty million more in their "solution to the Polish question."[129]

After conquering Poland, Hitler immediately planned his invasion of France. Germany first invaded Norway and Denmark in April 1940 followed by France, through neutral Belgium and the Netherlands, in May 1940. Within a couple of weeks, the Germans had reached the English Channel. The Germans captured Paris in June. Britain was now on its own as the U.S. had not yet entered the war and the Soviet Union had its non-aggression pact with Germany. Germany had hoped that Britain would negotiate for peace, but new British Prime Minister Winston Churchill vowed:

> "We shall not flag or fail. We shall go on to the end, we shall fight in France, we shall fight on the seas and oceans, we shall fight with growing confidence and growing strength in the air, we shall defend our Island, whatever the cost may be, we shall fight on the beaches, we shall fight on the landing grounds, we shall fight in the

fields and in the streets, we shall fight in the hills; we
shall never surrender, and even if, which I do not for a
moment believe, this Island or a large part of it were subjugated and starving, then our Empire beyond the seas,
armed and guarded by the British Fleet, would carry on
the struggle, until, in God's good time, the New World,
with all its power and might, steps forth to the rescue and
the liberation of the old."[130]

The Nazis had to punish such disobedience. In August 1940, the
German Luftwaffe began its attack on Britain's military assets. The
German attack failed to destroy Britain's air defenses and the British
refused to surrender or even agree to an armistice. Hitler admitted his
first serious defeat,[131] but he was not one to stop. The Blitz began in
September 1940 as Hitler targeted London and other British cities,
killing tens of thousands of British civilians in just a few months.

At the same time, Germany drew up plans to attack the Soviet Union, believing that victory would come easily.[132] To Hitler, this attack
was about more than just territory. Hitler claimed it would be "a battle
between world views" that would destroy the "Jewish-Bolshevik
intelligentsia."[133] The army was ordered to kill all Jews and decreed
that no German soldiers would be held accountable for crimes
committed against the enemy.[134] In drawing up their invasion plans,
the Nazis recognized that 30 million locals would have to be removed
from their land[135] and that millions would starve as a result.[136] Three
million German soldiers attacked the Soviet Union in June 1941.
Germany expected the war to last just three months, so it left no
reserves and did not prepare for the cold Russian winter.[137] Five
months later, a little behind schedule, but still quite successful, the
German army was just outside Moscow. Hitler's generals warned him
of impending disaster and urged him to sue for peace, but with victory
just miles away, Hitler continued the attack on Moscow. In December,
the Soviet Union counter-attacked and Germany was forced to retreat.
By March 1942, one million Germans had died in battle, disease, or

malnutrition in the Russian campaign. Confidence in the German army took a severe hit while Soviet morale improved.

With Japan's bombing of Pearl Harbor in December 1941, the United States officially entered World War II. The U.S. and Britain attacked Axis forces in North Africa in November 1942 and the German troops there surrendered in May 1943. The Allies invaded Sicily in July 1943, which led to the fall of Mussolini in Italy. Without its important Italian ally, Germany had to fight on three fronts, in France, Italy, and Russia, against the combined might of the Soviet Union, United States, and Britain. The odds were now against Hitler and Germany. Hitler could have offered peace and negotiated to keep part of Germany's territorial gains, but he instead decided to continue fighting. To Hitler, this was not just a war for land. It was primarily a war of ideologies. Hitler was willing to sacrifice himself, his country, and his people for his vision of the future.

Like Dionysius who destroyed Syracuse as his tyranny fell, Hitler ordered the destruction of Germany's economic infrastructure in March 1945. Albert Speer, Minister of Armaments and War Production, argued against this "Nero Order"* and, as the man in charge of implementing it, ensured that it was largely ignored as he did all he could to help save the German infrastructure and provide support to the suffering German people. On April 30, 1945, Hitler committed suicide, together with Eva Braun, his mistress whom he had married just hours before. A few days later, Germany unconditionally surrendered and the long years of Nazi tyranny were over.

THE FAILURE OF NAZISM

In their campaign for parliament back in the 1920s and early 1930s, the Nazis promised economic prosperity, though they never announced a specific plan to accomplish this. Initially under the

---

* This name derives from the theory that Nero started the Great Fire of Rome in 64 AD.

Nazis, Germany did experience an economic recovery, but the design of the Nazi economic system doomed Germany to failure from the start.

Unemployment fell sharply in the first years of the Nazi regime, thanks to huge government programs, including the construction of the Autobahn, new housing and government buildings, and military projects.[138] Although this put people to work, it did not improve their standard of living.[139] The government ran large deficits to fund these projects and acquired free labor from the 1935 introduction of six months of required labor service. Germany played a number of financial games to fund the deficit but, in the end, had to print more money to pay its bills. Currency reserves disappeared and Germany could not import the raw materials it needed.

While democratic principles and rule of law disappeared back in 1934, what was left of economic freedom was abolished with the Four Year Plan of 1936. Hjalmar Schacht, the man who saved the German economy in the 1920s and Minister of Economics beginning in 1934, warned in 1936 about inflation if rearmament was not slowed down. He also argued that Germany could recover its lost territories through negotiation instead of war. Schacht was ignored and the Four Year Plan of 1936 put the German economy under government control with Hermann Goering acting as economic dictator, though he knew little about economics. Seeing the impending economic disaster, Schacht resigned his post in 1937.

Schacht saw that Nazi economics could not work, especially as Hitler and Goering subordinated the economy to military preparations and warfare.[140] Hitler mistakenly believed that his confiscation of Jewish property and wars of conquest would pay for the military expenditures.[141] In fact, this strategy worked for a while, just as it had in ancient Rome. Hitler took over Austria with little difficulty while Britain and France gave him the German parts of the Sudetenland. Thus, at little expense, Germany gained valuable new territory with the wealth of many people and businesses to plunder. But when the German expansion hit resistance and all the easy booty had already been taken, the expenses of maintaining the empire exceeded the value of the tributes and raw materials that could be extorted from the new territories.

In Nazi thought, the persecution and extermination of Jews and other inferior races and nations also made for good economics. During World War II, Germany and the armies far from home faced food shortages and possible starvation. The Nazis therefore had to choose who would receive the available food and who would starve. The logical conclusion, for the Nazis, was to keep the food for themselves and exterminate the inferior Jews, Poles, Russians, and Gypsies.[142] As point seven of the Twenty-Five Points states, "If it should not be possible to feed the whole population, then aliens (noncitizens) must be expelled from the Reich."[143] In this case, the quickest way to expel them was to kill them.

The German economy failed to produce enough food because it was focusing too much of its resources toward producing weapons and too much of its labor force was fighting in the war instead of working on farms and in factories back home. Even as the German economy failed to produce enough for its own people, production in the conquered countries declined markedly from the destruction of the invading Nazis, plundering of its wealth, and imprisonment and murder of its citizens. Not only was Germany unable to support itself, countries like Poland were no longer able to support themselves.

To help alleviate the labor shortage in Germany because so many of the Germans were fighting at the front, the Nazis imported foreign workers. By the autumn of 1944, 8.5 million foreigners worked in Germany, including 2 million prisoners of war and 650,000 in concentration camps, mostly Jews.[144] The remaining were workers from the Soviet Union, Poland, France, and Italy who were forced to come work in Germany or have their ration books confiscated.[145] Although many of these workers earned the same wages as Germans, high tax rates and charges for room and board often left them with little extra to spend or save.[146] Thanks to these workers, arms production more than tripled between January 1942 and July 1944.[147] Without this forced labor, the German economy and war machine would have failed even earlier.

As in all tyrannies, many of the Nazi leaders used their power to amass vast wealth. Hermann Goering used his power as commander of the Luftwaffe, administrator of the Four Year Plan, and Hitler's designated successor to acquire mansions and create an enormous industrial enterprise called Hermann Goering Works. As Reichsminister of Propaganda, Joseph Goebbels received gifts from the media, including a house given to him by the film industry. He also used his power to seduce several female film stars.[148]

Going back at least as far as Plato, idealists have argued that a government of highly intelligent and well-intentioned individuals could effectively run the country for the well-being of the people. But giving such power to government officials is likely to attract people hungry for wealth or power. Furthermore, the power hungry will use violence and deception to gain power, making their assumption of power more likely and more dangerous.

One of the key principles of the Nazis was that a government run by superior men, Nietzsche's Ubermenschen, is better than a republic in which everybody, regardless of intelligence, has a say in government. However, when these supermen in government turn out to be fallible, just like everybody else, they take down the entire country with them. With the quick victory in France, Hitler believed himself to be a military genius, as did many of his deputies. As a result, he minimized the importance of his soldiers and ignored the advice of military advisors. By ignoring military experts and outside opinions, the German victories turned into military defeats.[149] Even as defeat was assured and Hitler prepared to commit suicide, Hitler refused to write a single word of regret in his last will and testament, not even for the 6.8 million Germans who died in the war.[150] Hitler and the Nazis came to power promising the German people an Aryan utopia. Instead, he brought death and destruction, yet he could not apologize for his errors. Hitler had sacrificed the German people for his Nazi ideology. In modern times, authoritarian leaders claim to use their power to benefit the people. Communism promised to bring equality to the working class. Fascism promised to bring glory back to Italy. Nazism promised German rebirth. In the end, these movements and their authoritarian leaders cared more about themselves and their ideologies than the people they supposedly served.

By relying on a plunder-based economy, diverting resources to "national interests" such as war and expansion of the borders, and centralizing power in fallible men, as all men are, the Nazis created a flawed system that was doomed to fail. These were the proposals of militarism, nationalism, authoritarianism, and "third way" economics that the Nazis campaigned on back in the 1920s and early 1930s and which the German people voted for. Although most of the world was shocked by the brutality of Nazism, a number of people predicted it. As far back as 1927, Austrian economist Ludwig von Mises predicted the coming end of freedom in central Europe.[151] Winston Churchill also spoke up against the Nazis. However, the vast majority of people ignored these warnings, ignorant of how centralized control of the economy and people's lives leads to tyranny.

THE WEST GERMAN ECONOMIC MIRACLE

The economic situation in Germany after World War II was terrible. Germany was bankrupt, millions were killed in the war and Holocaust, millions more were wounded, many of the remaining people were starving and homeless, and much of the country lay in ruin from the Allied bombing and invasion. Twenty percent of all housing was destroyed, food production had fallen in half between 1938 and 1947, and industrial production dropped by two-thirds.[152]

The Allies divided Germany into four occupation zones with the Soviets controlling the east, the British the northwest, the United States the southwest, and France along the French-German border in the west. Many former Nazis in the east made the transition from the Nazi to the Soviet dictatorship, but those who did not were thrown into the former Nazi concentration camps along with dissident communists, democrats, and capitalists. In contrast, the U.S., Britain, and France had difficulty finding qualified Germans to help administer their zones.[153] Thus, many ex-Nazis realized that they were more akin to the communist Soviets than the democratic and capitalist

West. Furthermore, the western zones of Germany received substantial support from Britain and the United States, whereas the Soviet Union exploited its zone.[154] The "greedy" capitalists thus helped the West Germans, while the Soviets further impoverished those in the East, despite their supposed goal of supporting the working class and spreading international brotherhood.

In 1945, Ludwig Erhard, a believer in free markets and opponent of the Nazis during their regime, was appointed Minister of Economics in West Germany, later becoming the director of the Office of Economic Opportunity and advisor to the military governor of the U.S. zone. Erhard pushed for currency reform and elimination of price controls and rationing. On June 20, 1948, Germany returned to capitalism. As Erhard bragged, "I have not relaxed rationing; I have abolished it! Henceforth, the only rationing ticket the people will need will be the deutschemark. And they will work hard to get these deutschemarks, just wait and see."[155] At the same time, tax rates were reduced dramatically, with the marginal rate for most people declining from 85 percent to 18 percent.[156] This encouraged people to return to work. Absenteeism dropped from 9.5 to 4.2 hours per week.[157] Industrial production increased by 50 percent in the six months following the June 1948 reintroduction of capitalism.[158]

In May 1949, Germany adopted a new constitution, its Basic Law, which guaranteed essential freedoms. The new Basic Law was designed to prevent the problems Germany experienced under the Weimar Republic. The rights of the people were made inviolable, undemocratic parties were banned, and parliament would be responsible for appointing a chancellor.[159] In the first election in West Germany in August 1949, the right-wing Christian Democratic Union received 31 percent of the vote, the left-wing Social Democratic Party won 29.2 percent, and the centrist Free Democratic Party earned 11.9 percent, with the remaining smaller parties totaling 27.9 percent.[160] Theodor Heuss of the Free Democratic Party became president and Konrad Adenauer of the Christian Democratic Union became chancellor. The Christian Democratic Union and Free Democratic

Party partnered with the right-wing German Party and controlled 208 of the new Bundestag's 402 seats.[161]

The economy in free West Germany boomed. People moved from the country to the cities and blue-collar jobs were replaced by white-collar jobs. The middle class grew substantially and the people's standard of living improved dramatically, in addition to enjoying freedom for the first time in nearly two decades. As a result of the improving economy, the Christian Democratic Union won 45.2 percent of the vote in the September 1953 election, a 14.2 percentage point increase.[162] The economy continued to grow and the Christian Democratic Union ran in 1957 with the slogan "NO EXPERI-MENTS!"[163] The German people voted for more of the same and the CDU won 50.2 percent of the vote, another five percent gain.[164]

By 1958, industrial production was four times its pre-capitalist levels of early 1948. In contrast, the communist East German economy was stagnant.[165] Although the tyranny of the Nazis left Germany physically and psychologically scarred, West Germany quickly became one of the world's wealthiest countries, just ten years after returning to capitalism.

CHAPTER EIGHT

THE UNITED STATES OF AMERICA

Two-hundred twenty years ago, starting with a blank slate but basing their grand experiment on a careful study of history and the ideas of those that came before them, the Founding Fathers of the United States created an extraordinary system designed to promote freedom and stability. Their invention encouraged liberty and free enterprise, thus enabling the United States of America to become the world's greatest economic and military superpower, an empire spreading liberty and capitalism across the globe. However, the political system they created, one of separation of powers and checks and balances, has deteriorated over time, especially in the last hundred years as both Republicans and Democrats adopted much of the progressive and socialist platforms. The desire for more democracy and larger, more centralized government has turned what once was a laissez-faire representative government into a large interventionist government.

CREATING THE CONSTITUTION

For years, the American colonies and the British government had argued over taxation and trade policy.[1] In 1775, fighting broke out in New England. In 1776, the American colonies announced their autonomy from Great Britain and Thomas Jefferson penned the Declaration of Independence. Though its composition is brilliant, it merely expressed the sentiments that already existed across the colonies.[2] In 1781, the American army led by General George Washington, with help from the French, defeated the British army commanded by General Lord Charles Cornwallis at Yorktown, effectively ending the war and winning the American colonies their independence.

After declaring their independence in 1776, the thirteen states formed a confederation. The Articles of Confederation were drafted in 1777 and ratified in March 1781, just six months prior to the victory at Yorktown. But the Confederation struggled under the Articles because the national government could not enforce its laws as it had "no authority," making its laws "mere recommendations which the States observe or disregard at their option."[3] Just six years after becoming the law of the land, many Americans realized the Articles of Confederation were not working as the states bickered, unable to reach consensus, unwilling to give money to the Congress of the Confederation, and unable to pay the soldiers, except with worthless paper money.[4]

An Assembly of Demigods

With this in mind, fifty-five delegates from the thirteen states met in Philadelphia in the summer of 1787. Their original intent was to amend the Articles of Confederation, but most of the delegates realized that the old system had to be scrapped. The delegates were free to create, from scratch, the best system they could conceive of. Their goal was to establish a system that avoided both a powerful government and anarchy. They also hoped to avoid the wars between the rich and the poor that afflict almost every society. Their goals were "to form a more perfect Union, establish Justice, insure domestic Tranquility, provide for the common defence, promote the general Welfare, and secure the Blessings of Liberty to ourselves and our Posterity."[5] Of course, this is easier said than done. Many nations have tried to accomplish this, but few have succeeded. To achieve this, something new had to be created. As James Madison wrote in Federalist No. 39, "Every previous national authority either had been centralized or else had been a confederation of sovereign states. The new American system was neither one nor the other; it was a mixture of both."[6]

These fifty-five delegates were highly educated college graduates and students of rhetoric.[7] Most of them held public offices and about half were lawyers or judges.[8] They were well-versed in the Bible[9] and had read the works of the ancient Greeks and Romans,[10] the histories of Greece and Rome, especially Montesquieu's *Considerations on the Causes of the Greatness of the Romans and their Decline*,[11] and the more modern works of political philosophy, especially from the English republicans.[12] In a letter to John Adams, Thomas Jefferson called the delegates at the Philadelphia Convention of 1787 "an assembly of demigods,"[13] even though many of the leading minds were absent with Thomas Jefferson in Paris, John Adams in London, Anti-Federalists Patrick Henry and Richard Henry Lee refusing to attend, and future Chief Justice of the Supreme Court John Jay not even appointed as a delegate, even though he would author a few of the Federalist Papers advocating ratification of the Constitution.[14]

The Founding Fathers were well aware that a constitution is just a legal guideline which, if ignored, is quite worthless. The Founders knew that a "virtuous" citizenry would be needed to prevent tyranny.[15] Jefferson writes that it is the people who are the "ultimate guardians of their own liberty."[16] To help the people maintain their liberty, the Founders believed that the Constitution should be short, easily understood, "concerned with first principles of government," and "conform" to the people's customs, morals, and beliefs,[17] so that the people will read it, respect it, follow it, and defend it.

The United States was fortunate that its Founding Fathers were so well versed in political philosophy and history. They understood that they had to design a system with checks and balances between the different branches of government and between the states and federal government. They knew that both centralized power and unfettered democracy led to tyranny and hoped to limit the power of government. At the Constitutional Convention, Alexander Hamilton said, "We are now forming a republican government. Real liberty is neither found in despotism, nor in the extremes of democracy, but in moderate governments."[18] To establish a system of checks and balances, they relied on the ideas and writings that came before them, British common law, and the various constitutions and political structures of the American states.[19]

After the Constitution was written, the Founding Fathers still had to convince the people and the state legislatures to ratify it. In their arguments for its ratification, the Founders demonstrated their knowledge of ancient history. John Adams, for example, in *A Defence of the Constitutions of Government of the United States of America*, "examined twelve ancient democratic republics, three ancient aristocratic republics, and three ancient monarchical republics."[20] In Federalist No. 63, James Madison examines the constitutions of Athens, Sparta, and Carthage.[21] In Federalist No. 6, Alexander Hamilton writes that "Sparta, Athens, Rome, and Carthage were all republics" and evaluates how they, along with Venice, Holland, and Britain, suffered as a result of the many wars they fought.[22] Adams, Hamilton, and Madison were not simply showing off their knowledge. Each used the examples of history to demonstrate how this new Constitution would surpass all others[23] by learning from the successes of previous societies and avoiding the mistakes that led to their downfalls.

Much had changed since the ancient days of Greece and Rome. Political thought advanced greatly since Aristotle wrote about majority rule versus rule by none and since Polybius described how government should include a system of checks and balances. While the Founders certainly read the political philosophies of the ancient Greeks and Romans,[24] they also studied and relied heavily on more recent political thinkers.

The most cited political thinker at the time of the American Revolution was Charles de Secondat Montesquieu.[25] The Frenchman was one of the few modern non-English writers the Founders studied and whose ideas they incorporated.[26] The Founders continued to read the classic histories of Plutarch, Livy, and Tacitus,[27] but they also read Montesquieu's *Considerations on the Causes of the Greatness of the Romans and their Decline*,[28] written in 1734.[*] Montesquieu also wrote *Spirit of the Laws* in 1748, which analyzes what type of constitution

---

[*] Edward Gibbon's *The History of the Decline and Fall of the Roman Empire* debuted in 1776, but only three of the six volumes had been published by the 1787 Constitutional Convention. Additionally, Gibbon focuses on the decline of Rome, starting in the year 180 AD, thus skipping the entire history of the Roman Republic and its transformation into the Roman Empire, which would have been of great value to the Founding Fathers.

would create the best environment for freedom and argues for the separation of powers, as exemplified by the English Constitution. He wrote this for the benefit of the French people, but the Founders adapted his ideas for their new nation.[29]

The second most cited political thinker at the time of the American Revolution was Sir William Blackstone, the English judge and professor.[30] Blackstone sided with the American colonies in its disagreements with England,[31] possibly making his works even more popular in the colonies. His 1765 book *Commentaries on the Laws of England* sold as well in America as in England, despite the colonies having just one-third the population of England.[32] Much of United States law comes from British common law and Blackstone's *Commentaries* were the best exposition of that law and was relied on heavily by the Founding Fathers.[33] Furthermore, Charles Cotesworth Pinckney, an influential delegate at the Constitutional Convention, studied under Blackstone at Oxford University.[34]

Sir William Blackstone was not alone in his defense of the American colonies. Edmund Burke, member of the British House of Commons as a Whig, was such a staunch defender of America that he was hired by the New York Assembly to represent the state in England.[35] Edmund Burke's *Speech on American Taxation* in 1774 argued against the taxes England enacted on the American colonies after the Boston Tea Party. His *Speech on Conciliation with the Colonies* in 1775 argued that England had to moderate its stance. About the Americans, Burke wrote, "This fierce spirit of liberty is stronger in the English colonies...than in any other people of the earth."[36]

Another extremely influential political thinker was John Locke, who had lived one hundred years prior to the American Revolution. In 1689, Locke wrote his *Two Treatises of Government*. In his *First Treatise*, Locke argues against the divine right of kings, an idea likely to have garnered much support in America during the Revolution. In his far more influential *Second Treatise*, Locke contends that the government's job is to protect the "natural rights of life, liberty, and estate,"[37] a precursor to the Declaration of Independence's "life, liberty, and pursuit of happiness."

The best guide, however, for the Founding Fathers was experience. Though they took inspiration from the Bible, Greece, Rome, and the political philosophers of their time, the system they created was largely derived from the colonial governments which, in turn, were based on England's political system.[38] Much of the U.S. Constitution, in fact, came from the state constitutions written after 1776. In 1780, John Adams was the chief architect of the Massachusetts Constitution, which employed a system of checks and balances, the first state constitution to do so. This constitution, which is still in force today, would be the basis for many states to follow and for the United States Constitution in 1787.[39] For example, the U.S. Constitution copied Massachusetts with the establishment of a bicameral legislature, known as Congress, which itself was a copy of the British House of Commons and House of Lords.[40]

Checks and Balances

The Founding Fathers created a constitution with a complex system of checks and balances designed to prevent tyranny. In Federalist No. 47, James Madison writes, "The accumulation of all powers, legislative, executive, and judiciary, in the same hands, whether of one, a few, or many, and whether hereditary, selfappointed, or elective, may justly be pronounced the very definition of tyranny."[41] By dividing powers between the three branches of government and keeping each branch independent of the others, in addition to dividing power between the federal government and the states, the Founders believe that tyranny could be prevented.

The Founding Fathers worried that the legislative branch would be the most powerful. James Madison writes in Federalist No. 51, "In republican government, the legislative authority necessarily predominates. The remedy for this inconveniency is to divide the legislature into different branches; and to render them, by different modes of election and different principles of action, as little connected with each other as the nature of their common functions and their common dependence on the society will admit."[42] Even as the delegates at the Constitutional Convention agreed that there should be two legislative bodies, they nevertheless disagreed regarding how they should represent the people. One group argued for an equal number of representatives for each state whereas another argued for representation proportional to population. Roger Sherman and Oliver Ellsworth, both of Connecticut, proposed a compromise wherein House seats would be allocated in proportion to the population of each state but each state would control an equal number of Senate seats. Additionally, representatives in the House would be directly elected by the people, whereas senators would be chosen by the state legislatures. The House, therefore, is to be close to the people and better represent them, whereas the Senate was to be a smaller, more exclusive body. The U.S. Senate was to be a check on the more democratic House of Representatives,[43] just as the Roman Senate checked the mob mentality that often swept through Rome.

Under this system, a coalition of large or small states could pass legislation in one house, but would have much more difficulty in passing bills in both houses. This also made it more difficult for a region to gain control of both houses. At a time when the South and North were often arguing with each other over slavery and tariffs, this system ensured, for the time being, that the North with its many small states would dominate the Senate and the more populous South would control the House.[44]

Although the Founders divided the power of the legislative branch, they did the exact opposite with the executive branch by choosing to give all its power to a single man, the President. In fact, the President is the only member of the executive branch explicitly mentioned in the Constitution.* In ancient Greece and Rome, the people often resorted to "temporary tyrants" to fight wars. By creating this strong President as "Commander in Chief of the Army and Navy of the United States, and of the Militia of the several States, when called into the actual Service of the United States,"[45] the President could act as a temporary

---

* Article II Section 2 of the *United States Constitution* states that the President "may require the Opinion, in writing, of the principal Officer in each of the executive Departments, upon any subject relating to the Duties of their respective Offices." This led to the creation of what we now call the Cabinet.

THE UNITED STATES OF AMERICA

tyrant in times of emergency to oversee the military plans of the country with "supreme command and direction of the military and naval forces."[46] Although the President would have complete authority in managing the war, the power to declare war remained with Congress.[47] The Founding Fathers chose to create a powerful President to streamline military decisions, but his powers were still limited in scope.

The Founding Fathers saw the benefits of keeping the three branches of government as independent of each other as possible. They therefore created the electoral college to choose the President. Instead of directly electing the President with majority rule or allowing Congress to select the President, each state held a number of "electoral votes" equal to its number of House and Senate seats. Originally, the candidate with the most votes became President and the person with the second most votes became Vice President. After the election of 1800, when no candidate received a majority and it took the House thirty-six ballots to elect Thomas Jefferson, the Twelfth Amendment altered the system so that votes for President and Vice President would be separate. Also in the original system, the electors were chosen by the states and those electors then decided which candidate to vote for. But the people began demanding that the electors vote for a specific candidate, so now the people vote for a Presidential candidate and the electors from each state are pledged to vote for that candidate.[48] This system makes the President totally independent of Congress because they have no say in his election, except in the rare situation in which no person receives a majority of electoral votes, which last occurred in 1824. Additionally, because a candidate becomes President by winning the most electoral votes, even if he does not win a majority of the popular vote, he is somewhat independent of the people, as well.[49] In this way, the President represents the entire country and not Congress, a single state or region, or even the majority of people over the minority.

The President was also given the power to veto legislation passed by Congress. The Founders believed that the legislative branch is inherently the most powerful and, therefore, many checks on its power had to be created. In Federalist No. 48, James Madison writes, "The legislative department is everywhere extending the sphere of its activity, and drawing all power into its impetuous vortex... The legislative department derives a superiority in our governments from other circumstances. Its constitutional powers being at once more extensive, and less susceptible of precise limits, it can, with the greater facility, mask, under complicated and indirect measures, the encroachments which it makes on the co-ordinate departments... The legislative department alone has access to the pockets of the people."[50] With the power to veto legislation, the President can stop a simple majority of Congress from passing legislation that he disagrees with. In this way, the President can stop Congress' most egregious bills from becoming law. On the other hand, a two-thirds majority of both houses of Congress can vote to overturn the Presidential veto,[51] thus preventing the President from blocking all legislation, which would have taken away all of Congress' power.

The third branch of government is the judicial branch. According to the United States Constitution, Supreme Court Justices are to be selected by the President "with the advice and consent of the Senate."[52] By dividing the power of selecting judges between the two other branches, the power of each of those branches is thus limited. Because Supreme Court Justices serve a lifelong term,[53] unless impeached and convicted,* they are entirely independent of the other branches.

Though not part of the Founding Fathers' plan, political parties emerged soon after the Constitution was written. Nevertheless, the Constitution was so designed to prevent groups of people, whether a regional group or a political faction, from gaining control of the entire government. By dividing powers between the different branches of government, splitting the legislature into two houses with different methods of election, and dividing the power between the national and state governments, a single political party rarely controls the entire

---

* The only Supreme Court Justice to be impeached was Samuel Chase in 1805, but he was acquitted. Abe Fortas resigned from the Court in 1969 in the face of possible impeachment hearings after he allegedly accepted a questionable fee from a financier under investigation for securities violations.

government. For example, when Jefferson's Democratic-Republicans controlled the legislative and executive branches from 1801 to 1824, the Federalist John Marshall dominated the Supreme Court. Furthermore, a political party often has different factions within itself pushing different agendas. During its twenty-four year reign, the Democratic-Republicans often lacked cohesiveness on issues such as tariffs, internal improvements, and the national bank,[54] as well as slavery.[55] In 1824, four Democratic-Republicans ran for President. Following the election, the party split into different factions with Andrew Jackson and Martin van Buren forming the Democratic Party while John Quincy Adams and Henry Clay formed what would become the Whig Party.

Even if it wanted to be a democracy, the United States was simply too large to be one. In the democracies of ancient Greece, all voters resided in one city and could easily be assembled to conduct government business. The U.S. was over a thousand mile long, far too large to have everybody vote on each piece of business. Therefore, representative government was needed to give the people the right to vote but enable the gathering of legislators and executives.[56] Additionally, the United States was so large that its people felt like citizens of their own states more than of a single country. While a citizen from Trenton, New Jersey may have had much in common with one from Philadelphia, Pennsylvania, just across the Delaware River, citizens from South Carolina and Massachusetts, on opposite ends of the country, felt little brotherhood, except when faced with a common enemy. Furthermore, the people believed that a far away government in New York City, Philadelphia, or Washington would not understand their needs and could not represent them. Therefore, a system of dual sovereignty needed to be created.[57]

This federalist system of divided power between the national and state government would be difficult to design. Although the United States generally used Greece, Rome, and England as guides to create its political system and governmental institutions, no country had ever created a strong federal government while leaving most power with the individual states.[58] To help create this balance between the states and the federal government, the state legislatures were given the power to select the Senators representing their states,* making the federal government, or a part of it, directly answerable to the states.[59]

A good constitution must be permanent and provide the nation with legal and political stability, but it must still be flexible enough to allow changes without abolishing the entire document.[60] The Founding Fathers, therefore, provided a method of amending the Constitution that is difficult enough to prevent constant alteration but still allows vital updates to be made. Constitutional amendments require a two-thirds vote in each house of Congress and ratification by three-quarters of the states. After ratification of the Constitution in 1789, the Anti-Federalists raised concerns about the people's civil liberties and the possibility of the federal government infringing upon them.[61] As a result, just months after the Constitution was ratified, a Bill of Rights containing twelve Amendments was proposed to guarantee the rights of the people and the states. Ten of these proposals were ratified in 1791.† These first ten Amendments did little to change the Constitution; they simply clarified it without increasing or decreasing the government's powers.[62] Over the following 220 years, only seventeen Amendments have been added to the Constitution, making it a remarkably stable document.

An Effective System

The structure of the United States government, as established by the Founding Fathers in the Constitution, makes tyranny much less likely. It is nearly impossible for a dictator to gain control because the President has limited power. Individual states and regions are countered by other states and regions, making domination by one group unlikely. The rich cannot gain control because the House and the Senate, since 1913, are elected by the people, as is the President,

---

* Until the Seventeenth Amendment was ratified in 1913, providing for the direct election of Senators.

† One of the remaining two proposed Amendments was finally ratified in 1992, more than 200 years after Congress submitted it to the states for ratification.

though indirectly. In its original design, the poor were not able to use government to redistribute wealth because the federal government had no legal authority to directly tax the people.*

One of the brilliant methods of maintaining liberty that the Founders included in the Constitution was the different methods of selecting government officials. Representatives are elected by geographic districts, Senators were chosen by the state legislatures, the President elected by the Electoral College, and Supreme Court Justices appointed by the President but confirmed by the Senate.[63] Furthermore, each official serves for a different length of time. The Representative has a two-year term, Presidents are elected for four years, Senators serve for six, and Supreme Court Justices have life tenure. This staggered system prevents the sudden takeover of power by one man or group. Although the House of Representatives can quickly change sides in just one election, it normally takes two or three elections for the Senate to change. The Supreme Court moves even more slowly, often taking decades to change its complexion. For example, when Franklin Roosevelt was President with big majorities in both houses of Congress, the Democrats pushed through a large number of new programs, much of it within the President's famous first hundred days. However, the Supreme Court later ruled that much of the legislation was unconstitutional. Though the country had given overwhelming majorities to the Democrats, the more slowly changing judicial branch defended the Constitution and prevented the executive and legislative branches from imposing their wills.

An important result of the federal system is competition among the states. According to the Constitution, most of the power of government remains with the states. By enabling each state to pursue its own goals and strategies, other states can copy successful projects and avoid those that have failed elsewhere. As Supreme Court Justice Louis Brandeis wrote in 1932, "It is one of the happy incidents of the federal system that a single courageous State may, if its citizens choose, serve as a laboratory; and try novel social and economic experiments

---

* Until the Sixteenth Amendment was ratified in 1913, creating the income tax.

without risk to the rest of the country."[64] Today, states compete to create the most efficient tax structure, attract businesses, provide the highest quality education and health care at the lowest cost, fight crime without infringing on civil rights, and provide other valuable services. Each state tries to provide its citizens with the best living environment and, thereby, attract new residents. Instead of limiting the country to one grand experiment, the states provide fifty experiments, all occurring at the same time. Each American can then choose which state best fits his needs.

The United States has seen this competition at work in recent years. Low tax states have seen a huge influx of people coming from states with higher tax rates. For example, Massachusetts residents have fled to New Hampshire,[65] which has no sales tax and no tax on earned income. Recently, New York Governor David Paterson said, "You heard the mantra, "Tax the rich, tax the rich." We've done that. We've probably lost jobs and driven people out of the state."[66] According to a recent study, 1.5 million New York residents left the state between 2000 and 2008. Furthermore, these emigrants earned 13 percent more than the immigrants replacing them. As a result, New York has lost $4.3 billion in taxable income.[67] In an opinion piece for the *Los Angeles Times*, William Voegeli writes that government spending in California is 47 percent higher than in Texas, but the roads are of equal quality and schools are better in Texas. As a result, California has a net out-migration of over 3,000 people per week whereas Texas has a net in-migration of about 1,500 people per week.[68]

In total, the states with the lowest tax rates have seen their population and economy grow dramatically while high tax states have seen slower economic growth and negative domestic migration.[69] The nine states that have no income tax gained 235,000 new residents in 2007 and 2.6 million from 1997 to 2007 from other states, whereas the ten states with the highest tax burden lost 441,000 residents in 2007 and over three million people from 1997 to 2007 to other states.[70] Competition between the states has given American citizens the ability to choose from among fifty options on how much to pay in taxes and how much to receive in services at the state level. Under this competitive system, states making poor decisions are punished by seeing their people leave while states making good decisions see increased demand for residency. More important, states can copy the successful and learn from the mistakes of the unsuccessful, thus making each state's government more efficient.

For two hundred twenty years, the Unites States Constitution has been successful in preventing the tyranny that the Founders worried about. The system of checks and balances not only gave each branch of government separate powers, but also gave each branch some power over the others. James Madison states that "ambition must be made to counteract ambition... to control the abuses of government."[71] That men of ambition may attempt to seize control of the government should not be surprising. By preventing men from serving in more than one branch of government, creating checks and balances between the three branches, and limiting the power of the federal government, the Founders prevented the rise of tyranny and oligarchy.[72] As a result of this success, the U.S. Constitution is a model for countless other countries.[73]

THE LOSS OF STATES RIGHTS

The Constitution created a federalist system, wherein the national government has supreme power in foreign affairs and defense, but most other governmental powers are left to the states. The Tenth Amendment granted the states all powers not delegated to the federal government, but this was implied by the Constitution from the start.[74] However, over the years, much of the power of the states has been taken away by the national government.

In Federalist No. 17, Alexander Hamilton argues, "It will always be far more easy for the State governments to encroach upon the national authorities than for the national government to encroach upon the State authorities."[75] James Madison makes the same argument in Federalist No. 45: "The State governments will have the advantage of the Federal government, whether we compare them in respect to the immediate dependence of the one on the other; to the weight of personal influence which each side will possess; to the powers respectively vested in them; to the predilection and probable support of the people; to the disposition and faculty of resisting and frustrating the measures of each other."[76] History has proven them wrong as the federal government has become superior to the states.[77]

It did not take long for the federal government to exert itself upon the states. Madison recognized his error and began arguing against the growing federal government. In response to the Alien and Sedition Acts of 1798, which sought to restrict dissent against government policies and expel aliens with suspected foreign loyalties,[78] James Madison penned the Virginia Resolutions and Thomas Jefferson wrote the Kentucky Resolutions, in which they argued that the states had the right to interpose between the federal government and the people and also to nullify unconstitutional laws.[79]

In 1828, Congress passed and President John Quincy Adams signed into law a protective tariff, which the South called the "Tariff of Abominations" because it was designed not to generate needed revenue, but had the purpose of "the protection of one branch of industry at the expense of others."[80] With the election of Andrew Jackson that same year, the tariff was replaced by a lower one, but South Carolina thought that even this one was too harsh and declared both tariffs "unconstitutional, unequal, and oppressive."[81] Finally, an even lower tariff was passed and South Carolina was appeased. The threat of ignoring federal law and possible secession forced the national government into action. States rights had acted as a check on the federal government.

The states rights claim was not just a Southern argument designed to protect the institution of slavery. The 1798 Resolutions were about freedom of speech and due process, not slavery. The tariff argument of 1828 also had nothing to do with slavery; it concerned the requirement that taxes be "in Proportion to the Census or enumeration herein before directed to be taken."[82] Furthermore, during the War of 1812, many in the North proposed seceding from the Union because they disagreed with the war and the resulting restrictions on trade, which were hurting Northern commercial interests.[83]

This argument about interposition, nullification, and secession was put to rest with the Civil War and the case of *Texas v. White* in 1869, in which the Supreme Court ruled that the Union is "indissoluble," states cannot secede, and that, legally, the Confederate States never left the Union.[84] As a result of the Civil War, the subsequent Supreme Court ruling, and the federal government's occupation of the South during Reconstruction, the states lost their right to question the federal government and this important check on the federal government's power was lost.

WAR POWERS

The Civil War resulted in the exact opposite of what the South wanted. The South lost the war, their slaves were freed, hundreds of thousands died, and the South was occupied by the North. Worse yet, the South had seceded and fought the war, in part, to protest the growth of the federal government, but the war only enabled the federal government to increase its power.

On April 27, 1861, just two weeks after the Civil War began at Fort Sumter, President Abraham Lincoln suspended habeas corpus. Habeas corpus, Latin for "you have the body," granted a prisoner the right to appear before a court to determine the legality of his imprisonment. The Constitution provides for the suspension of due process "when in Cases of Rebellion or Invasion the public safety may require it,"[85] but this power was given to Congress, not the President. Initially, Lincoln only suspended habeas corpus in the area between Philadelphia and Washington, D.C., but in 1863 it was suspended throughout the United States. Lincoln's opponents called him a tyrant[86] and Roger Taney, Chief Justice of the Supreme Court, ruled that the President did not have the power to suspend habeas corpus. In 1863, Congress voted to suspend habeas corpus, thus confirming Lincoln's dictatorial power. In total, it is estimated that over thirteen thousand civilians were arrested without the right to habeas corpus.[87] Lincoln also censored the newspapers and assemblies "when they may be working palpable injury to the Military," but warned his generals "to exercise great caution, calmness, and forbearance."[88]

Running out of money, the United States paid creditors and soldiers with Demand Notes. These "greenbacks" were not backed by gold or silver and quickly declined in value.[89] Printing money caused prices to rise[90] and people did not want to use the declining greenbacks,[91] forcing the government to look for other means of raising funds. In 1862, Congress passed and President Lincoln signed into law the country's first income tax at a rate of three percent on incomes over six hundred dollars and five percent on incomes over ten thousand. This income tax was eliminated in 1872, but was revived in the 1890s, at which time the Supreme Court ruled it was unconstitutional because it was not apportioned according to the census as required by the Constitution.[92]

Lincoln also instituted the nation's first military draft in 1863, leading to draft riots in New York City. Only 46,000 draftees and 118,000 hired substitutes served in the army, just eight percent of the Union's 2.1 million troops.[93] However, the draft was a successful fundraising tool because it allowed drafted men to opt out by paying three-hundred dollars. It raised $600 million in funds for the war.[94]

These same powers were used by President Woodrow Wilson in World War I. Woodrow Wilson believed that, in times of war, disloyal Americans should be dealt with firmly.[95] In 1917, Wilson tried to make it illegal to publish information the President deems useful to the enemy.[96] The press protested and Representative William Wood called this provision "an instrument of tyranny" and Representative Martin Madden said "we ought not to do the thing that will establish autocracy in America."[97] This provision was defeated in the House but Congress passed a scaled back version, the Espionage Act of 1917, giving the Postmaster General the authority to exclude any mailings advocating illegal behavior and also made it illegal to "cause or attempt to cause insubordination, disloyalty, mutiny, or refusal of duty."[98] In 1918, Wilson got his censorship of both the press and the general population with the passage of the Sedition Act, which made it illegal to write or say anything "abusive" about the government, military, Constitution, flag, or uniforms of the United States.[99]

Like Lincoln, President Wilson initiated a draft but, unlike during the Civil War, there were no major protests and many Americans were enthusiastic about joining the armed services.[100] Nevertheless, a large percentage opposed this forced conscription. Although a total of 2,180,296 conscripts were inducted in to the military,[101] 337,649 did not show up when ordered to report for duty.[102] In addition to this thirteen percent of draftees who absconded, it is impossible to know how many served only under fear of imprisonment and how many more unwilling draftees convinced the draft board that they were unfit for duty.

Thanks to the 16th Amendment, the income tax had already become legal by the beginning of World War I. Whereas Abraham Lincoln struggled to raise money for his war, Woodrow Wilson had the income tax to raise funds. The 1916 Revenue Act raised the minimum tax rate from 1 percent to 2 percent and the top tax rate went from 7 percent to 15 percent. It also created new taxes on estates and corporate profits. By 1918, the top tax rate had risen to 77 percent and the lowest tax rate was up to 6 percent, though only 5 percent of the population paid any income taxes.[103]

The peace and prosperity of the Roaring Twenties enabled Congress to cut taxes five times with the top rate declining to 25 percent and the lowest rate falling all the way to 1 percent. The lower taxes, in turn, further strengthened the economy.[104] Then the Great Depression hit America and tax revenues dropped sharply. In response, both President Herbert Hoover and President Franklin Roosevelt raised taxes, weakening the economy even further.[105] By 1939, the top tax rate was back up to 79 percent and the lowest rate up to 4 percent. World War II required even more tax revenue and the top tax rate rose to an unbelievable 94 percent while the lowest tax rate jumped to 23 percent and applied to people with income of just five hundred dollars.[106]

World War II was the United States' closest encounter with socialism. In addition to the record high tax rates, government took over most of the nation's economy. Federal government spending had already risen from 3.7 percent of GDP in 1929 to 10.9 percent in 1936 and 11.2 percent in 1941 as the government attempted to spend its way out of the Great Depression. But federal government spending exploded during World War II, rising to 47.9 percent of GDP in 1945, 88 percent of which was military spending. Federal, state, and local governments combined spent a record 53.0 percent of GDP in 1945.[107] Government thus directly controlled the majority of U.S. economic output and indirectly controlled much of the remaining through regulatory oversight, rationing, and price controls.

Like Lincoln and Wilson before him, Franklin Roosevelt censored the media and initiated a draft. President Roosevelt also suspended the right of habeas corpus. With his signing of Executive Order 9066, nearly all 120,000 Japanese Americans living on the West Coast, two-thirds of whom were American citizens,[108] were moved from their homes to internment camps where they would spend the next two or three years. Francis Biddle, Roosevelt's Attorney General, summarized the President's thinking: "What must be done to defend the country must be done... The Constitution has never greatly bothered any wartime President."[109]

Like the tyrants of Greece and temporary dictators of Rome, the President takes for himself or receives from Congress additional powers during times of war. Like the tyrants and dictators of Greece and Rome, Presidents Lincoln, Wilson, and Roosevelt conscripted young men into the military, raised taxes, increased the government's control of the economy, and violated the rights of many in defense of their country.

However, the power of the President must be limited even in times of war. The system of checks and balances ensures that the President, even if Congress is of the same party, will be limited in his power as his political opponents voice their dissent and attempt to block legislation in Congress. Additionally, the Supreme Court can rule the President's actions unconstitutional. Though the three branches will often work together, especially in wartime, to diminish civil rights, the system does ensure that the worst acts will be prevented. Even though

President Roosevelt interned the Japanese Americans, they were treated very well compared to how the Germans or Japanese treated their enemy non-combatants.

Another key restriction on the President and Congress is that they must still stand for reelection, even in times of war. Though Lincoln and Roosevelt may have acted like tyrants in many respects, they certainly would have stepped down had they lost the election campaigns they ran during their wars. Presidents during times of war must limit their tyranny or the people will vote them out of office.

The most important factor though is that these war powers must be temporary. After the war ends, the government must give up its extraordinary powers and the people's rights must be fully restored. Furthermore, the growth in government necessary to execute the war must be scaled back after peace is achieved.

After World War I, Congress and President Wilson immediately scaled back federal government spending from 24.1 percent of GDP in 1919 to just 7.7 percent in 1920. Military spending dropped from 14.4 percent of GDP in 1919 to 3.0 percent in 1920, on its way to a low of 1.3 percent in 1926. Likewise, after World War II, President Harry Truman reduced the federal government from 47.9 percent of GDP in 1945 to 13.2 percent in 1948 and military spending declined from 42.0 percent of GDP in 1945 to 7.3 percent in 1948.[110]

Though military spending is now a relatively small part of the economy compared to previous wartimes, in many respects the United States is in a permanent state of war. Prior to World War II, the most the military ever spent in peacetime was 2.9 percent of GDP in 1932. But in 2009, the U.S. spent 5.6 percent of GDP on the military. Even in 1999, when the U.S. was enjoying the "peace dividend" after the fall of the Soviet Union, military spending was at 3.6 percent, a fifty-nine year low. But even this was higher than the pre-World War II peacetime record and more than the United States spent during any single year of the War of 1812, Mexican-American War, or Spanish-American War.[111] This semi-permanent state of war is reminiscent of the incessant warfare conducted by the tyrants of ancient Greece designed to keep the people busy, distracted, and loyal.

The relatively high level of military spending since the end of World War II was initially caused by the Cold War. The United States spent significant sums containing the Soviet threat and fighting communism in Korea and Vietnam. When the Soviet Union collapsed due to the failures of communism and their inability to maintain military and economic parity with the West, the United States became the world's lone superpower and, therefore, assumed the role of global policeman. More recently, after the September 11, 2001 attacks on the United States, the U.S. military has waged a war against terrorism, overthrowing the Taliban regime in Afghanistan and Saddam Hussein in Iraq. With this permanent state of war, the government has kept many of its wartime powers, including spying on those suspected of being involved in terrorism and imprisoning military combatants without the right of habeas corpus. Obviously, these powers do not nearly approach those of the previous wars, but certainly exceed those of normal peacetime.

Seeing the usefulness of war to expand government and gain powers not enumerated in the Constitution, politicians and bureaucrats often use war terminology to advance their agendas. The War on Drugs, War on Poverty, and War on Cancer were not real wars, but by creating a sense of urgency, proponents of these issues hoped to receive government funding before public sentiment shifted to other causes. Many argue the War on Terrorism should also be on this list of fictitious wars, but it at least involves real military conflict. To some extent, the War on Drugs also requires military support, but it remains primarily a job for law enforcement and public education. The wars on poverty and cancer though require neither the military nor law enforcement and, therefore, the use of the war metaphor is simply a deceptive tool used to gain support for increased government spending.

DEPENDENCY ON GOVERNMENT

More than two thousand years ago, the Greeks and Romans wrote about the evils of democracy, as did the Founding Fathers just two hundred years ago. James Madison writes in Federalist No. 10, "Democracies have ever been spectacles of turbulence and contention; have ever been found incompatible with personal security or the rights of property; and have in general been as short in their lives as they have been violent in their deaths."[112] Nevertheless, Americans have ignored these warnings and history's examples. Since the adoption of the Constitution, the United States has trended toward more democracy, exemplified by the direct election of Senators and increased use of referendum and initiative. One effect of this democracy has been the growing demand for the government to provide for the people.

In 1941, President Franklin Roosevelt made his Four Freedoms speech, in which he argued that all people "everywhere in the world" should have freedom of speech and expression, freedom of religion, freedom from want, and freedom from fear.[113] The first two freedoms are guaranteed by the Constitution, but the latter two were new. In his 1944 State of the Union Address, Roosevelt proposed an "economic bill of rights" including the right to work at a living wage, "freedom from unfair competition and domination by monopolies," the right "to a decent home," the right to medical care, "protection from the economic fears of old age, sickness, accident, and unemployment," and "the right to a good education."[114]

There is a most obvious difference between the original Bill of Rights and this second one. The original enumerates rights "to prevent misconstruction or abuse" of the government's powers.[115] Franklin Roosevelt's new freedoms and rights though are the exact opposite. They are powers given to the government to provide economic benefits to the people. These new freedoms and rights only cheapen the real rights that people need to live in civilized society. In fact, society has survived and thrived for millennia without these new "rights." But when the people lose their basic rights, those of life, liberty, and property, society is no longer free.

Just after listing his new bill of rights in his 1944 State of the Union Address, Roosevelt said, "All of these rights spell security."[116] But Benjamin Franklin had already warned us, "They who can give up essential liberty to obtain a little temporary safety, deserve neither liberty nor safety."[117] To alleviate their "economic fears," many Americans are willing to sacrifice some of their liberty to receive the new benefits Roosevelt outlined. Friedrich Hayek explains the real purpose of these new freedoms and rights: "The demand for the new freedom was thus only another name for the old demand for an equal distribution of wealth."[118]

After World War II, total spending at all levels of government had fallen to 20.5 percent of GDP by 1948 from a record high of 53.0 percent in 1945. But in the sixty years to follow, government spending has risen fairly consistently to hit 42.7 percent in 2009, a level exceeded only by the World War II years of 1943, 1944, and 1945. Nonmilitary spending has risen from 11.0 percent of GDP in 1945 to a record high 37.1 percent in 2009.[119]

Health care was the largest spending category in 2009 at 16.6 percent of government spending. Government health care consists primarily of Medicare at 42.6 percent of the total, Medicaid at 29.7 percent, and government-operated hospitals and health administration at 18.9 percent.[120] Medicare currently consumes 3.5 percent of GDP, a manageable amount. But the Congressional Budget Office estimates Medicare will consume 9.0 percent of GDP in 2050 and 13.5 percent of GDP in 2080.[121]

The second largest budget category is pensions at 15.3 percent of all government spending.[122] This consists of Social Security along with government employee retirement plans. Social Security had outlays equaling 4.4 percent of GDP in 2008, but that figure is expected to grow to 6.1 percent by 2033. Social Security ran a surplus of 0.5 percent of GDP in 2008, but is predicted to run a deficit of 1.2 percent in 2033.[123] Had the government put the Social Security money in a trust fund, as it promised, the past surpluses would have been saved to pay future deficits. But the government has already spent that money, leaving nothing to pay out future benefits. The result is that taxes will have to rise or benefits will have to be cut. This would not be the first time the government raised the Social Security tax or cut benefits. The original Social Security tax in 1935 was 2 percent, half paid by the employee and half by the employer, on the first three thousand dollars of income. From the 2 percent rate that lasted from 1935 to 1949, the rate went up regularly until it reached the current 12.4 percent rate in 1990.[124]

At the same time, Social Security benefits, which were non-taxable, became taxable. Now, individual retirees with income of $25,000 to $34,000 and couples with income of $32,000 to $44,000 pay income taxes on half their Social Security benefits. Individuals and couples with higher incomes pay income taxes on 85 percent of their benefits.[125] Though low-income retirees see no change in benefits or taxes paid, somebody in the top tax bracket of 35 percent sees a decrease in after-tax benefits of nearly 30 percent. Additionally, the "normal retirement age" is slowly being raised from 65 to 67.[126] As life expectancy rises, it only makes sense for people to retire at a later age. However, it is unfair and immoral to alter the agreement under which taxpayers were paying into the system. If this were a private corporation changing the terms of an established contract, they would certainly be the subject of a class action lawsuit and likely an investigation by the federal and state governments.

Health care and pensions, combined, comprise 31.9 percent of government spending,[127] a figure that is expected to rise dramatically in the future.[128] Welfare, including payments to the poor and disabled, unemployment benefits, housing assistance, and non-monetary assistance such as food stamps, makes up another 9.7 percent of government spending, bringing entitlement spending to 41.6 percent of government spending.[129] In the first quarter of 2009, Social Security, Medicare, welfare, and other benefits provided by the government accounted for 16.2 percent of all personal income, a record high.[130] Americans have become dependent on the government, something the Founders did not intend. After paying tens or hundreds of thousands of dollars into Social Security and Medicare, only the very rich would be able forego the benefits promised them. Every election, retirees and people approaching retirement vote for candidates who promise not to touch their retirement or health care programs. This has made fixing the structural problems behind these programs virtually impossible, but it has accomplished the goal of modern liberals and socialists of making Americans dependent on the government.

Many are calling for free health care as well. Why work if the government will provide free food, subsidized housing, free health care, and a welfare check? With the high rates of taxation, increased regulation, and welfare for not working, Americans are starting fewer new businesses.[131] For many, the risk of starting a small business is too high, whereas one can work for a big corporation that is required by law to provide a minimum wage, limited work hours, good working conditions, insurance against injury, health care, retirement plans, and other benefits. Additionally, if somebody working as an employee is laid off, the government will be there to help them out. The small business owner receives no such support from the government.

Even better than working for a large corporation is working for the government. As of January 2010, 22.5 million Americans worked for the government, 17.3 percent of the workforce. Back in 1948, just 13.1 percent worked for the government.[132] Government employees also receive higher salaries. In 1948, the average government employee was paid the same as one working for a private firm, but in 2008, the average salary of a government employee was 11.7 percent higher than in the private sector. Even more impressive, a federal employee who received 4.8 percent more income than a private employee in 1948 now receives 40.8 percent more, as of 2008.[133] And these employment figures do not include all the jobs created by the 529 billion dollars worth of contracts given out by the federal government each year,[134] two-thirds of which were for defense programs.[135] As of 2006, government contracts to private defense companies employed an additional 1.4 million people.[136]

Americans have also become dependent on the government to protect them from employers, manufacturers, retailers, and themselves. The National Relations Labor Board, created in 1935, "guarantees the right of employees to organize and to bargain collectively with their employers, and to engage in other protected concerted activity with or without a union, or to refrain from all such activity."[137] In 1971, the Occupational Safety and Health Administration was created "to prevent work-related injuries, illnesses, and deaths" by inspecting workplaces for health and safety violations.[138] The Food and Drug Administration monitors the safety of food and drugs in the United States. The Federal Trade Commission and Department of Justice enforce the many consumer protection laws. The Environmental Protection Agency safeguards the country's air, water, and land. The state and local governments often have departments to conduct many of the same tasks. They also regulate and often set prices for utilities and insurance. Thus, in addition to its direct control over 43 percent of the American economy, the government also indirectly controls where people work, where they live, and what they consume.

As the American people become more dependent on the government, it becomes increasingly difficult to stop the growth of government. Although many or even most people want smaller government, big government does not require a majority supporting it. All that is needed is for a majority to support each individual project. If a majority supports Social Security, a majority supports Medicare, and a majority supports welfare, all three will exist even if a majority opposes "big government." In other words, a bill proposing all three programs may fail to achieve majority support, but by breaking it into three separate bills, each will pass individually as special interest groups convince the public of their program's necessity. Thus, the United States ends up with the big government that very few people want, but each individual program has enough support to be created and preserved.

WE ARE ALL CRIMINALS NOW

Tyrants and totalitarians often keep the laws a secret to oppress the average citizen and imprison, exile, or kill their political opponents. The tyrant or totalitarian can easily change the law to attack specific individuals or groups and, without them knowing of the law change, find them guilty of committing the new crime. But free societies will not stand for such devious actions. Instead, the politicians must keep the people repressed by making the law so complex that nobody can understand it. The government has prohibited so many activities that virtually all Americans are now criminals. If an American buys goods over the Internet without paying sales tax, buys medicine from Canada or Mexico, makes a mistake on his taxes, or downloads music or movies without paying, he is a criminal. There are now over four thousand federal crimes[139] and there are thousands more state and local crimes as well. The government does not prosecute most of these "innocent" crimes, but the penalty can be severe, including years in jail, if they decide to prosecute to the full extent of the law.

Based on the Fifth and Sixth Amendments to the U.S. Constitution, all Americans are presumed innocent until proven guilty by an impartial jury. But the government often treats its citizens like criminals, with one set of rules for government officials and another set for the common people. And with so many laws to follow, each American is already a criminal, justifying the government's often condescending attitude toward the people.

Take the tax code, for instance. Tens of thousands of pages long, including well over a thousand different forms, and constantly growing. The tax code is so complicated that nobody understands it all, not even the IRS. Of course, nobody needs to understand all of it because most tax laws apply to so few people. Nevertheless, the instructions for the standard personal income tax form 1040 is now 174 pages long. Furthermore, many people with higher incomes will have to recalculate their taxes using the Alternative Minimum Tax. There are additional forms that each person may be required to complete to report income they received during the year or to take tax deductions. Even somebody trying to be honest may accidentally record an unqualified dividend as a qualified dividend, mix up short-term and long-term capital gains, deduct ineligible expenses or dependants, or fail to claim credits he is not even aware of. It is no surprise that so many use professional tax preparers or software, even though they are also far from perfect. As a result, the IRS conducts 1.4 million audits per year,[140] most of which are likely the result of simple mistakes or ignorance of complicated tax laws.

The IRS is also a tool to be used by corrupt Presidents against their enemies. President Franklin Roosevelt ordered the Bureau of Internal

Revenue, predecessor to the IRS, to audit Andrew Mellon, the former Secretary of the Treasury. President Roosevelt also intervened in a tax case against Brown & Root, a defense contractor that had funded Lyndon Johnson's campaign for Senate, a scandal that might have ended the future President's political career. President John F. Kennedy used the IRS to audit right-wing extremist groups. President Richard Nixon used the IRS to investigate his political opponents and critics. President Bill Clinton has also been accused of misusing the IRS and the FBI, but an official investigation found no wrong-doing by the President.

The vast majority of Americans are unlikely to feel the wrath of the President or the IRS, but the government watches each person's every move, ready to prosecute if someone becomes an enemy of the state. ECHELON, for example, is capable of intercepting phone calls, e-mails, faxes, and other data traffic. Though its purpose is to spy on terrorists and other enemies of the free world, it has reportedly been used for corporate espionage as well.[141]

The government has also increased its supervision of financial transactions. With the passage of the Money Laundering Control Act in 1986, banks are required to report to the government all transactions exceeding ten thousand dollars, a small sum that enables the government to monitor every major transaction, from transferring funds between one's bank and brokerage account or withdrawing money to buy a house or car. Though this is designed to catch money laundering schemes and the average person's information is seen only by a computer, the information can be easily retrieved and used against somebody who happens to make it on the President's enemies list or is being charged with tax evasion, money laundering, or terrorism. Following the 2001 terrorist attacks, the government initiated Know Your Customer rules. Financial institutions must collect information from its customers and verify that they are not money launderers or terrorists. The government has thus enlisted the banks, brokerages, and insurance companies to do some of its spying for it. In addition to simply checking the account holder's name against lists of known terrorists and money launderers, the financial institutions must monitor customer transactions and report to the government any possible fraud and links to terrorist or mob organizations. Besides adding untold costs onto the financial institutions, it does little to stop the terrorists because they can just move their banking overseas. But it does enable the government to keep an eye on its citizens. Again, most of this information is collected and never used, but should one become suspected of a serious crime, the government has reams of information on every American at its disposal. Along with the government's army of lawyers, the average American stands little chance when accused of a crime.

There is one area in which the government's monitoring of the public's activities is constantly felt by the average American. In recent years, the police have more actively gone after speeders and illegal parkers, partly to generate revenue. Furthermore, many cities and states have installed photo radar cameras to photograph speeders and send them a ticket without even involving the police. While this frees up the police to fight real crime, if that was the intention, this has created a new set of problems.

A basic tenet of law is the right to face one's accuser. However, when a speeding ticket is issued by a machine, this is impossible. To work around this legal issue, many states have turned the crimes of speeding and running red lights into civil offenses. By doing so, states can send out a ticket and collect the revenue without going to court for each case. Additionally, with no criminal penalty or points against one's driver's license, most just pay the fine because it is cheaper to do so than to lose a day's wages challenging the ticket in court. Many places have made fighting these tickets even more costly by adding on administrative or court fees just to challenge the ticket.[142]

While the photo radar systems are currently being used to give out tickets and generate a new revenue stream for the government, these cameras could be used by the police to investigate crimes. The United Kingdom already has a vast network of over a million CCTV cameras watching the streets for crime and invading the privacy of its citizens. The U.S. is moving in that direction. Cities and states are buying license-plate scanners that can capture, analyze, and store 1,500 license plates per minute.[143] While this can be useful in capturing wanted felons and stolen vehicles, just a few cameras positioned in the correct locations can gather information on millions of Americans. Unscrupulous employees may already be using the system to stalk spouses, friends, and enemies, possibly using the information to commit crimes.

With the plethora of laws that nobody can know or obey in its entirety and the government spying and recording details about each American, it should come as no surprise that Presidents often have difficulty finding clean nominees to fill cabinet positions. Timothy Geithner worked at the International Monetary Fund and then was president of the Federal Reserve Bank of New York before he was nominated as the Secretary of the Treasury. Obviously, he is a financial expert, yet somehow he forgot to pay his self-employment taxes, even though he received money from the IMF specifically for that purpose. It appears like Geithner evaded his taxes, but he claims to have been careless and that the mistake was unintentional. Similarly, Charles Rangel, chairman of the House Ways and Means Committee, which writes the country's tax laws, did not pay property taxes on some land he owns in New Jersey[144] nor pay taxes from rental income on a beach house he owns in the Dominican Republic,[145] yet he is still in office. The Secretary of the Treasury, who oversees the IRS, and the man heading the tax-writing committee in the House of Representatives either cannot properly pay their taxes or choose to evade them. The tax system is either too complicated or it is administered by corrupt politicians, or both.

Geithner is not the only recent nominee to run into legal problems. Within the first hundred days, ten Barack Obama nominees withdrew their candidacies for issues including corruption, taxes, ethics, conflicts of interest, fraud, incompetence, embezzlement, cronyism, and the old excuse of "personal reasons."[146] This problem predates President Obama. President Bill Clinton's first choice for attorney general, Zoë Baird, was forced to withdraw when it was revealed that she failed to pay social security taxes for two illegal immigrants she hired as nannies. Clinton's second choice for Attorney General, Kimba

Wood, was also forced to withdraw for hiring a babysitter who was in the country illegally. President George W. Bush had a similar problem when Linda Chavez withdrew after it became known that she provided free room and board to an illegal immigrant. President Bush's choice for Homeland Security Secretary, Bernard Kerik, was also forced to withdraw because he too hired an illegal immigrant and failed to pay the proper taxes. Either the government has become extremely corrupt or it has simply become impossible for anybody, even those who write and enforce the laws, to avoid illegal or unethical activity.

The impossible-to-follow tax code along with monitoring of financial transactions and commonly ignored laws such as speeding, buying goods over the Internet without paying sales tax, buying medicines from overseas, and downloading music and movies have turned us all into criminals. The government normally ignores these minor crimes, but has started cracking down on some, such as tax evasion and speeding, whose enforcement will also bring in much needed revenue. Occasionally, the government, especially a state attorney general with political ambitions, will want to make an example of somebody and prosecute the person for one of these minor crimes.

All this may sound paranoid, but do not say that to Joe Wurzelbacher, a plumber who had the nerve to ask Democratic presidential nominee Barack Obama a simple question on taxes. Barack Obama's lengthy response concluded with "I think when you spread the wealth around, it's good for everybody," a response not too popular with many taxpayers. As a result of Joe the Plumber's new found fame, and infamy with Democrats, the Director of the Ohio Department of Job and Family Services initiated a search for information on Joe Wurzelbacher using state computers, the very thing those who build and control these databases said would not happen. This misuse of government databases to spy on Joe the Plumber leads one to wonder how often local, state, and federal governments misuse official government information without the public's knowledge.

Between 1989 and 1994, over a thousand IRS employees were investigated for snooping into the files of friends, neighbors, relatives, and celebrities.[147] Aware of the problem, the IRS vowed to stop this breach of privacy. But in 1997, it was reported that the IRS investigated another 1,500 such cases in the previous two years and fired 23 employees.[148] The problem continues to this day with a Treasury Department investigator testifying before Congress that 521 cases were investigated in 2007, up from 430 cases in 1998.[149] In June 2009, an employee of the California Franchise Tax Board was charged with unauthorized access to an IRS computer and unauthorized inspection of tax returns.[150] Similarly, the State Department has a problem with employees "snooping into the passport files of famous Americans."[151] Yet, some people also want to grant the government access to each American's medical files.

Our government has created too many laws and constantly changes them, thus entrapping the people. Additionally, many crimes are so minor that they are ignored by the people. Furthermore, the government pries into every aspect of our lives by monitoring financial transactions and spying, both legally and illegally. As a result, we are all criminals now.

THE POLITICAL CLASS

The United States of America is largely a classless society. Yes, there are the upper class, middle class, and lower class, but nobody is forced into one of those classes and people quite frequently move between them. The United States never had royalty or a landed aristocracy, and the Founding Fathers hoped to create a meritocracy. Alexander Hamilton argues in Federalist No. 36: "There are strong minds in every walk of life that will rise superior to the disadvantages of situation, and will command the tribute due to their merit, not only from the classes to which they particularly belong, but from the society in general."[152] The Founders would be extremely disappointed to discover that a political class has emerged that, to a large extent, controls the government. This political class lives off the largesse of government and, in many respects, has their own set of rules, which they write for themselves.

Throughout history, politics has been a family affair. In most mon-archies, kingship passed from father to son or another close relative. While there is no heredity of power in democratic republics, a famous last name often helps gain fame and power. Roman politicians often used their names and ancestry to push their careers. The Gracchi brothers, tribunes who tried to redistribute the land, were the grand-sons of the famous general Scipio Africanus who defeated Hannibal. Marcus Junius Brutus, the powerful politician and member of the conspiracy to kill Julius Caesar, was a descendent of Lucius Junius Brutus, founder of the Roman Republic, and also a descendent of Cato the Elder. Cato the Elder was also an ancestor of Cato the Younger, another opponent of Julius Caesar. Marcus Aemilius Lepidus, who formed the Second Triumvirate with Octavian and Mark Antony, was also a descendant of Cato the Elder. Mark Antony was also Julius Caesar's second cousin. Julius Caesar came from an important family as well, with his father reaching the rank of praetor. For centuries, the name Caesar would be taken by the Roman Emperors and would later be adapted for the German Kaisers and the Russian Czars.

A famous name and famous relatives certainly seems to help. It should come as no surprise that the United States has seen the same kind of hereditary advantage in politics. In fact, the first President not to be a Founding Father was John Quincy Adams, the son of President John Adams, second cousin once removed of Samuel Adams, and holder of one of the most famous last names in America. There have been many other presidential families. President Benjamin Harrison was the grandson of President William Henry Harrison. Franklin Delano Roosevelt and Theodore Roosevelt were fifth cousins and Theodore was also uncle to Franklin's wife Eleanor. More important, the popular Roosevelt name likely helped Franklin Roosevelt advance his political career. The Kennedy family produced three brothers who served in the Senate. One became President. Another was Attorney General before becoming a Senator, but was assassinated just after winning California's Democratic presidential primary. The third served as Senator for forty-six years. Recently, George H. W. Bush served a single term as President. His son George W. Bush served as

President for eight years and another son, Jeb Bush, was governor of Florida. Hilary Clinton was elected to the Senate after husband Bill Clinton's two terms as President, and is currently Secretary of State. There are also numerous distant relationships between the Presidents, which have played little role in their elections, but the important connections may have helped them start their political careers. For example, President Barack Obama is a direct descendant of King Edward I, who ruled England from 1272 to 1307. President Obama is also distantly related to former Presidents James Madison, Harry Truman, Lyndon Johnson, Gerald Ford, and both Bushes, in addition to many other famous politicians.[153] After the 2005 election, Dana Milbank of the Washington Post summarized the situation: "With at least 18 senators, dozens of House members and several administration officials boosted by family legacies, modern-day Washington sometimes resembles the court of Louis XIV without the powdered wigs."[154] The United States was meant to be a "government of the people, by the people, for the people,"[155] but instead, the government is full of career politicians, primarily from well-connected upper-class families and often with a famous last name.

Ideally, government would be a place where men of good character go to affect positive change. Instead, for many it is a place to gain fame, sell influence, and accumulate wealth. In 2006, fifty-eight percent of Senators and forty-four percent of Representatives were millionaires, compared with just one percent of all American adults.[156] Many, of course, were rich before joining government and used their wealth to finance their campaigns, but they too use their political status and power to amass even more wealth or funnel government funds to friends and family.

In 2006, Newt Gingrich said, "There is $2.6 trillion spent in Washington, with the authority to regulate everything in your life. Guess what? People will spend unheard-of amounts of money to influence that. The underlying problems are big government and big money."[157] By 2009, that figure had grown to $3.5 trillion, or 24.7 percent of Gross Domestic Product, making lobbying even more attractive than it was just a few years ago. And that is just the federal government.

State governments spent another $1.3 trillion or 9.4 percent of GDP and local governments spent $1.7 trillion or 12.2 percent of GDP in 2009. After adjusting for intergovernmental transfers, government spending totaled $6.1 trillion in 2009, 42.7 percent of GDP.[158]

All this government spending has made lobbying a very profitable venture for corporations and interest groups. Furthermore, lobbying has become necessary for many companies who rely on government spending to survive. Defense contractors need lobbyists to push their projects or they will lose their funding and go bankrupt. Finance and health care firms need lobbyists to keep the government out of their way or to shape legislation to their advantage. Lobbying is, in many ways, a means of bribing government officials in exchange for favorable treatment, but it also is a means of extortion whereby government officials threaten to hurt the corporation or interest group if they don't build projects in their districts, give jobs to friends and family members, and hire them when they retire or lose their reelection bids.

If one corporation or interest group decides not to play the lobbying game, it will receive no government contracts while its competitors receive favorable tax treatment and other government freebies. Effectively, a company that tries to take the high road will be at a severe competitive disadvantage. In addition to lobbying, corporations and interest groups must contribute money to political campaigns to receive the politician's help in political and legislative matters. Actually, they must donate money to both candidates to ensure that they have some influence regardless who wins. If a corporation or interest group gives to just one party but the other wins, it could become a target of government cutbacks, higher taxes, or simply not receive any government contracts.

Lobbying is a big business. More than 14,000 lobbyists in Washington spend $3 billion per year.[159] At the local level, as of 2006, there were another 59,000 lobbyists spending $1.3 billion per year buying political influence.[160] Obviously, these lobbyists expect a return on their "investment"—they expect the politicians to give them back more than they spend.

One way politicians benefit from all this lobbying is through family members acting as lobbyists. Although lobbyists cannot legally lobby their relatives, it occurs quite frequently. A *USA Today* investigation found that 53 relatives of lawmakers and top aides worked at lobbying firms and they sought $750 million in appropriations from family members 30 times in 2005.[161] It is also likely, though nearly impossible to investigate, that other politicians will be more receptive to these family lobbyists. The spouse of a Congressman acting as a lobbyist is likely to be friendly with many other Congressmen. Furthermore, a Congressman may grant a lobbyist an appropriation in expectation of that lobbyist's relative, who is also a Congressman, doing the same for his relative who is a lobbyist. Congressmen and other government officials really see the benefits when they too become lobbyists after leaving political office. A recent study found "more than 2,200 former federal employees had registered as federal lobbyists, as had nearly 275 former White House aides and nearly 250 former members of Congress."[162] This is a growing problem for the United States government. Back in the 1970s, just 3 percent of lawmakers went to work as lobbyists, but the number had risen to 22 percent in the 1990s.[163]

Former Congressmen have a major advantage in the lobbying game because they are given access to the floors of Congress, the dining rooms, and the gym. This type of access cannot be purchased at any price, putting former Congressmen very much in demand with their pay going up commensurately. As more politicians and bureaucrats become lobbyists, the potential for conflicts of interest grows. Congressmen in Washington are supposed to represent their constituents, but it appears as if they are simply positioning themselves for lucrative lobbying jobs after they are defeated or retire.

Look at how Congressmen use their power to help the special interests that they favor. In October 2008, Congress passed and President Bush signed the Emergency Economic Stabilization Act of 2008, which included $700 billion to purchase distressed assets, thus helping banks recover some of their recent losses. The financial industry is a major contributor to political campaigns and Congress had no problem giving them hundreds of billions of the taxpayers' money even though the average American received little to no help from the government, even as unemployment was rising rapidly. In May 2009, Congress included the "cash for clunkers" program within its Supplemental Appropriations Act, providing one billion dollars, later raised to three billion, for consumers to trade in their old vehicles for new more fuel efficient cars. The government helped out the auto industry while it ignored other industries, possibly because General Motors was already being taken over by the U.S. government and, therefore, part of the government's "stimulus program" was being funneled into a government-owned corporation. Giving the money straight to consumers would have been much more helpful to the average American, more efficient because it would not need a new bureaucracy to administer the program, and fairer as all Americans would have received help and not just those who were in the market for a new car and happened to have a "clunker." Additionally, a tax cut or stimulus check would have avoided destroying hundreds of thousands of cars, even though these cars still worked. The primary job of government officials is supposed to be to protect the rights of all Americans, but instead they used their legislative power to help certain industries and certain Americans. And then they turn the bill over to the American public.

Another perk the political class receives is free travel. Congressmen and other government officials travel on political junkets, fact finding missions, and speaking tours that are often nothing more than covers for free trips to exotic locations, paid for by the taxpayer. In fact, politicians often combine official travel with fundraising tours. They will give a speech or two during the day and host a fundraising dinner in the evening. By giving those speeches, the government picks up the tab, even though the real reason for the trip is the fundraising.

In September 2009, President Barack Obama flew Air Force One to Copenhagen where he tried to win the 2016 Olympics for Chicago. Michelle Obama flew on a separate Air Force 757 earlier in the week, even though she has no official position within the U.S. government. Although they spent millions of dollars of taxpayer money to travel on unofficial business,[164] Michelle Obama reminds the American people of the "sacrifice" she made on behalf of Chicago and the United States.[165] Only the political class can claim that spending other people's money so they can fly around the world is a sacrifice.

At least there are excuses for this travel on the federal level. Congressmen have to travel between their home districts and Washington, D.C. while the President, Secretary of State, and trade representatives must meet with foreign leaders to maintain good relationships with their governments. But at the state and local level, except in extremely large states, travel expenses should be insignificant. Even though all foreign relations are conducted by the federal government, there is a growing trend of governors and mayors traveling to foreign countries promoting their states and towns. The most outrageous example is that of South Carolina Governor Mark Sanford's travels to Argentina, where he was having an extra-marital affair. One such trip in 2008 was a "Latin American trade mission," which the taxpayers paid for.[166] Thus, the American people are paying for the vacations and affairs of the politicians. In contrast, many Congressmen have vilified corporate executives for their travels to expensive hotels on private jets when the members of the political class do the same.

Many politicians take their family with them on their travels, that is when the trip is not a cover for an extra-marital affair. When a President travels overseas on official business, his spouse is often right by his side and, sometimes, other family members travel with him as well. Although this may help form a closer bond between the President and other world leaders, the First Lady and other family members have no official government positions, yet the taxpayer pays for their travel expenses. The average corporate executive does not travel the world doing business with his or her family coming along at the company's expense. But politicians are in their own class and the taxpayer does not notice the millions spent on this when trillions are spent elsewhere.

Another big perk enjoyed by the political class is the use of their office for non-government business, such as running for reelection. Congressmen and the President have the franking privilege, allowing them to correspond with their constituents at the government's expense. Technically, they cannot use this for campaign purposes, but sending a letter to potential voters telling them about all the legislation he proposed in Congress or signed into law is perfectly legal, even if the real purpose is to boast of a job well done and convince the voters to reelect him. Incumbents therefore have a major advantage over their opponents and the political class is largely able to keep power for themselves.

GOVERNMENT BUREAUCRACY

The political class is much too busy enriching themselves and running for reelection to govern the country. Besides, a government spending four trillion dollars cannot possibly be administered by just 535 Congressmen and the President. Therefore, both the President and Congress have delegated administrative authority of numerous government programs to bureaucrats. Bureaucrats have also taken over much of the legislative process. Representatives, Senators, and the President no longer write or read the bills they vote on. Legislative assistants, with help from lobbyists and lawyers, write and read the bills for the Representatives and Senators, who are too busy making speeches and campaigning for office to do their jobs. None of them have time to read thousand-page bills, such as the health care bills proposed in 2009. As House Judiciary Chairman John Conyers said, "I love these members, they get up and say, "Read the bill." What good is reading the bill if it's a thousand pages and you don't have two days and two lawyers to find out what it means after you read the bill?"[167] So in reality, the government is being run by unelected and often unknown bureaucrats.

Congress has created agencies to regulate most aspects of the American economy. There are agencies to regulate energy production, education, banks, financial markets, homeland security, transportation, labor, safety, parks, agriculture, food, drugs, the media, and countless other areas. In addition to administering their industries, they write many of the laws for the government. For example, the tax code as written by Congress is about 8,500 pages long, but another 100,000 pages of tax rules, regulations, and manuals come from the IRS.[168] Congress may set tax rates, but often it is the Treasury Department and IRS that determine what is taxable income.

The President also has a number of "czars" to ensure his orders are followed. Presidents like creating these czar positions because they do not have to go through the long and difficult Senate confirmation process required of cabinet nominees. On May 30, 2009, Senator John McCain tweeted, "Obama has more czars than the Romanovs — who ruled Russia for 3 centuries. Romanovs 18, cyberczar makes 20."[169] Checking the facts, PolitiFact counted twenty-eight at that time, with czars for Afghanistan, AIDS, Border, Car, Climate, Drug, Economic, Energy, Faith-based, Great Lakes, Green Jobs, Guantanamo Closure, Health, Information, Intelligence, Mideast Peace, Mideast Policy, Pay, Regulatory, Science, Stimulus Accountability, Sudan, TARP, Technology, Terrorism, Urban Affairs, Weapons, and WMD.[170] The list has since expanded.

One of the largest effects from this growing bureaucratization has been the decline of individual and states rights and the increasing power of the federal government.[171] Powers that previously had been left to the states and individuals, as specified by the Ninth and Tenth Amendments to the Constitution, have been given over to these regulatory agencies. The United States now has hundreds of thousands of unelected bureaucrats making and administering laws that often have little to no constitutional foundation.

DEMOCRACY AND DEMAGOGUERY IN ARIZONA*

In the late nineteenth and early twentieth centuries, the Progressives pushed for public voting on legislation. Initiatives give the public the right to propose and pass legislation while referendums enable

---

* I will be looking at my home state of Arizona as an example. Twenty-four states, the District of Columbia, and many county and city governments allow ballot initiatives.

them to veto a bill passed by the legislature. These ballot propositions take control out of the hands of the legislature and governor, giving it directly to the people instead. Arizona included initiative and referendum in its constitution upon becoming a state in 1912, along with recall, which enables the people to remove public officials from office. The Founding Fathers and other political thinkers warned about the evils of direct democracy, and we choose to ignore their advice at great risk.

Initiatives and referendums have often been used in Arizona to fool the people. Back in 1990, Arizona had two propositions on the ballot establishing a Martin Luther King, Jr./Civil Rights Day. One proposition would have retained the Columbus Day holiday and the other would not. If both propositions were to pass, the one with more votes would become law. As a result of this setup, many people voted for one but not the other. As a result of splitting the "yes" vote between two different choices, both propositions failed, Arizona became the victim of many jokes, and the National Football League took away the Super Bowl. Many suspect that the second proposition was added for the sole purpose of confusing the public, splitting the vote, and blocking the new MLK holiday.

Recently, ballot propositions have been successfully used to raise sales tax rates for all sorts of new spending, including roads, schools, police, fire, and parks. Every year, the voters face a number of small sales tax increases. Some fail and some pass. Over time, these small tax increases add up. Most recently, on May 18, 2010, Arizona voters approved by a nearly 2-to-1 margin a one percentage point increase in the sales tax rate. When I moved to Arizona in 1986, the sales tax in Phoenix was 6.7 percent. Today, it stands at 9.3 percent. Additionally, Phoenix recently approved a two percent sales tax on food.

The standard reply is that these programs need more money because the city and state are growing. This argument is ridiculous because a growing population would generate proportionally more tax money. Tax rates do not need to be raised to keep the number of police officers, teachers, or roads per capita at a steady level. By raising tax rates, the amount of government revenue per capita is growing, even after adjusting for inflation, and the money does not always go into the primary functions of government. Instead, it has gone into stadiums, multi-billion dollar trolleys, and expensive modern school buildings that, though they look nice, do little to improve education.

The biggest problem with these sales tax propositions is that they are often a bait-and-switch technique used by the government and special interest groups. By putting popular items on the ballot, they can be funded by special sales taxes, allowing more money within the general fund to be spent on less popular items. For example, on September 11, 2007, Phoenix voters approved by a 68 to 32 margin a new 0.2 percent sales tax to hire 500 more police officers and 100 more fire fighters. However, just a few months later, Phoenix announced they will reduce funds to police and fire due to falling tax revenue. In reality, the money from the new sales tax was simply replacing the money no longer coming out of the general budget.

Similarly, in 2000, Arizona passed Proposition 301 establishing a 0.6 percent sales tax to fund education. Unlike many states, Arizona does not rely entirely on property taxes to fund education. With no dedicated source of funds for schools, there is no way to ensure the new sales tax money is going toward education.

Roads and public transportation are another big issue in Arizona. In general, gas taxes are used to build and maintain roads, but Maricopa County voted for a 0.5 percent sales tax to build more roads and expand mass transit, including the building of a new light rail system. This project, if it is needed at all, should be funded from the gas tax or out of general revenue. With the growth in Phoenix's population and economy, Maricopa County's tax collection increased substantially each year until the most recent recession. Furthermore, a gas tax for road building makes the most sense because gas consumption is a very good proxy for road usage. Sales taxes apply to everybody, whether the payer drives or not. Taxes, if possible, should be paid by those who benefit from them.

Taxes with assigned spending items are a good idea, when such spending is necessary. In reality, all taxes should work this way, as the gas tax does in theory. However, by adding these special taxes on top of the general taxes, government can hide unpopular spending within the general budget while admonishing the people to vote for new or increased directed taxes because, as the politicians claim, the government needs more money to fund the popular items.

Liberals claim that these taxes and spending are necessary to maintain civilized society and help the poor. That argument is feasible concerning items such as roads, police, and education, but that does not stop the government from spending vast amounts of money on other less necessary projects. For years, local governments have been involved in the business of building stadiums and leasing them to their local sports teams. This is not a job for the government. It does not help the poor or protect the rights of the people. In fact, it is a gift to the owners of the sports franchises and local merchants near the stadium site. If the owners of a baseball team want a new stadium, they should build it themselves. The only reason the sports franchise is unwilling to build their own stadiums is because it would be unprofitable. The theory the government uses to build stadiums for the sports franchises is that because the local merchants benefit from increased sales and the government benefits from increased tax revenue, it may be unprofitable for the sports franchise to build the stadium but worthwhile for the government. In reality, all the stadium does is shift business from one sector to another. Money spent at the stadium or the surrounding businesses is money not spent elsewhere. A number of studies have been conducted demonstrating that even though some sectors may benefit from new stadiums, the net effect is neutral or even negative.[172]

Years ago, almost all stadiums were multi-purpose. Outdoor stadiums were used for both football and baseball while indoor arenas were used for both hockey and basketball. In those days, the local government would build the stadium and rent it out to both sports franchises. Of course the two sports teams could have formed a partnership and built the stadium themselves, but at least there was some logic to the public funding. Today, with only one franchise using most stadiums, there is even less reason for the government to build stadiums costing hundreds of millions of dollars, or $1.6 billion in the case of the new Yankee Stadium, of which New York City taxpayers financed half the cost.[173] The vast majority of the time, the stadium sits empty as the sports team travels and during the off-season, though the stadium may host a few concerts, Ice Capades, or the circus a few times a year. It is reassuring to know that the government is in the business of providing Americans with a circus, just like the "bread and circuses" of ancient Rome.

Every voter in Arizona knows to expect the same or similar propositions on the ballot each year. The philosophy of the special interest groups is to keep putting these proposals on the ballot until they are approved. This goes beyond just taxes. Both sides of the gay marriage and immigration issues put their proposals on the ballot every year or two. When one side's bill is finally approved by the people, after numerous attempts and slight rewording of the proposal to appease the last voters needed to make a majority, the opposing side then puts the opposite on the ballot while those supporting the new status quo claim, "we already voted on this." Of course, when this new bill is passed, the roles reverse. The United States has a representative system to avoid all this.

The Founding Fathers warned about the evils of democracy. Today the politicians and special interest groups use propositions to trick the voters into constantly growing government. We have to rid ourselves of the democracy in our midst and return to our republican roots.

THE UNITED STATES TODAY AND TOMORROW

In 2009, the federal government ran a record peacetime deficit of 9.9 percent on spending of 24.7 percent of GDP.[174] The deficit is expected to narrow and spending as a percent of GDP should decline as the economy recovers, the temporary stimulus spending ends, and the Bush tax cuts expire. The Congressional Budget Office (CBO) projects a deficit of between 2.3 and 7.4 percent on spending of 22.6 to 26.0 percent of GDP in 2020. But the deficit will start rising thereafter thanks to the entitlement programs that have already been created and the interest to cover the debts created by them. By 2035, the federal government will be spending 27.4 to 33.9 percent of the country's GDP and the deficit will be back up to 5.6 to 14.6 percent of GDP. By 2080, the deficit will be between 17.8 and 42.8 percent of GDP as spending by the federal government alone rises to between 43.7 and 64.7 percent of GDP.[175] Simply adding in the current state and local government spending of 18.0 percent of GDP,[176] total government spending would be between 61.7 and 82.7 percent of GDP in 2080. Clearly, that would be unsustainable.

Obviously, these large deficits create an even larger debt. As of 2009, the federal debt held by the public was 55 percent of GDP,[177] a large but manageable amount. The debt was just 41 percent at the end of 2008 and the 40-year average is 36 percent.[178] The problem though lies in the future, not the present. By 2035, the debt is projected to be between 79 and 181 percent of GDP and, by 2080, it is predicted to be between 283 and 716 percent of GDP.[179] The United States is clearly on the road to bankruptcy if the situation does not improve. Given that the deterioration intensifies just after 2020, we have just ten years to fix our government. Ten years may sound like a long time, but barring a real revolution, one with guns and violence, governments rarely change that quickly. It has taken the progressives and modern liberals a hundred years to produce our large government, but we have just one-tenth the time to reverse the trend. Not just stop new spending programs, but actually reduce the current commitments of the U.S. government.

State and local governments, though, may go bankrupt much more quickly if they do not improve their situations. The federal government can temporarily stave off bankruptcy by printing money. This will devalue the dollar and make Americans poorer, but it will buy some time before the day of reckoning. However, state and local governments cannot print money. The fifty states recorded a record $110 billion deficit in 2009, equal to 15.2 percent of their budgets. These deficits are expected to rise even higher in 2010 and stay at extremely elevated levels for the next few years.[180] The state and local governments will have no choice but to cut back on services, lay off employees, and raise taxes, or face bankruptcy.

Many are in favor of soaking the rich even more to close the budget gap. However, according to the Organisation for Economic Co-operation and Development (OECD), the United States has the most progressive tax system, with the richest ten percent of households paying 45.1 percent of all taxes. After adjusting for the concentration of income, the United States still has the second most progressive tax system, behind Ireland.[181] Raising taxes on the wealthy may drive them overseas or into hiding. The burden will then fall on the middle class, who will also be forced to leave when their tax burden becomes unbearable and jobs become scarce as the wealthy take their spending and jobs-producing capital with them. This occurred in ancient Rome and could just as easily take place in the United States.

In fact, the extremely rich are already avoiding the United States' high taxes. Billionaire George Soros moved his trading operations to Curacao of Netherlands Antilles to avoid U.S. taxes and regulatory supervision.[182] Marc Rich, another billionaire, moved to Switzerland after being indicted for market manipulation, trading with Iran, and tax evasion, but was later pardoned by President Bill Clinton.[183] The extremely wealthy also set up tax exempt foundations to avoid estate taxes and taxes on capital gains. Bill Gates and Warren Buffett, the world's richest and second richest men,[184] have given the vast majority of their wealth to the Bill & Melinda Gates Foundation,[185] thus avoiding taxes on their billions. The average wealthy person, though, has a job and cannot just leave the country, but he can retire early or cut back his work hours if he believes that his time is better spent in leisure than working and giving over a majority of his income to the government.

Corporations are also leaving the United States. The U.S. has the second highest corporate tax rate among OECD countries at 39.25 percent, just behind Japan's 39.54 percent. The U.S.'s corporate tax rate has held steady for the last twenty years while the OECD average has declined from over 45 percent to 26.6 percent.[186]

As a result, a number of U.S. corporations have moved overseas in recent years, a number of them to Ireland and Switzerland.[187] In 2007, Halliburton moved to Dubai in the United Arab Emirates. With little development of newly discovered oil fields in the United States, Halliburton simply moved closer to its center of business. Furthermore, Halliburton has been demonized by many on the left,[188] making the decision to leave easier.

The United States is repeating the mistakes of the past: redistributing wealth through a progressive tax system, expanding the size of government, creating fictional wars where none exist, enriching the political class, establishing an army of unelected bureaucrats to control the lives of the people, and promoting democracy at the expense of the republic. The United States government is approaching bankruptcy and there are two likely outcomes if the current direction is maintained.

First, the wealthy will leave the United States and go to countries with lower taxes and less burdensome regulation. This is already occurring as some extremely wealthy individuals set up tax exempt foundations and move overseas. Additionally, corporations are fleeing the United States to more favorable environments.

Second, as the problems of the United States become more pronounced and it becomes obvious that the current political system cannot fix the problem, the public will call for giving a single individual or group the power to restructure the government and country. Though we may be fortunate enough to get a Solon or a Cincinnatus, the more likely result, as history demonstrates, is tyranny.

Clearly, we should avoid that uncertainty by reversing the trend toward bigger government. The real problem is that it is the nature of politicians and bureaucrats to support bigger government, regardless of their political party. For six years, the United States saw the size of government grow dramatically under President Bush and a Republican Congress. The voters threw out the free-spending Republicans only to see the Democratic Congress with President Obama spend at an even faster pace. It is obvious that the current political system favors ever larger government. The supporters of small government have not been able to create a permanent political majority and simply throwing out one party in favor of another is not enough to fix the problem. Furthermore, there is nowhere to escape to because there are no large countries with small government philosophies. Most large advanced countries are in the same situation as the U.S., some even worse. Though it will be difficult and time consuming, the only solution is to sway the hearts and minds of the people back to liberty. Only then can political change be accomplished.

How do we fight for freedom and oppose the approaching tyranny? Obviously, we must vote in elections and support those in politics who defend our liberty and the Constitution. But that will not be enough. Most important of all, each of us must act as a modern-day Samuel, Solon, Socrates, Cicero, Cato, James Madison, Pyotr Stolypin, Hjalmar Schacht, or Ludwig Erhard, persuading people of the advantages of liberty and informing them of the evils of big government.

The recent "tea party" protests that have spread across the country are a positive sign. It is reassuring to see so many people defending liberty. Although these protests will not change the opinion of an ideological politician, it will influence undecided voters and politicians will be forced to bend their wills to the people's, for fear of losing their next election. We can only rely on politicians to do what is right if the people demand it of them. We must vote for candidates who support liberty, vote out those who oppose it, and convince the public that freedom is more beneficial than the temporary gain from larger government.

ACKNOWLEDGEMENTS

I could not have written this book alone. First, I would like to thank my family who supported me throughout this project. I would like to thank my parents, Ray and Leah Newton, and my grandparents, Arnold and Helene Newton, who provided feedback and criticism throughout this project and read through each chapter, often more than once. I would like to thank Doctor Louis Feldman, the Abraham Wouk Family Professor of Classics and Literature at Yeshiva University, for his advice and constructive criticism, especially on the ancient Greece chapter. I would like to thank Rabbi Zvi Holland, director of the Phoenix Community Kollel, for his assistance with the chapter on ancient Israel. I would also like to thank Bentley Erdwurm, who read through the chapter on Communist Russia and provided advice throughout the project. Despite all the help I received, any errors in this book are mine alone.

CITATIONS

CHAPTER ONE
FREE SOCIETIES AND TYRANNIES

1. Santayana, *The Life of Reason* Volume 1 Chapter 12.
2. *United States Declaration of Independence*, Preamble.
3. Hamilton, Jay, and Madison, *The Federalist Papers* No. 51.
4. *Ethics of the Fathers* 3:2.
5. Paine, *Common Sense* 1.
6. Compania De Tabacos v. Collector.
7. Adams, *The Works of John Adams*. Vol. 6 page 9.
8. Bulwer-Lytton, *Richelieu; Or, the Conspiracy: A Play, in Five Acts* 43.
9. Douglass, "A Plea for Free Speech in Boston."
10. Aristotle, *Politics* Book 3 Part 7.
11. Aristotle, *Politics* Book 5 Part 10.
12. Hayek, *The Road to Serfdom* xxxii.
13. Harris, *Upton Sinclair, American Rebel* 351.
14. Polybius, *The Histories* 6.9.7-8.

CHAPTER TWO
ANCIENT GREECE

1. Hall, "Dorians," *Encyclopedia of Ancient Greece* 241.
2. Hammond, *A History of Greece to 322 B.C.* 75-82; Hall, "Dorians," *Encyclopedia of Ancient Greece* 240; Stearns, *Encyclopedia of World History* 58. See also Thucydides, *The Peloponnesian War* 1.12.
3. Stearns, *Encyclopedia of World History* 58.
4. Hammond, *A History of Greece to 322 B.C.* 140-143.
5. Hammond, *A History of Greece to 322 B.C.* 145-151.
6. Plutarch, *Parallel Lives* Solon 14.1.
7. Plutarch, *Parallel Lives* Solon 22.1.
8. Plutarch, *Parallel Lives* Solon 24.2.
9. Plutarch, *Parallel Lives* Solon 25.4.
10. Schmitz, "Eleutheria," *A Dictionary of Greek and Roman Antiquities* 454-455.
11. Aristotle, *Politics* Book 6 Part 2.

12. Aristotle, *Politics* Book 6 Part 2.
13. Aristotle, *Politics* Book 3 Part 7.
14. Plato, *Republic* 557a.
15. Plato, *Republic* 558c.
16. Plato, *Republic* 562b.
17. Plato, *Republic* 563b.
18. Plato, *Republic* 564a.
19. Aristotle, *Politics* Book 6 Part 2.
20. Engen, "The Economy of Ancient Greece," *EH.Net Encyclopedia*.
21. Finley, *The Ancient Economy* 151.
22. Finley, *The Ancient Economy* 152.
23. Finley, *The Ancient Economy* 152.
24. Smith, *Dictionary of Greek and Roman Antiquities* 448-450.
25. Tocqueville, *Democracy in America* 60-61.
26. Tocqueville, *Democracy in America* 61.
27. Tocqueville, *Democracy in America* 61.
28. Weerakkody, "Inheritance."
29. Plutarch, *Parallel Lives* Solon 21.2.
30. Plutarch, *Parallel Lives* Themistocles 4.1-2.
31. Euripides, *Hecuba* lines 291-292.
32. Xenophon, *The Polity of the Athenians and the Lacedaemonians* Chapter 1.
33. Babler, "Slavery," *Encyclopedia of Ancient Greece* 665.
34. Babler, "Metics," *Encyclopedia of Ancient Greece* 469-470.
35. Babler, "Slavery," *Encyclopedia of Ancient Greece* 664.
36. Babler, "Slavery," *Encyclopedia of Ancient Greece* 665.
37. Babler, "Slavery," *Encyclopedia of Ancient Greece* 664.
38. Boeckh, *The Public Economy of Athens* 657.
39. Babler, "Slavery," *Encyclopedia of Ancient Greece* 665.
40. Thucydides, *The Peloponnesian War* 7.27.5.
41. Momigliano, "Freedom of Speech in Antiquity," *The Dictionary of the History of Ideas*.
42. Plutarch, *Parallel Lives* Dion 34.1.
43. Plutarch, *Parallel Lives* Dion 34.2.
44. Plutarch, *Parallel Lives* Dion 34.4-35.1.
45. Stenudd, *Cosmos of the Ancients: The Greek Philosophers on Myth and Cosmology* 48.
46. Xenophanes, *Fragments and Commentary* 67.
47. Xenophanes, *Fragments and Commentary* 67.
48. Stenudd, *Cosmos of the Ancients: The Greek Philosophers on Myth and Cosmology* 48.
49. Hammond, *A History of Greece to 322 B.C.* 418.
50. Curd, "Anaxagoras," *Stanford Encyclopedia of Philosophy*.
51. Smith, *Dictionary of Greek and Roman Biography and Mythology Vol 1*, 998.
52. Plato, *Apology* 30e.
53. Smith, *Dictionary of Greek and Roman Antiquities* 781.
54. Babler, "Slavery," *Encyclopedia of Ancient Greece* 664.
55. Demosthenes, "Speeches" 1.4.
56. Demosthenes, "Speeches" 10.20.

57. Lewis, *Ancient Tyranny* 5.
58. Lewis, *Ancient Tyranny* 5.
59. Aristotle, *Politics* Book 3 Part 7.
60. Aristotle, *Politics* Book 5 Part 10.
61. McGlew, *Tyranny and Political Culture in Ancient Greece* 184.
62. Thucydides, *The Peloponnesian War* 2.63.2.
63. Thucydides, *The Peloponnesian War* 3.37.2.
64. Aristotle, *Politics* Book 5 Part 10.
65. Plutarch, *Parallel Lives* Dion 44.7-9.
66. Aristotle, *Politics* Book 5 Part 10.
67. Aristotle, *Politics* Book 5 Part 10.
68. Aristotle, *Politics* Book 5 Part 10.
69. Xenophon, *Hellenica* 7.1.44.
70. Xenophon, *Hellenica* 7.1.45.
71. Xenophon, *Hellenica* 7.3.12.
72. Xenophon, *Hellenica* 7.1.46.
73. Plutarch, *Parallel Lives* Pericles 9.1.
74. Aristotle, *Politics* Book 5 Part 11.
75. Xenophon, *Hellenica* 7.1.46.
76. Aristotle, *Politics* Book 5 Part 10.
77. Xenophon, *Hellenica* 7.1.46.
78. Diodorus Siculus, *The Library of History* 15.70.3.
79. Plutarch, *Parallel Lives* Agis 10-11.
80. Machiavelli, *Prince* 57-58.
81. Aristotle, *Politics* Book 5 Part 11.
82. Aristotle, *Politics* Book 5 Part 11.
83. Aristotle, *Politics* Book 5 Part 11.
84. Xenophon, *Hellenica* 7.1.46.
85. Xenophon, *Hellenica* 7.3.8.
86. Diodorus Siculus, *The Library of History* 15.70.3.
87. Aristotle, *Politics* Book 5 Part 11.
88. Aristotle, *Politics* Book 5 Part 11.
89. Thucydides, *The Peloponnesian War* 1.99.3.
90. McGlew, *Tyranny and Political Culture in Ancient Greece* 184.
91. Thucydides, *The Peloponnesian War* 2.40.4-5.
92. Plutarch, *Parallel Lives* Pericles 39.4.
93. "Cleon," *Encyclopædia Britannica*.
94. Herodotus, *The Histories* 1.59.6.
95. Aristotle, *The Athenian Constitution* Part 16.
96. Herodotus, *The Histories* 5.62.2.
97. Thucydides, *The Peloponnesian War* 6.57.3 and Aristotle, *The Athenian Constitution* Part 18.
98. Thucydides, *The Peloponnesian War* 6.59.2.
99. Aristotle, *The Athenian Constitution* Part 19.
100. Aristotle, *Politics* Book 5 Part 12.
101. Lewis, *Ancient Tyranny* 8 based on Aristotle, *Politics* Book 5 Part 10.
102. Plutarch, *Parallel Lives* Solon 30.5.
103. Plutarch, *Parallel Lives* Solon 14.5.

104. Plutarch, *Parallel Lives* Solon 30.5. See also Aristotle, *The Athenian Constitution* Part 14.
105. Demosthenes, "Speeches" 9.65.
106. Plutarch, *Parallel Lives* Demosthenes 20.2
107. Aristotle, *Politics* Book 5 Part 10.
108. Aristotle, *Politics* Book 5 Part 10.
109. Aristotle, *Politics* Book 5 Part 11.
110. Plato, *Apology* 32b-32c.
111. Xenophon, *Memorabilia* 1.2.12.
112. Plato, *Apology* 32c.
113. Plato, *Republic* 865e-866a.
114. Thucydides, *The Peloponnesian War* 1.17.1.

CHAPTER THREE
ANCIENT ROME

1. Livy, *History of Rome* 1.59.
2. Livy, *History of Rome* 2.1.
3. Livy, *History of Rome* 2.1.
4. Polybius, *The Histories* 6.4.7-13.
5. Polybius, *The Histories* 6.9.7-9.
6. Livy, *History of Rome* 2.41.
7. Livy, *History of Rome* 2.42.
8. Livy, *History of Rome* 2.48 and 2.63.
9. Polybius, *The Histories* 6.10.6-10.
10. Polybius, *The Histories* 6.10.13-14.
11. Polybius, *The Histories* 6.13.
12. Polybius, *The Histories* 6.14.
13. Polybius, *The Histories* 6.12.
14. Polybius, *The Histories* 6.12.9.
15. Polybius, *The Histories* 6.18.
16. Montesquieu, *Considerations on the Causes of the Greatness of the Romans and their Decline* Chapter 8.
17. Cicero, *Political Works* 237.
18. Plutarch, *Parallel Lives* Sulla 31-33.
19. Montesquieu, *Considerations on the Causes of the Greatness of the Romans and their Decline* Chapter 11.
20. Montesquieu, *Considerations on the Causes of the Greatness of the Romans and their Decline* Chapter 11.
21. Livy, *History of Rome* 4.5.
22. *Twelve Tables.*
23. *Twelve Tables* 2.11.
24. *Twelve Tables* 5.1.
25. *Twelve Tables* 7.1, 7.2, 7.6.
26. *Twelve Tables* 7.4, 7.6.
27. *Twelve Tables* 7.4.
28. *Twelve Tables* 6.1.

29. *Twelve Tables* 7.17.
30. *Twelve Tables* 8.1.
31. *Twelve Tables* 9.1.
32. *Twelve Tables* 9.2.
33. Bartlett, "How Excessive Government Killed Ancient Rome."
34. "The Roman Gladiator History & Origins."
35. Wiedemann, *Emperors and Gladiators* 8.
36. Phillips, *Slavery from Roman Times to the Early Transatlantic Trade* 19.
37. Dionysius, *Roman Antiquities* 2.16.1.
38. Livy, *History of Rome* 8.28.
39. *Twelve Tables* 2.5.
40. Dionysius, *Roman Antiquities* 2.27.
41. *Twelve Tables* 6.7.
42. Seneca, *Moral Epistles* 47.
43. *Twelve Tables* 6.2.
44. Livy, *History of Rome* 7.16.
45. Harbottle, *Dictionary of Quotations* 116 from Cicero, *Philippics* 3.35.
46. *Twelve Tables* 7.8.
47. Cicero, *Philippics* 2.64.
48. Montesquieu, *Considerations on the Causes of the Greatness of the Romans and their Decline* Chapter 20.
49. *Twelve Tables* 10.2.
50. Lucretius, *Of The Nature of Things* Book II Atomic Forms and their Combinations.
51. Plutarch, *Parallel Lives* Caesar 14.2.
52. Plutarch, *Parallel Lives* Caesar 14.4-6.
53. Plutarch, *Parallel Lives* Caesar 57.1.
54. Plutarch, *Parallel Lives* Caesar 57.8.
55. Plutarch, *Parallel Lives* Caesar 58.1.
56. Dickinson, *Death of a Republic* 365-366.
57. Plutarch, *Parallel Lives* Caesar 59.6.
58. Suetonius, *The Lives of the Twelve Caesars* Julius Caesar 80.1.
59. Plutarch, *Parallel Lives* Cicero 48.6.
60. Cicero, *De Officiis* 1.25.
61. Cicero, *De Officiis* 2.73.
62. Cicero, *De Officiis* 2.78.
63. Cicero, *De Officiis* 1.43.
64. Cicero, *De Officiis* 2.60.
65. Cicero, *De Officiis* 2.84.
66. Cicero, *De Officiis* 2.77.
67. Plutarch, *Parallel Lives* Cato 3.3.
68. Plutarch, *Parallel Lives* Cato 17.4-5.
69. Plutarch, *Parallel Lives* Cato 19.1-2.
70. Plutarch, *Parallel Lives* Cato 33.1.
71. Plutarch, *Parallel Lives* Cato 33.3.
72. Plutarch, *Parallel Lives* Cato 70.4-7.
73. Suetonius, *The Lives of the Twelve Caesars* Julius Caesar 82.2.
74. Suetonius, *The Lives of the Twelve Caesars* Julius Caesar 83.2.

75. Suetonius, *The Lives of the Twelve Caesars* Julius Caesar 83.2.
76. Montesquieu, *Considerations on the Causes of the Greatness of the Romans and their Decline* Chapter 13.
77. Suetonius, *The Lives of the Twelve Caesars* Augustus 37.
78. Suetonius, *The Lives of the Twelve Caesars* Augustus 30.
79. Suetonius, *The Lives of the Twelve Caesars* Augustus 41.1.
80. Suetonius, *The Lives of the Twelve Caesars* Augustus 43.1.
81. Suetonius, *The Lives of the Twelve Caesars* Tiberius 24.1.
82. Suetonius, *The Lives of the Twelve Caesars* Tiberius 30.
83. Suetonius, *The Lives of the Twelve Caesars* Tiberius 32.2.
84. Suetonius, *The Lives of the Twelve Caesars* Tiberius 33.
85. Tacitus, *Annals* 4.1.
86. Tacitus, *Annals* 4.33.
87. Tacitus, *Annals* 6.19.
88. Montesquieu, *Considerations on the Causes of the Greatness of the Romans and their Decline* Chapter 14.
89. Tacitus, *Annals* 6.36.
90. Suetonius, *The Lives of the Twelve Caesars* Tiberius 75.
91. Suetonius, *The Lives of the Twelve Caesars* Caligula 13-14.
92. Suetonius, *The Lives of the Twelve Caesars* Caligula 22.1.
93. Suetonius, *The Lives of the Twelve Caesars* Caligula 24.1.
94. Suetonius, *The Lives of the Twelve Caesars* Caligula 26.1.
95. Suetonius, *The Lives of the Twelve Caesars* Caligula 26.2-5.
96. Suetonius, *The Lives of the Twelve Caesars* Caligula 27, 30, 32.
97. Suetonius, *The Lives of the Twelve Caesars* Caligula 36.
98. Suetonius, *The Lives of the Twelve Caesars* Caligula 37.
99. Suetonius, *The Lives of the Twelve Caesars* Caligula 38.1.
100. Suetonius, *The Lives of the Twelve Caesars* Caligula 40-41.1.
101. Suetonius, *The Lives of the Twelve Caesars* Claudius 10.4.
102. Suetonius, *The Lives of the Twelve Caesars* Claudius 18-19.
103. Suetonius, *The Lives of the Twelve Caesars* Claudius 20.1.
104. Suetonius, *The Lives of the Twelve Caesars* Claudius 21.1-3.
105. Suetonius, *The Lives of the Twelve Caesars* Claudius 29.2.
106. Suetonius, *The Lives of the Twelve Caesars* Claudius 34.
107. Tacitus, *Annals* 14.31.
108. Suetonius, *The Lives of the Twelve Caesars* Claudius 44-45.
109. Tacitus, *Annals* 15.44.
110. Tacitus, *Annals* 15.44.
111. Suetonius, *The Lives of the Twelve Caesars* Nero 38.
112. Tacitus, *Annals* 15.39.
113. Suetonius, *The Lives of the Twelve Caesars* Nero 26-34.
114. Cassius Dio, *Roman History* 63.22.
115. Suetonius, *The Lives of the Twelve Caesars* Nero 49.2.
116. Suetonius, *The Lives of the Twelve Caesars* Nero 57.1.
117. Cassius Dio, *Roman History* 65.2.5.
118. Cassius Dio, *Roman History* 65.10.
119. Suetonius, *The Lives of the Twelve Caesars* Vespasian 18.
120. Cassius Dio, *Roman History* 65.12 and 65.13.

121. Suetonius, *The Lives of the Twelve Caesars* Vespasian 18.
122. Suetonius, *The Lives of the Twelve Caesars* Vespasian 9.
123. Suetonius, *The Lives of the Twelve Caesars* Vespasian 15.
124. Suetonius, *The Lives of the Twelve Caesars* Vespasian 25.
125. Suetonius, *The Lives of the Twelve Caesars* Titus 6-7.
126. Suetonius, *The Lives of the Twelve Caesars* Titus 7.
127. Suetonius, *The Lives of the Twelve Caesars* Titus 7.
128. Suetonius, *The Lives of the Twelve Caesars* Titus 8.3-4.
129. Suetonius, *The Lives of the Twelve Caesars* Domitian 1.3.
130. Suetonius, *The Lives of the Twelve Caesars* Domitian 2.3.
131. Suetonius, *The Lives of the Twelve Caesars* Domitian 4.1.
132. Suetonius, *The Lives of the Twelve Caesars* Domitian 5.
133. Suetonius, *The Lives of the Twelve Caesars* Domitian 12.1-2.
134. Suetonius, *The Lives of the Twelve Caesars* Domitian 10.2-5.
135. Suetonius, *The Lives of the Twelve Caesars* Domitian 14.1.
136. Suetonius, *The Lives of the Twelve Caesars* Domitian 23.1.
137. Cassius Dio, *Roman History* 68.1.
138. Cassius Dio, *Roman History* 68.2.
139. Cassius Dio, *Roman History* 68.3.
140. Tocqueville, *Democracy in America* 803-804.
141. Gibbon, *The History of the Decline and Fall of the Roman Empire* Vol 1 85-86.
142. Cassius Dio, *Roman History* 73.10.
143. Cassius Dio, *Roman History* 73.4.
144. Cassius Dio, *Roman History* 73.15.
145. Montesquieu, *Considerations on the Causes of the Greatness of the Romans and their Decline* Chapter 9.
146. Bartlett, "How Excessive Government Killed Ancient Rome."
147. Mises, *Economic Policy, Thoughts for Today and Tomorrow* 102-103.
148. Montesquieu, *Considerations on the Causes of the Greatness of the Romans and their Decline* Chapter 15.
149. Bartlett, "How Excessive Government Killed Ancient Rome."
150. Montesquieu, *Considerations on the Causes of the Greatness of the Romans and their Decline* Chapter 18.
151. Bartlett, "How Excessive Government Killed Ancient Rome."

CHAPTER FOUR
ANCIENT ISRAEL

1. Exodus 33:11.
2. Number 27:15-23.
3. Judges 3:15-29.
4. Judges 4-5.
5. Judges 6-8.
6. Judges 11.
7. Judges 16.
8. Judges 17:6 and 21:25.
9. Exodus 18.

10. Number 11:16.
11. *Mishnah: Sanhedrin* 1:1.
12. Leviticus 16.
13. Exodus 28:15 and Number 27:21.
14. *Talmud Bavli: Yoma* 73b.
15. Scherman, *The Chumash: The Stone Edition* 470; Judges 1:1-2, 20:18-28; I Samuel 14:36-37, 23:1-5, 28:6, 30:7-8; and II Samuel 5:23.
16. Scherman, *The Chumash: The Stone Edition* 471; Joshua 9:14; I Samuel 10:20-22; and II Samuel 2:1.
17. Deuteronomy 20:1-4 and Maimonides and Touger, *Mishneh Torah: Hilchot Melachim U'Milchamoteihem* 7:3.
18. I Samuel 23:1-5.
19. See Scherman, *Tanach: The Stone Edition* Appendix A Timelines 3 and 4.
20. Maimonides and Touger, *Mishneh Torah: Hilchot Melachim U'Milchamoteihem* 2:5.
21. Maimonides and Touger, *Mishneh Torah: Hilchot Melachim U'Milchamoteihem* 2:5.
22. Maimonides and Touger, *Mishneh Torah: Hilchot Melachim U'Milchamoteihem* 3:8.
23. Maimonides and Touger, *Mishneh Torah: Hilchot Melachim U'Milchamoteihem* 3:4.
24. Maimonides and Touger, *Mishneh Torah: Hilchot Melachim U'Milchamoteihem* 3:4.
25. Maimonides and Touger, *Mishneh Torah: Hilchot Melachim U'Milchamoteihem* 2:6.
26. Maimonides and Touger, *Mishneh Torah: Hilchot Melachim U'Milchamoteihem* 4:1.
27. Maimonides and Touger, *Mishneh Torah: Hilchot Melachim U'Milchamoteihem* 4:3.
28. Maimonides and Touger, *Mishneh Torah: Hilchot Melachim U'Milchamoteihem* 5:1-2.
29. I Kings 16:29-33.
30. I Kings 18:40.
31. I Kings 19.
32. Judges 8:1-3.
33. Judges 12:1-6.
34. Judges 19-20.
35. II Samuel 2-5.
36. Exodus 20:7.
37. Exodus 14:11, 15:24, 16:317:2-3; Numbers 11:1, 11:4-6, and 14:1-3.
38. Deuteronomy 17:14-20.
39. I Samuel 8:5.
40. I Samuel 8:5.
41. I Samuel 8:7.
42. I Samuel 15.
43. II Samuel 12.
44. I Kings 22.
45. Jeremiah 20:2, 32:1-5, 37:15-16, and 38:6.
46. Judges 8:1.
47. Judges 8:2-3.
48. Judges 12:1.
49. Judges 12:4-6.
50. Joshua 14:1-5.
51. Number 25:9-15.
52. Leviticus 25:13-16.
53. Leviticus 25:16.
54. Leviticus 25:31.

55. Leviticus 25:29-30.
56. Exodus 23:14-19; Deuteronomy 12:5-27, 16:1-17, and 26:1-4.
57. I Kings 21:2.
58. I Kings 21:3.
59. I Kings 21:4.
60. Deuteronomy 7:26.
61. Karo and Isserles, *Shulchan Aruch: Yoreh Deah* 117.
62. See Massekhet Nezikin (Tractate of Damages) of the Talmud.
63. Karo and Isserles, *Shulchan Aruch: Yoreh Deah* 249-251.
64. Exodus 23:10-11; Leviticus 25:1-7 and 25:21-22.
65. Leviticus 25:6.
66. Leviticus 25:21.
67. Genesis 12:10.
68. Genesis 26:1.
69. Genesis 41:25-57.
70. Ruth 1:1.
71. II Samuel 21:1.
72. I King 18:2.
73. II Kings 4:38 and 6:25.
74. Humphrey, *Greek and Roman Technology: A Sourcebook* 96.
75. Deuteronomy 21:16.
76. Numbers 27:8-11.
77. *Mishna: Ketuboth* 4:11-12 and Maimonides and Touger, *Mishneh Torah: Hilchot Ishut* 20:3.
78. Tocqueville, *Democracy in America* 61.
79. Deuteronomy 23:20-21.
80. Leviticus 25:39.
81. Leviticus 25:39-43.
82. Deuteronomy 16:14.
83. Deuteronomy 15:12.
84. Deuteronomy 15:13-14.
85. *Talmud Bavli: Kiddushin* 20b.
86. Numbers 18:21.
87. See *Talmud Bavli: Bava Basra* 7b-8a.
88. I Kings 12:4.
89. Judges 10:6.
90. Judges 17:6 and 21:25.
91. Judges 16:29-30.
92. I Samuel 4-6.
93. I Samuel 7:13.
94. I Samuel 8:1-3.
95. Scherman, *The Prophets: Samuel* 49.
96. Scherman, *The Prophets: Samuel* 49.
97. I Samuel 7:16.
98. I Samuel 8:5.
99. I Samuel 8:20.
100. I Samuel 8:5.
101. I Samuel 8:10.

102. I Samuel 8:11-18.
103. I Samuel 8:11.
104. I Samuel 8:12-13.
105. I Samuel 8:15.
106. I Samuel 8:17.
107. I Samuel 8:14.
108. I Samuel 8:16.
109. I Samuel 8:14.
110. I Samuel 8:15.
111. I Samuel 8:17-18.
112. I Samuel 8:18.
113. I Samuel 8:19-20.
114. I Kings 5:15-6:38.
115. I Kings 7:1-8.
116. I Kings 3:1 and 9:15.
117. I Kings 9:15-19.
118. I Kings 7:8 and 9:24.
119. I Kings 10:16-17.
120. I Kings 10:18-20.
121. I Kings 7:48-50.
122. I Kings 10:26-28.
123. I Kings 5:27-28.
124. I Kings 5:29-30.
125. I Kings 9:20-22.
126. Scherman, *The Prophets: Kings* 47.
127. I Kings 4:6, 5:21, 9:15, and 10:15.
128. Exodus 36:5-7.
129. Joshua 18:1.
130. Scherman, *Tanach: The Stone Edition* 558.
131. I Kings 12:25-33.
132. I Kings 12:4.
133. I Kings 12:4.
134. I Kings 12:14.
135. I Kings 12:18.
136. I Kings 12:19.
137. I Kings 12:21-24.
138. I Kings 14:25-26.
139. I Kings 12:28.
140. I Kings 12:28-33.
141. I Kings 12:31.
142. II Kings 15:9.
143. II Kings 15:18.
144. I Kings 20:34, 22:29; and II Kings 3:7.
145. II Kings 12:19 and 15:19.
146. II Kings 15:19.
147. II Kings 15:20.
148. II Samuel 5:11 and I Kings 5:15.
149. I Kings 10:2 and 10:25.

150. I Kings 12:25-33.
151. II Kings 17.
152. II Kings 24-25.

CHAPTER FIVE
COMMUNIST RUSSIA

1. Langworth, *Churchill by Himself: The Definitive Collection of Quotations* 145.
2. Kort, *A Brief History of Russia* 93.
3. Wallace, *Russia* 475.
4. Kort, *A Brief History of Russia* 99-100.
5. Kort, *A Brief History of Russia* 102.
6. Kort, *A Brief History of Russia* 104.
7. Kort, *A Brief History of Russia* 106.
8. Ascher, *Russia: A Short History* 125.
9. Kort, *A Brief History of Russia* 107-108.
10. Ascher, *Russia: A Short History* 125.
11. Ascher, *Russia: A Short History* 125.
12. Ascher, *Russia: A Short History* 104.
13. Ascher, *Russia: A Short History* 104-105.
14. Ascher, *Russia: A Short History* 131 and Kort, *A Brief History of Russia* 109.
15. Ascher, *Russia: A Short History* 132.
16. Ascher, *Russia: A Short History* 133.
17. Ascher, *Russia: A Short History* 134.
18. Ascher, *Russia: A Short History* 135.
19. Kort, *A Brief History of Russia* 115.
20. Kort, *A Brief History of Russia* 115-116.
21. Kort, *A Brief History of Russia* 111.
22. Ascher, *Russia: A Short History* 137.
23. Kort, *A Brief History of Russia* 117.
24. Ascher, *Russia: A Short History* 139.
25. Kort, *A Brief History of Russia* 120.
26. Ascher, *Russia: A Short History* 140-141.
27. Ascher, *Russia: A Short History* 143-144.
28. Waldron, *Between Two Revolutions: Stolypin and the Politics of Renewal in Russia* 184.
29. Hayek, *The Road to Serfdom* 153.
30. Ascher, *Russia: A Short History* 143-148.
31. Waldron, *Between Two Revolutions: Stolypin and the Politics of Renewal in Russia* 67.
32. Kort, *A Brief History of Russia* 121.
33. Kort, *A Brief History of Russia* 121.
34. Ascher, *Russia: A Short History* 151.
35. Jacob, *Six Thousand Years of Bread Its Holy and Unholy History* 318.
36. Kort, *A Brief History of Russia* 122.

37. Service, *A History of Modern Russia: From Nicholas II to Vladimir Putin* 16 and Waldron, *Between Two Revolutions: Stolypin and the Politics of Renewal in Russia* 92.
38. Ascher, *Russia: A Short History* 150.
39. Kort, *A Brief History of Russia* 123.
40. Ascher, *Russia: A Short History* 151.
41. Ascher, *Russia: A Short History* 154.
42. Ascher, *Russia: A Short History* 155.
43. Ascher, *Russia: A Short History* 156.
44. Ascher, *Russia: A Short History* 156.
45. Ascher, *Russia: A Short History* 156.
46. Kenez, *A History of the Soviet Union from the Beginning to the End* 15.
47. Service, *A History of Modern Russia: From Nicholas II to Vladimir Putin* 35.
48. Kort, *A Brief History of Russia* 152.
49. Kort, *A Brief History of Russia* 154.
50. Kort, *A Brief History of Russia* 154.
51. Ascher, *Russia: A Short History* 166.
52. Ascher, *Russia: A Short History* 166.
53. Mises, *Liberalism: The Classical Tradition* 24.
54. Kort, *A Brief History of Russia* 158.
55. Ascher, *Russia: A Short History* 169.
56. Kort, *A Brief History of Russia* 159.
57. Kort, *A Brief History of Russia* 162.
58. Ascher, *Russia: A Short History* 171.
59. Kort, *A Brief History of Russia* 163.
60. Ascher, *Russia: A Short History* 171-172.
61. Kort, *A Brief History of Russia* 163.
62. Ascher, *Russia: A Short History* 172.
63. Kort, *A Brief History of Russia* 161.
64. Kort, *A Brief History of Russia* 161.
65. Kort, *A Brief History of Russia* 161.
66. Ascher, *Russia: A Short History* 174.
67. Ascher, *Russia: A Short History* 174.
68. Hayek, *The Road to Serfdom* 165.
69. Kort, *A Brief History of Russia* 164-165.
70. Kort, *A Brief History of Russia* 163.
71. Kort, *A Brief History of Russia* 164.
72. Ascher, *Russia: A Short History* 176.
73. Kort, *A Brief History of Russia* 165.
74. Kort, *A Brief History of Russia* 170.
75. Kort, *A Brief History of Russia* 166.
76. Aristotle, *Politics* Book 5 Part 10.
77. Ascher, *Russia: A Short History* 183.
78. Kort, *The Soviet Colossus: History and Aftermath* 200.
79. Kort, *A Brief History of Russia* 177.
80. Kort, *A Brief History of Russia* 175-176.
81. Kort, *A Brief History of Russia* 177.
82. Kort, *A Brief History of Russia* 182.

83. Ascher, *Russia: A Short History* 183-184.
84. Kort, *A Brief History of Russia* 173.
85. Kort, *A Brief History of Russia* 174.
86. Kort, *A Brief History of Russia* 174-175.
87. Ascher, *Russia: A Short History* 194.
88. Kort, *A Brief History of Russia* 176.
89. Kort, *A Brief History of Russia* 176.
90. Kort, *A Brief History of Russia* 167.
91. Ascher, *Russia: A Short History* 190.
92. Australian Associated Press, "Death of Leo Trotsky."
93. Ascher, *Russia: A Short History* 191 and Kort, *A Brief History of Russia* 183.
94. Kort, *A Brief History of Russia* 183-184.
95. Kort, *A Brief History of Russia* 179.
96. Ascher, *Russia: A Short History* 191-192.
97. Kort, *A Brief History of Russia* 180-181.
98. Tocqueville, *Democracy in America* 405.
99. Tocqueville, *Democracy in America* 405.
100. Tocqueville, *Democracy in America* 405.
101. Kort, *A Brief History of Russia* 192.
102. Kort, *A Brief History of Russia* 189.
103. Kort, *A Brief History of Russia* 189.
104. Ascher, *Russia: A Short History* 198.
105. Kort, *A Brief History of Russia* 192.
106. Kort, *A Brief History of Russia* 161.
107. Sanford, *Poland: The Conquest of History* 14.
108. Kort, *The Columbia Guide to the Cold War* 13.
109. Parkinson, *The Encyclopedia of Modern War* 80.
110. Kort, *A Brief History of Russia* 200.
111. Kenez, *A History of the Soviet Union from the Beginning to the End* 238.
112. Kenez, *A History of the Soviet Union from the Beginning to the End* 239.
113. Williams, *The Prague Spring and its aftermath: Czechoslovak politics, 1968-1970* 112.
114. Williams, The Prague Spring and its aftermath: Czechoslovak politics, 1968-1970 158.
115. Gaddis, *The Cold War: A New History* 150.
116. White, "Death Tolls for the Major Wars and Atrocities of the Twentieth Century" <users.erols.com/mwhite28/warstat2.htm#North>.
117. White, "Death Tolls for the Major Wars and Atrocities of the Twentieth Century" <users.erols.com/mwhite28/warstat2.htm#North>.
118. Kort, *The Columbia Guide to the Cold War* 14.
119. Rummel, *Death by Government* 98.
120. Rummel, *Death by Government* 98.
121. Rummel, *Death by Government* 97.
122. Kenez, *A History of the Soviet Union from the Beginning to the End* 210.
123. Garthoff, *Reflections on the Cuban Missile Crisis* 86.
124. White, "Minor Atrocities of the Twentieth Century" <users.erols.com/mwhite28/warstat6.htm#Cuba59>.
125. Amstutz, *Afghanistan: The First Five Years of Soviet Occupation* 168.

126. Hilali, *US-Pakistan Relationship: Soviet Invasion of Afghanistan* 78.
127. Hilali, *US-Pakistan Relationship: Soviet Invasion of Afghanistan* 198.
128. Hilali, *US-Pakistan Relationship: Soviet Invasion of Afghanistan* 198.
129. United States CIA, *Intelligence Memorandum: Communist Military Aid Deliveries to North Vietnam*.
130. Associated Press, "Soviet Involvement in the Vietnam War."
131. Kenez, *A History of the Soviet Union from the Beginning to the End* 233.
132. Kort, *A Brief History of Russia* 222-223.
133. Kort, *A Brief History of Russia* 223.
134. Tarasulo, *Gorbachev and Glasnost: Viewpoints from the Soviet Press* 329.
135. Kort, *A Brief History of Russia* 227.
136. Kort, *A Brief History of Russia* 227.
137. "Excerpts From Yeltsin's Speech to Lawmakers."
138. Hayek, *The Road to Serfdom* 29.
139. Langworth, *Churchill by Himself: The Definitive Collection of Quotations* 13.
140. "National Accounts Main Aggregates Database," *United Nations Statistics Division*.
141. Hagen, "East Germany: Transition with Unification, Experiments, and Experiences," *Transition The First Decade* 88.
142. "National Accounts Main Aggregates Database," *United Nations Statistics Division*.
143. "National Accounts Main Aggregates Database," *United Nations Statistics Division*.
144. "National Accounts Main Aggregates Database," *United Nations Statistics Division*.
145. "Russia," *The World Factbook*.
146. Hayek, *The Road to Serfdom* xxxiv.
147. Gott, *Hugo Chavez and the Bolivarian Revolution* 67.
148. Gott, *Hugo Chavez and the Bolivarian Revolution* 134.
149. Furshong, "What is Bolivarian Socialism? And When?"
150. Sojo, "Venezuela's Chavez Closes World Social Forum with Call to Transcend Capitalism."
151. Daniel, "Food, farms the new target for Venezuela's Chavez."
152. Gott, *Hugo Chavez and the Bolivarian Revolution* 135-136.
153. "Chavez promises a socialist Venezuela as he starts new 6-year term," *USA Today*.
154. "Chavez promises a socialist Venezuela as he starts new 6-year term," *USA Today*.
155. "Chavez promises a socialist Venezuela as he starts new 6-year term," *USA Today*.
156. Lustig, "Hugo Chavez: Charming provocateur."
157. Gott, *Hugo Chavez and the Bolivarian Revolution* 137.
158. "Chavez promises a socialist Venezuela as he starts new 6-year term," *USA Today*.
159. Daniel, "Food, farms the new target for Venezuela's Chavez."
160. Barillas, "Expropriations in Venezuela threaten oil supply."
161. Morsbach, "Venezuelan shoppers face food shortages."
162. Daniel, "Food, farms the new target for Venezuela's Chavez."
163. Barillas, "Expropriations in Venezuela threaten oil supply."
164. "Showering With Hugo," *Investors.com*.
165. "Water rationing for Venezuela's capital city," *Breitbart.com*.
166. "Showering With Hugo," *Investors.com*.
167. "Water rationing for Venezuela's capital city," *Breitbart.com*.
168. "Showering With Hugo," *Investors.com*.
169. "Venezuela: Oil," *Energy Information Administration: Official Energy Statistics from the U.S. Government*.

170. Barillas, "Expropriations in Venezuela threaten oil supply."
171. Barillas, "Expropriations in Venezuela threaten oil supply."
172. Clendenning, ""Axis of Good" for Brazil, Cuba and Venezuela?"

CHAPTER SIX
FASCIST ITALY

1. Wilson, *War Message to Congress*, April 3, 1917.
2. "Statuto Albertino," *Encyclopædia Britannica*.
3. De Grand, *Italian Fascism* 4.
4. De Grand, *Italian Fascism* 6.
5. De Grand, *Italian Fascism* 4.
6. De Grand, *Italian Fascism* 5.
7. De Grand, *Italian Fascism* 12.
8. De Grand, *Italian Fascism* 5.
9. De Grand, *Italian Fascism* 5.
10. De Grand, *Italian Fascism* 5.
11. De Grand, *Italian Fascism* 13.
12. De Grand, *Italian Fascism* 12.
13. De Grand, *Italian Fascism* 17.
14. De Grand, *Italian Fascism* 17-18.
15. Kedward, *Fascism in Western Europe* 1900-1945 40.
16. Sadkovich, "Isonzo, Battles of, Nos. 1-4 (1915)," *The European Powers in the First World War: An Encyclopedia* 365.
17. White, "Source List and Detailed Death Tolls for the Twentieth Century Hemoclysm" <users.erols.com/mwhite28/warstat1.htm#WW1>.
18. Fry, Goldstein, and Langhorne, *Guide to International Relations and Diplomacy* 178-179.
19. De Grand, *Italian Fascism* 25-26.
20. Eatwell, *Fascism: A History* 49.
21. Eatwell, *Fascism: A History* 48.
22. De Grand, *Italian Fascism* 22.
23. De Grand, *Italian Fascism* 24.
24. Kedward, *Fascism in Western Europe* 1900-1945 36.
25. Eatwell, *Fascism: A History* 51.
26. Morgan, *Italian Fascism: 1919-1945* 32.
27. De Grand, *Italian Fascism* 24.
28. Kedward, *Fascism in Western Europe* 1900-1945 42.
29. Eatwell, *Fascism: A History* 14.
30. Lubasz, *Fascism: Three Major Regimes* 3.
31. Payne, *A History of Fascism, 1914-1945* 10.
32. Payne, *A History of Fascism, 1914-1945* 10.
33. Eatwell, *Fascism: A History* 15.
34. Eatwell, *Fascism: A History* xxv.
35. Kedward, *Fascism in Western Europe* 1900-1945 209-212.
36. Eatwell, *Fascism: A History* 14.
37. Eatwell, *Fascism: A History* 10.

38. Eatwell, *Fascism: A History* 44.
39. Eatwell, *Fascism: A History* 44.
40. Kedward, *Fascism in Western Europe* 1900-1945 196-197.
41. Payne, *A History of Fascism, 1914-1945* 5.
42. De Grand, *Italian Fascism* 30; Eatwell, *Fascism: A History* 45; and Payne, *Fascism: Comparison and Definition* 45.
43. Kedward, *Fascism in Western Europe* 1900-1945 40.
44. Eatwell, *Fascism: A History* 44.
45. Eatwell, *Fascism: A History* 44-45.
46. Polybius, *The Histories* 6.9.8.
47. De Grand, *Italian Fascism* 31.
48. De Grand, *Italian Fascism* 32.
49. De Grand, *Italian Fascism* 32.
50. Payne, *Fascism: Comparison and Definition* 47-48.
51. Payne, *Fascism: Comparison and Definition* 48-49.
52. De Grand, *Italian Fascism* 35.
53. Eatwell, *Fascism: A History* 49.
54. De Grand, *Italian Fascism* 35.
55. De Grand, *Italian Fascism* 35.
56. De Grand, *Italian Fascism* 36.
57. De Grand, *Italian Fascism* 36.
58. Payne, *Fascism: Comparison and Definition* 49.
59. De Grand, *Italian Fascism* 20.
60. De Grand, *Italian Fascism* 42.
61. Lubasz, *Fascism: Three Major Regimes* 6.
62. De Grand, *Italian Fascism* 51.
63. Morgan, *Italian Fascism: 1919-1945* 90.
64. De Grand, *Italian Fascism* 53.
65. Bini, "Umberto Ricci: profile of a militant economist," *European Economists of the Early 20th Century: Studies of Neglected Continental Thinkers of Germany and Italy* 274.
66. De Grand, *Italian Fascism* 47.
67. Di Scala, *Italy from Revolution to Republic: 1700 to the present* 258.
68. Zamagni, *The Economic History of Italy: 1860-1990 Recovery after Decline* 244.
69. De Grand, *Italian Fascism* 61.
70. De Grand, *Italian Fascism* 59.
71. De Grand, *Italian Fascism* 64.
72. De Grand, *Italian Fascism* 64.
73. De Grand, *Italian Fascism* 66.
74. De Grand, *Italian Fascism* 66.
75. De Grand, *Italian Fascism* 66.
76. De Grand, *Italian Fascism* 81.
77. De Grand, *Italian Fascism* 82.
78. Duggan, *The Force of Destiny: A History of Italy Since 1796* 508-509.
79. De Grand, *Italian Fascism* 83 and 107.
80. Duggan, *The Force of Destiny: A History of Italy Since 1796* 491.
81. De Grand, *Italian Fascism* 100-101.
82. De Grand, *Italian Fascism* 100.

83. De Grand, *Italian Fascism* 101-102.
84. Payne, *Fascism: Comparison and Definition* 53.
85. Lee, *European Dictatorships: 1918-1945* 106-107.
86. De Grand, *Italian Fascism* 119 and Morgan, *Italian Fascism: 1919-1945* 180.
87. Aristotle, *Politics* Book 3 Part 7.
88. Payne, *Fascism: Comparison and Definition* 73-76.
89. De Grand, *Italian Fascism* 105.
90. De Grand, *Italian Fascism* 106.
91. De Grand, *Italian Fascism* 106.
92. De Grand, *Italian Fascism* 108.
93. De Grand, *Italian Fascism* 113.
94. De Grand, *Italian Fascism* 113.
95. De Grand, *Italian Fascism* 112.
96. De Grand, *Italian Fascism* 113.
97. De Grand, *Italian Fascism* 123.
98. De Grand, *Italian Fascism* 123.
99. De Grand, *Italian Fascism* 126-129.
100. Duggan, *The Force of Destiny: A History of Italy Since 1796* 554.
101. Duggan, *The Force of Destiny: A History of Italy Since 1796* 556.
102. Payne, *Fascism: Comparison and Definition* 105-106.
103. Payne, *A History of Fascism, 1914-1945* 5.
104. Payne, *A History of Fascism, 1914-1945* 8.
105. Eatwell, *Fascism: A History* 6-7.
106. Payne, *Fascism: Comparison and Definition* 141.
107. Payne, *Fascism: Comparison and Definition* 141-142.
108. Payne, *Fascism: Comparison and Definition* 152.
109. Payne, *Fascism: Comparison and Definition* 142.
110. Payne, *A History of Fascism, 1914-1945* 254.
111. Payne, *Fascism: Comparison and Definition* 143.
112. Kedward, *Fascism in Western Europe* 1900-1945 103-104.
113. Payne, *Fascism: Comparison and Definition* 149.
114. Payne, *Fascism: Comparison and Definition* 149.
115. White, "Secondary Wars and Atrocities of the Twentieth Century" <users.erols.com/mwhite28/warstat3.htm#Spanish>.
116. White, "Secondary Wars and Atrocities of the Twentieth Century" <users.erols.com/mwhite28/warstat3.htm#Spanish>.
117. See Kedward, *Fascism in Western Europe* 1900-1945 99-106; Payne, *Fascism: Comparison and Definition* 141-157; and Payne, *A History of Fascism, 1914-1945* 252-267 for more details on fascism in Spain.
118. Payne, *Fascism: Comparison and Definition* 107.
119. Bukey, *Hitler's Austria: Popular Sentiment in the Nazi Era, 1938-1945* 10.
120. See Bukey, *Hitler's Austria: Popular Sentiment in the Nazi Era, 1938-1945* 10-11; Gellott, "Austria," *World Fascism A Historical Encyclopedia* 67-71; Humphreys, *The Rough Guide to Vienna* 353-354; Payne, *Fascism: Comparison and Definition* 107-110; and Payne, *A History of Fascism, 1914-1945* 245-252 for more details on fascism in Austria.
121. Payne, *Fascism: Comparison and Definition* 173.
122. Payne, *Fascism: Comparison and Definition* 173.

123. Coppa, "Peron, Juan Domingo," *Encyclopedia of Modern Dictators: From Napoleon to the Present* 232 and Chirot, *Modern Tyrants: The Power and Prevalence of Evil in Our Age* 275.
124. Coppa, "Peron, Juan Domingo," *Encyclopedia of Modern Dictators: From Napoleon to the Present* 233 and Chirot, *Modern Tyrants: The Power and Prevalence of Evil in Our Age* 275.
125. *Elections in the Americas: A Data Handbook Volume 2: South America* 110.
126. Buchrucker, "Interpretations of Peronism: Old Frameworks and New Perspectives," *Peronism and Argentina* 5.
127. Payne, *Fascism: Comparison and Definition* 173.
128. Chirot, *Modern Tyrants: The Power and Prevalence of Evil in Our Age* 278.
129. Chirot, *Modern Tyrants: The Power and Prevalence of Evil in Our Age* 277.
130. Chirot, *Modern Tyrants: The Power and Prevalence of Evil in Our Age* 277.
131. Coppa, "Peron, Juan Domingo," *Encyclopedia of Modern Dictators: From Napoleon to the Present* 232-233.
132. *Elections in the Americas: A Data Handbook Volume 2: South America* 110.
133. Rock, *Argentina, 1516-1987: From Spanish Colonization to Alphonsín* 311.
134. Payne, *Fascism: Comparison and Definition* 173.
135. See Chirot, *Modern Tyrants: The Power and Prevalence of Evil in Our Age* 275-279; Coppa, "Peron, Juan Domingo," *Encyclopedia of Modern Dictators: From Napoleon to the Present* 232-234; Crassweller, *Peron and the Enigmas of Argentina*; Payne, *Fascism: Comparison and Definition* 172-175; Payne, *A History of Fascism, 1914-1945* 346-349; and Rock, *Argentina, 1516-1987: From Spanish Colonization to Alphonsín* 262-319 for more details on fascism in Argentina.

CHAPTER SEVEN
NAZI GERMANY

1. Morris, *Weimar Republic and Nazi Germany* 183.
2. Payne, *Fascism: Comparison and Definition* 53.
3. Morris, *Weimar Republic and Nazi Germany* 26.
4. Kitchen, *A History of Modern Germany* 209.
5. Kitchen, *A History of Modern Germany* 209.
6. Kitchen, *A History of Modern Germany* 206-207.
7. Kitchen, *A History of Modern Germany* 205.
8. Kitchen, *A History of Modern Germany* 213-214.
9. Kitchen, *A History of Modern Germany* 218.
10. Kitchen, *A History of Modern Germany* 218.
11. Kitchen, *A History of Modern Germany* 212.
12. Shirer, *The Rise and Fall of the Third Reich: A History of Nazi Germany* 56.
13. Kitchen, *A History of Modern Germany* 224.
14. Kitchen, *A History of Modern Germany* 224.
15. O'Kane, *Paths to Democracy: Revolution and Totalitarianism* 106.
16. Kitchen, *A History of Modern Germany* 230 and 233.
17. Kitchen, *A History of Modern Germany* 232.
18. Kitchen, *A History of Modern Germany* 234.
19. Eatwell, *Fascism: A History* 123 and Kitchen, *A History of Modern Germany* 236.

20. Kitchen, *A History of Modern Germany* 239.
21. Kitchen, *A History of Modern Germany* 235.
22. Kitchen, *A History of Modern Germany* 238.
23. Eatwell, *Fascism: A History* 130.
24. Eatwell, *Fascism: A History* 129.
25. Kitchen, *A History of Modern Germany* 240 and 244.
26. Hayek, *The Road to Serfdom* 184.
27. Hayek, *The Road to Serfdom* 68.
28. Davidson, *The Making of Adolf Hitler: The Birth and Rise of Nazism* 285.
29. Payne, *Fascism: Comparison and Definition* 52.
30. "The 25 Points of Hitler's Nazi Party," *The History Place.*
31. Ellul, *Autopsy of Revolution* 288.
32. Toland, *Adolf Hitler: The Definitive Biography* 224-225.
33. Payne, *Fascism: Comparison and Definition* 56.
34. Payne, *Fascism: Comparison and Definition* 52.
35. Pipes, *Property and Freedom* 221-222.
36. Payne, *Fascism: Comparison and Definition* 89.
37. Hayek, *The Road to Serfdom* 35.
38. Eatwell, *Fascism: A History* 132.
39. "The 25 Points of Hitler's Nazi Party," *The History Place.*
40. Payne, *Fascism: Comparison and Definition* 56.
41. Eatwell, *Fascism: A History* 133.
42. Kitchen, *A History of Modern Germany* 245.
43. Kitchen, *A History of Modern Germany* 241.
44. Kitchen, *A History of Modern Germany* 241.
45. Eatwell, *Fascism: A History* 136-137.
46. Eatwell, *Fascism: A History* 142.
47. "The 25 Points of Hitler's Nazi Party," *The History Place.*
48. Eatwell, *Fascism: A History* 166-167 and Payne, *Fascism: Comparison and Definition* 57.
49. Payne, *Fascism: Comparison and Definition* 56.
50. Eatwell, *Fascism: A History* 119.
51. Payne, *Fascism: Comparison and Definition* 56-57 and 67.
52. Paxton, *The Anatomy of Fascism* 216.
53. Eatwell, *Fascism: A History* 132.
54. Eatwell, *Fascism: A History* 145.
55. Payne, *Fascism: Comparison and Definition* 67.
56. Eatwell, *Fascism: A History* 145.
57. Kitchen, *A History of Modern Germany* 247.
58. Eatwell, *Fascism: A History* 137 and Kitchen, *A History of Modern Germany* 248.
59. Kitchen, *A History of Modern Germany* 249.
60. Eatwell, *Fascism: A History* 135 and Kitchen, *A History of Modern Germany* 251.
61. Eatwell, *Fascism: A History* 134 and Kitchen, *A History of Modern Germany* 251.
62. Kitchen, *A History of Modern Germany* 252.
63. Kitchen, *A History of Modern Germany* 252.
64. Kitchen, *A History of Modern Germany* 252.
65. Eatwell, *Fascism: A History* 138.
66. Kitchen, *A History of Modern Germany* 253.

67. Eatwell, *Fascism: A History* 138.
68. Kitchen, *A History of Modern Germany* 254 and Lubasz, *Fascism: Three Major Regimes* 7.
69. Kitchen, *A History of Modern Germany* 255.
70. Eatwell, *Fascism: A History* 141 and Kitchen, *A History of Modern Germany* 256.
71. Kitchen, *A History of Modern Germany* 259.
72. Kitchen, *A History of Modern Germany* 260.
73. Kitchen, *A History of Modern Germany* 260.
74. Kitchen, *A History of Modern Germany* 260.
75. Kitchen, *A History of Modern Germany* 257.
76. Kitchen, *A History of Modern Germany* 259.
77. Kitchen, *A History of Modern Germany* 260.
78. Kitchen, *A History of Modern Germany* 259.
79. Kitchen, *A History of Modern Germany* 261.
80. Morris, *Weimar Republic and Nazi Germany* 183.
81. Kitchen, *A History of Modern Germany* 261.
82. Kitchen, *A History of Modern Germany* 261.
83. Kitchen, *A History of Modern Germany* 262.
84. Eatwell, *Fascism: A History* 144.
85. Eatwell, *Fascism: A History* 165.
86. Eatwell, *Fascism: A History* 151.
87. Kitchen, *A History of Modern Germany* 264-265.
88. Eatwell, *Fascism: A History* 162 and Kitchen, *A History of Modern Germany* 265.
89. Bendersky, *A History of Nazi Germany: 1919-1945* 148 and Kitchen, *A History of Modern Germany* 288-290.
90. Kitchen, *A History of Modern Germany* 289.
91. Kitchen, *A History of Modern Germany* 314.
92. Kitchen, *A History of Modern Germany* 289.
93. Eatwell, *Fascism: A History* 162-163.
94. Kitchen, *A History of Modern Germany* 267.
95. Kitchen, *A History of Modern Germany* 278.
96. Kitchen, *A History of Modern Germany* 268-269.
97. Kitchen, *A History of Modern Germany* 269.
98. Kitchen, *A History of Modern Germany* 269.
99. Kitchen, *A History of Modern Germany* 269-270.
100. Kitchen, *A History of Modern Germany* 270.
101. Eatwell, *Fascism: A History* 159 and Kershaw, *The "Hitler Myth": Image and Reality in the Third Reich* 1.
102. Eatwell, *Fascism: A History* 159.
103. Kitchen, *A History of Modern Germany* 272.
104. Eatwell, *Fascism: A History* 160.
105. Eatwell, *Fascism: A History* 160.
106. Eatwell, *Fascism: A History* 149 and Kitchen, *A History of Modern Germany* 273.
107. Kitchen, *A History of Modern Germany* 279.
108. Kitchen, *A History of Modern Germany* 279.
109. Kitchen, *A History of Modern Germany* 279.
110. Kitchen, *A History of Modern Germany* 279.
111. Kitchen, *A History of Modern Germany* 281.

112. Eatwell, *Fascism: A History* 165-166 and 181.
113. Kitchen, *A History of Modern Germany* 281-282.
114. Kitchen, *A History of Modern Germany* 280.
115. Kitchen, *A History of Modern Germany* 280.
116. Kitchen, *A History of Modern Germany* 290.
117. Kitchen, *A History of Modern Germany* 293.
118. Kitchen, *A History of Modern Germany* 295.
119. Kitchen, *A History of Modern Germany* 296.
120. Kitchen, *A History of Modern Germany* 296.
121. Kitchen, *A History of Modern Germany* 296.
122. Self, *Neville Chamberlain: A Biography* 382.
123. Shirer, *The Collapse of the Third Republic: An Inquiry into the Fall of France in 1940* 529.
124. Kitchen, *A History of Modern Germany* 299.
125. Kitchen, *A History of Modern Germany* 304-305.
126. Eatwell, *Fascism: A History* 182.
127. Kitchen, *A History of Modern Germany* 306.
128. Hamerow, *Why We Watched: Europe, America, and the Holocaust* 325-327.
129. Kitchen, *A History of Modern Germany* 306-307.
130. Langworth, *Churchill by Himself: The Definitive Collection of Quotations* 5.
131. Kitchen, *A History of Modern Germany* 301.
132. Eatwell, *Fascism: A History* 177 and Kitchen, *A History of Modern Germany* 301.
133. Kitchen, *A History of Modern Germany* 301.
134. Kitchen, *A History of Modern Germany* 302-303.
135. Kitchen, *A History of Modern Germany* 301.
136. Kitchen, *A History of Modern Germany* 303.
137. Kitchen, *A History of Modern Germany* 303.
138. Kitchen, *A History of Modern Germany* 284.
139. Kitchen, *A History of Modern Germany* 286.
140. Payne, *A History of Fascism, 1914-1945* 93.
141. Kitchen, *A History of Modern Germany* 294.
142. Kitchen, *A History of Modern Germany* 307.
143. "The 25 Points of Hitler's Nazi Party," *The History Place*.
144. Kitchen, *A History of Modern Germany* 308.
145. Kitchen, *A History of Modern Germany* 309.
146. Kitchen, *A History of Modern Germany* 309.
147. Eatwell, *Fascism: A History* 187.
148. Eatwell, *Fascism: A History* 148.
149. Eatwell, *Fascism: A History* 178-179 and 189. See Victor Davis Hanson's *Carnage and Culture* about the superiority of Western armies due to their culture of individual liberty.
150. Eatwell, *Fascism: A History* 193.
151. Skousen, *The Making of Modern Economics: The Lives and Ideas of the Great Thinkers* 297.
152. Henderson, "German Economic Miracle."
153. Kitchen, *A History of Modern Germany* 317.
154. Kitchen, *A History of Modern Germany* 320.
155. Henderson, "German Economic Miracle."

156. Henderson, "German Economic Miracle."
157. Henderson, "German Economic Miracle."
158. Henderson, "German Economic Miracle."
159. Kitchen, *A History of Modern Germany* 324.
160. Kitchen, *A History of Modern Germany* 324.
161. Kitchen, *A History of Modern Germany* 324.
162. Kitchen, *A History of Modern Germany* 331.
163. Kitchen, *A History of Modern Germany* 333.
164. Kitchen, *A History of Modern Germany* 333.
165. Henderson, "German Economic Miracle."

CHAPTER EIGHT
THE UNITED STATES OF AMERICA

1. McClellan, *Liberty, Order, and Justice* 111-112.
2. Jefferson, *The Works of Thomas Jefferson* Vol 12 408-409.
3. Hamilton, Jay, and Madison, *The Federalist Papers* No. 15.
4. McClellan, *Liberty, Order, and Justice* 158-160.
5. *United States Constitution*, Preamble.
6. Hamilton, Jay, and Madison, *The Federalist Papers* No. 39.
7. McClellan, *Liberty, Order, and Justice* 253.
8. McClellan, *Liberty, Order, and Justice* 32.
9. Lutz, *A Preface to American Political Theory* 135-136.
10. McClellan, *Liberty, Order, and Justice* 16-17.
11. McClellan, *Liberty, Order, and Justice* 18.
12. McClellan, *Liberty, Order, and Justice* 32.
13. Bernstein, *Thomas Jefferson* 71.
14. McClellan, *Liberty, Order, and Justice* 253.
15. McClellan, *Liberty, Order, and Justice* 4.
16. Jefferson, *Notes on the State of Virginia Query* 14.
17. McClellan, *Liberty, Order, and Justice* 8.
18. Hamilton, *The Works of Alexander Hamilton* Vol. 2, 416.
19. McClellan, *Liberty, Order, and Justice* 49-50.
20. McClellan, *Liberty, Order, and Justice* 16.
21. Hamilton, Jay, and Madison, *The Federalist Papers* No. 63.
22. Hamilton, Jay, and Madison, *The Federalist Papers* No. 6.
23. McClellan, *Liberty, Order, and Justice* 5.
24. McClellan, *Liberty, Order, and Justice* 16-17.
25. Lutz, *A Preface to American Political Theory* 136-138.
26. McClellan, *Liberty, Order, and Justice* 48.
27. McClellan, *Liberty, Order, and Justice* 46.
28. McClellan, *Liberty, Order, and Justice* 18.
29. McClellan, *Liberty, Order, and Justice* 48-49.
30. Lutz, *A Preface to American Political Theory* 136-138.
31. McClellan, *Liberty, Order, and Justice* 31.
32. Thomas, *Industrial Revolution and the Atlantic Economy* 36.
33. McClellan, *Liberty, Order, and Justice* 32-33.

34. McClellan, *Liberty, Order, and Justice* 251.
35. McClellan, *Liberty, Order, and Justice* 31.
36. McClellan, *Liberty, Order, and Justice* 31-32.
37. McClellan, *Liberty, Order, and Justice* 251.
38. McClellan, *Liberty, Order, and Justice* 21.
39. McClellan, *Liberty, Order, and Justice* 91.
40. McClellan, *Liberty, Order, and Justice* 24-25.
41. Hamilton, Jay, and Madison, *The Federalist Papers* No. 47.
42. Hamilton, Jay, and Madison, *The Federalist Papers* No. 51.
43. McClellan, *Liberty, Order, and Justice* 25.
44. McClellan, *Liberty, Order, and Justice* 264-265.
45. *United States Constitution*, Article II Section 2.
46. Hamilton, Jay, and Madison, *The Federalist Papers* No. 69.
47. *United States Constitution*, Article I Section 8.
48. McClellan, *Liberty, Order, and Justice* 314-315.
49. McClellan, *Liberty, Order, and Justice* 314.
50. Hamilton, Jay, and Madison, *The Federalist Papers* No. 48.
51. *United States Constitution*, Article I Section 7.
52. *United States Constitution*, Article II Section 2.
53. *United States Constitution*, Article III Section 1.
54. Watson, *Liberty and Power: The Politics of Jacksonian America* 61-62
55. Howe, *What Hath God Wrought: The Transformation of America* 155.
56. McClellan, *Liberty, Order, and Justice* 16-18.
57. McClellan, *Liberty, Order, and Justice* 298-299.
58. McClellan, *Liberty, Order, and Justice* 22.
59. McClellan, *Liberty, Order, and Justice* 579.
60. McClellan, *Liberty, Order, and Justice* 9.
61. McClellan, *Liberty, Order, and Justice* 381-382.
62. McClellan, *Liberty, Order, and Justice* 406.
63. McClellan, *Liberty, Order, and Justice* 331-332.
64. Treisman, *The Architecture of Government: Rethinking Political Decentralization* 222.
65. Johnson, *The Changing Faces of New Hampshire: Recent Trends in the Granite State* 3.
66. Gormley, "Paterson: Taxing the rich backfired; the rich left the state."
67. Soltis, "Tax refugees staging escape from New York."
68. Voegeli, "The Golden State isn't worth it."
69. Laffer, Moore, and Williams, *Rich States, Poor States: ALEC-Laffer State Economic Competitiveness Index* 36-37.
70. Ciesielska, *Cost of Government Day 2009* 20-21.
71. Hamilton, Jay, and Madison, *The Federalist Papers* No. 51.
72. McClellan, *Liberty, Order, and Justice* 336.
73. "Constitution of the United States of America," *Encyclopædia Britannica*.
74. McClellan, *Liberty, Order, and Justice* 406.
75. Hamilton, Jay, and Madison, *The Federalist Papers* No. 17.
76. Hamilton, Jay, and Madison, *The Federalist Papers* No. 45.
77. McClellan, *Liberty, Order, and Justice* 322.
78. McClellan, *Liberty, Order, and Justice* 492.

79. McClellan, *Liberty, Order, and Justice* 492-493.

80. Calhoun, *South Carolina Exposition and Protest*.

81. Calhoun, *South Carolina Exposition and Protest*.

82. *United States Constitution*, Article I Section 9.

83. McClellan, *Liberty, Order, and Justice* 494-495.

84. McClellan, *Liberty, Order, and Justice* 494.

85. *United States Constitution*, Article I Section 9.

86. McGovern, *Abraham Lincoln* 60.

87. Neely, *The Fate of Liberty: Abraham Lincoln and Civil Liberties* 23.

88. Lincoln, *Speeches and Writings* 518.

89. Mitchell, *A History of the Greenbacks* 136.

90. Mitchell, *A History of the Greenbacks* 136.

91. Mitchell, *A History of the Greenbacks* 143-144.

92. *United States Constitution*, Article I Section 9.

93. Chambers, *The Oxford Companion to American Military History* 181.

94. Chambers, *The Oxford Companion to American Military History* 181.

95. Stone, *War and Liberty: An American Dilemma 1790 to the Present* 42.

96. Stone, *War and Liberty: An American Dilemma 1790 to the Present* 45.

97. Stone, *War and Liberty: An American Dilemma 1790 to the Present* 46.

98. Stone, *War and Liberty: An American Dilemma 1790 to the Present* 48.

99. Stone, *War and Liberty: An American Dilemma 1790 to the Present* 57.

100. Farwell, *Over There: The United States in the Great War* 50-52.

101. Farwell, *Over There: The United States in the Great War* 53.

102. Farwell, *Over There: The United States in the Great War* 52.

103. "History of the U.S. Tax System," *United States Department of The Treasury*.

104. "History of the U.S. Tax System," *United States Department of The Treasury*.

105. "History of the U.S. Tax System," *United States Department of The Treasury*.

106. "History of the U.S. Tax System," *United States Department of The Treasury*.

107. "Time Series Chart of US Government Spending."

108. Stone, *War and Liberty: An American Dilemma 1790 to the Present* 66.

109. Stone, *War and Liberty: An American Dilemma 1790 to the Present* 74.

110. "Time Series Chart of US Government Spending."

111. "Time Series Chart of US Government Spending."

112. Hamilton, Jay, and Madison, *The Federalist Papers* No. 10.

113. Roosevelt, "The Four Freedoms."

114. Roosevelt, "State of the Union Address."

115. *United States Constitution*, Preamble to the Bill of Rights.

116. Roosevelt, "State of the Union Address."

117. Franklin, *Memoirs of the Life and Writings of Benjamin Franklin* 270.

118. Hayek, *The Road to Serfdom* 30.

119. "Time Series Chart of US Government Spending."

120. "United States Federal State and Local Government Spending."

121. Congressional Budget Office, *The Long-Term Budget Outlook* 6.

122. "United States Federal State and Local Government Spending."

123. Congressional Budget Office, *CBO's Long-Term Projections for Social Security: 2009 Update* 23.

124. "FICA & SECA Tax Rates."

125. "Benefits Planner: Taxes and your Social Security benefits."

126. "The Full Retirement Age is Increasing."

127. "United States Federal State and Local Government Spending."

128. Congressional Budget Office, *The Long-Term Budget Outlook* 6.

129. "United States Federal State and Local Government Spending."

130. Cauchon, "Benefit spending soars to new high."

131. Shane, "Are We Becoming Less Entrepreneurial?"

132. "Employment, Hours, and Earnings from the Current Employment Statistics survey (National)."

133. "National Income and Product Accounts Table: Table 6.6D. Wage and Salary Accruals Per Full-Time Equivalent Employee by Industry."

134. "Top 100 Recipients of Federal Contract Awards for FY 2008."

135. "Federal Contract Awards by Major Agency."

136. "Defense-Related Employment and Spending statistics."

137. National Labor Relations Board website at www.nlrb.gov.

138. "OSHA's Frequently Asked Questions."

139. Baker, "Measuring the Explosive Growth of Federal Crime Legislation" 23.

140. Internal Revenue Service, *Fiscal Year 2008 Enforcement Results.*

141. Asser, "Echelon: Big brother without a cause?"

142. *15 Reasons to Oppose Photo Radar.*

143. Barr, "Government Surveillance Targets License Plates."

144. Hurt and Chiarmonte, "Tax Chief Charlie a Tax 'Cheat,' Too."

145. Kocieniewski, "Rangel Tries to Explain Back Taxes on Villa."

146. Malkin, "Obama's team is corrupt."

147. Hershey, "I.R.S. Staff Is Cited in Snoopings."

148. Hershey, "Snooping by I.R.S. Employees Has Not Stopped, Report Finds."

149. Poulsen, "Five IRS Employees Charged With Snooping on Tax Returns."

150. "Investigation Highlights," *U.S. Treasury Inspector General for Tax Administration (TIGTA).*

151. Pickler, "Fifth person pleads guilty to passport snooping."

152. Hamilton, Jay, and Madison, *The Federalist Papers* No. 36.

153. Roberts, "Notes on the Ancestry of Senator Barack Hussein Obama, Jr."

154. Milbank, "Family Ties Playing A Big Role On the Hill."

155. Lincoln, "Gettysburg Address."

156. "Congress Has Wealth to Weather Economic Downturn."

157. Purdum, "Go Ahead, Try to Stop K Street."

158. "Time Series Chart of US Government Spending."

159. "Lobbying Database."

160. "State Lobbying Totals, 2004-2006."

161. Kelley and Eisler, "Lobbying a family matter: Relatives have 'inside track' in lobbying for tax dollars."

162. Purdum, "Go Ahead, Try to Stop K Street."

163. Abramson, "The Business of Persuasion Thrives in Nation's Capital."

164. Knoller, "Obama's $3M Chicago Olympics Pitch Falls Short of the Gold."

165. York, "Michelle Obama: It's a 'sacrifice' to travel to Europe to pitch for the Olympics. But I'm doing it for the kids."

166. Vogel, "Sanford had trade mission rendezvous."

167. Ballasy, "Conyers Sees No Point in Members Reading 1,000-Page Health Care Bill."

168. Daily, *Stand Up to the IRS* 42.
169. Farley, "McCain says Obama has more czars than the Romanovs."
170. Farley, "McCain says Obama has more czars than the Romanovs."
171. McClellan, *Liberty, Order, and Justice* 344.
172. Jasina and Rotthoff, "The Impact of a Professional Sports Franchise on County Employment and Wages."
173. "Bonus Season for Baseball," *The New York Times*.
174. "Time Series Chart of US Government Spending."
175. Congressional Budget Office, *The Long-Term Budget Outlook* 6.
176. "United States Federal State and Local Government Spending."
177. Congressional Budget Office, *The Long-Term Budget Outlook* 6.
178. Congressional Budget Office, *The Long-Term Budget Outlook* 11.
179. Congressional Budget Office, *The Long-Term Budget Outlook* 6.
180. Lav and McNichol, "New Fiscal Year Brings No Relief From Unprecedented State Budget Problems."
181. Hodge, "News To Obama: The OECD Says the United States Has the Most Progressive Tax System."
182. Engdahl, "The Secret Financial Network Behind "Wizard" George Soros."
183. "World's Billionaires 2009: #468 Marc Rich."
184. "World's Billionaires 2009."
185. Noguchi, "Gates Foundation to Get Bulk of Buffett's Fortune."
186. Hodge, "U.S. Corporate Taxes Now 50 Percent Higher than OECD Average."
187. McGregor, "U.S. Companies Seek New Tax Havens."
188. Tremoglie, "The Facts on Halliburton."

BIBLIOGRAPHY

15 Reasons to Oppose Photo Radar. CameraFraud.com. 28 July 2009. <files.meetup.com/1275333/Updated%20Cheat%20sheet.doc>.

"1860 Census Results." *The Civil War Home Page.* <www.civil-war.net/pages/1860_census.html>.

Abramson, Jill. "The Business of Persuasion Thrives in Nation's Capital." *The New York Times* 29 Sept. 1998, sec. A: 1. <www.nytimes.com/1998/09/29/us/the-business-of-persuasion-thrives-in-nation-s-capital.html?pagewanted=all>.

Adams, John, and Charles Francis Adams. *The Works of John Adams. Vol. 6.* Boston: Charles C. Little and James Brown, 1851.

Adams, Michael C. C. *The Best War Ever: America and World War II.* New York: The Johns Hopkins University Press, 1993.

Amstutz, J. Bruce. *Afghanistan: The First Five Years of Soviet Occupation.* Washington: National Defense University, 1986.

Aristophanes. *The Knights. The Complete Greek Drama, vol. 2.* Ed. Eugene O'Neill, Jr. New York. Random House. 1938. *Perseus Digital Library Project.* Tufts University. <www.perseus.tufts.edu/cgi-bin/ptext?lookup=Aristoph.+Kn.+toc>.

Aristophanes. *The Wasps. The Complete Greek Drama, vol. 2.* Ed. Eugene O'Neill, Jr. New York. Random House. 1938. *Perseus Digital Library Project.* Tufts University. <www.perseus.tufts.edu/cgi-bin/ptext?lookup=Aristoph.+Wasps+toc>.

Aristotle. *Politics.* Trans. Benjamin Jowett. *The Constitution Society.* <www.constitution.org/ari/polit_00.htm>.

Aristotle. *The Athenian Constitution.* Trans. Sir Frederic G. Kenyon. *The Internet Classics Archive.* <classics.mit.edu/Aristotle/athenian_const.html>.

Arkenberg, J. S. "The Law Code of Gortyn (Crete), c. 450 BCE." *Internet Ancient History Sourcebook.* Aug. 1998. <www.fordham.edu/halsall/ancient/450-gortyn.html>.

Ascher, Abraham. *Russia: A Short History.* Oxford: Oneworld, 2009.

Asser, Martin. "Echelon: Big brother without a cause?" *BBC News.* 6 July 2000. <news.bbc.co.uk/2/hi/europe/820758.stm>.

Associated Press. "Soviet Involvement in the Vietnam War." *Historical Text Archive.* <historicaltextarchive.com/sections.php?op=viewarticle&artid=180>.

Australian Associated Press. "Death of Leo Trotsky." *The Age* 23 Aug. 1940. <150.theage.com.au/view_bestofarticle.asp?straction=update&inttype=1&intid=1188>.

Babler, Balbina. "Metics." *Encyclopedia of Ancient Greece.* Comp. Nigel Guy Wilson. New York: Routledge, 2006. 469-470.

Babler, Balbina. "Slavery." *Encyclopedia of Ancient Greece.* Comp. Nigel Guy Wilson. New York: Routledge, 2006. 664-665.

Baker, John S., Jr. "Measuring the Explosive Growth of Federal Crime Legislation." Engage 5.2: 23-32. *The Federalist Society.* 1 Oct. 2004. <www.fed-soc.org/publications/pubID.940/ pub_detail.asp>.

Ballasy, Nicholas. "Conyers Sees No Point in Members Reading 1,000-Page Health Care Bill--Unless They Have 2 Lawyers to Interpret It for Them." *CNSNews.com* 27 July 2009. <www.cnsnews.com/public/content/article.aspx?RsrcID=51610>.

Barillas, Martin. "Expropriations in Venezuela threaten oil supply." *Spero News.* 10 May 2009. <www.speroforum.com/a/19251/Expropriations-in-Venezuela-threaten-oil-supply>.

Barr, Bob. "Government Surveillance Targets License Plates." *The Barr Code.* AJC Blogs. 14 Aug. 2009. <blogs.ajc.com/bob-barr-blog/2009/08/14/government-surveillance-targets-license-plates/?cxntfid=blogs_bob_barr_blog>.

Bartlett, Bruce. "How Excessive Government Killed Ancient Rome." *Cato Journal* Volume 14 Number 2 (Fall 1994). *Cato Institute.* <www.cato.org/pubs/journal/cjv14n2-7.html>.

Bendersky, Joseph W. *A History of Nazi Germany: 1919-1945.* Chicago: Rowman & Littlefield Publishers, 2000.

"Benefits Planner: Taxes and your Social Security benefits." *Social Security Online.* 03 Sept. 2009 <www.ssa.gov/planners/taxes.htm>.

Berend, Ivan T. "Contemporary Hungary, 1956-1984." A *History of Hungary.* New York: Indiana University Press, 1994. 384-400.

Bernstein, Richard B. *Thomas Jefferson.* Oxford University Press US, 2005.

Bessel, Richard. *Nazism and War.* New York: Modern Library, 2006.

Best, Heinrich, and Maurizio Cotta, eds. *Parliamentary Representatives in Europe, 1848-2000.* Oxford: Oxford University Press, 2000.

Bini, Piero. "Umberto Ricci: profile of a militant economist." *European Economists of the Early 20th Century: Studies of Neglected Continental Thinkers of Germany and Italy.* Ed. Warren J. Samuels. Grand Rapids: Edward Elgar, 2003. 257-80.

Bloomfield, Maxwell H. *Peaceful Revolution: Constitutional Change and American Culture from Progressivism to the New Deal.* Cambridge, Mass: Harvard University Press, 2000.

Boeckh, August. *The Public Economy of Athens: To which is Added, a Dissertation on the Silver Mines of Laurion.* Trans. George Cornewall Lewis. Second ed. London: John W. Parker, 1842.

"Bonus Season for Baseball." The New York Times 17 Jan. 2002, sec. A: 28. <www.nytimes.com/2002/01/17/opinion/bonus-season-for-baseball.html>.

Buchrucker, Christian. "Interpretations of Peronism: Old Frameworks and New Perspectives." *Peronism and Argentina.* Ed. James P. Brennan. Wilmington, Del: Scholarly Resources, 1998. 3-28.

Bukey, Evan Burr. *Hitler's Austria: Popular Sentiment in the Nazi Era, 1938-1945.* Chapel Hill: The University of North Carolina Press, 2002.

Bulwer-Lytton, Edward. *Richelieu; Or, the Conspiracy: A Play, in Five Acts.* Paris: Baudry's European Library, 1839.

Burnham, David. "MISUSE OF THE I.R.S.: THE ABUSE OF POWER." *The New York Times* 3 Sept. 1989. <www.nytimes.com/1989/09/03/magazine/misuse-of-the-irs-the-abuse-of-power.html?pagewanted=all>.

Byrd, Robert. *The Senate of the Roman Republic.* Washington: U.S. Government Printing Office, 1994.

Calhoun, John C. *South Carolina Exposition and Protest*. Wikisource. 19 Dec. 1928. <en.wikisource.org/wiki/South_Carolina_Exposition_and_Protest>.

Cassius Dio. *Roman History*. Trans. Earnest Cary. Loeb Classical Library, 9 volumes. New York: Harvard University Press, 1914-1927. *LacusCurtius*. Bill Thayer. <penelope.uchicago.edu/Thayer/E/Roman/Texts/Cassius_Dio/home.html>.

Cauchon, Dennis. "Benefit spending soars to new high." *USA TODAY* 4 June 2009. <www.usatoday.com/news/washington/2009-06-03-benefits_N.htm#>.

Chambers, John Whiteclay, II. *The Oxford Companion to American Military History*. USA: Oxford University Press, 2000.

"Chavez promises a socialist Venezuela as he starts new 6-year term." *USA Today*. 10 Jan. 2007. <www.usatoday.com/news/world/2007-01-10-chavez-venezuela_x.htm?csp=34>.

Chirot, Daniel. *Modern Tyrants: The Power and Prevalence of Evil in Our Age*. Princeton, N.J: Princeton University Press, 1994.

Chrissanthos, Stefan G. "Freedom of Speech and the Roman Republican Army." *Free Speech in Classical Antiquity*. By Penn-Leiden Colloquium. Leiden: Brill, 2004. 341-68.

Cicero. *De Officiis*. Trans. Walter Miller. Loeb end. Cambridge: Harvard University Press, 1913. *The Constitution Society*. <www.constitution.org/rom/de_officiis.htm>.

Cicero. *Philippics. The Orations of Marcus Tullius Cicero*, literally translated by C. D. Yonge. London. George Bell & Sons. 1903. *Perseus Digital Library Project*. Tufts University. <www.perseus.tufts.edu/cgi-bin/ptext?lookup=Cic.+Phil.+toc>.

Cicero. *The Political Works of Marcus Tullius Cicero: Comprising his Treatise on the Commonwealth; and his Treatise on the Laws*. Translated from the original, with Dissertations and Notes in Two Volumes. By Francis Barham, Esq. (London: Edmund Spettigue, 1841-42). Vol. 1. *Online Library of Liberty*. <oll.libertyfund.org/546>.

Ciesielska, Monika. *Cost of Government Day 2009*. Washington: Americans for Tax Reform Foundation / Center for Fiscal Accountability, 2009. <www.fiscalaccountability.org/index.php?content=cogd-teas>.

Clendenning, Alan. ""Axis of Good" for Brazil, Cuba and Venezuela?" *Common Dreams*. 3 Jan. 2003. <www.commondreams.org/headlines03/0103-01.htm>.

"Cleon." *Encyclopædia Britannica*. 2009. *Encyclopædia Britannica Online*. 26 Jun. 2009 <www.britannica.com/EBchecked/topic/121210/Cleon>.

Compania De Tabacos v. Collector. No. 275 U.S. 87. U.S. Supreme Court. 21 Nov. 1927.

"Congress Has Wealth to Weather Economic Downturn." *Capital Eye Blog*. 13 Mar. 2008. OpenSecrets.org. <www.opensecrets.org/news/2008/03/congress-has-wealth-to-weather.html>.

Congressional Budget Office. *CBO's Long-Term Projections for Social Security: 2009 Update*. August 2009. <www.cbo.gov/ftpdocs/104xx/doc10457/08-07-SocialSecurity_Update.pdf>.

Congressional Budget Office. *The Long-Term Budget Outlook*. June 2009. <www.cbo.gov/ftpdocs/102xx/doc10297/06-25-LTBO.pdf>.

"Constitution of the United States of America." *Encyclopædia Britannica*. 2009. *Encyclopædia Britannica Online*. <www.britannica.com/EBchecked/topic/134197/Constitution-of-the-United-States-of-America/219004/The-Constitution-as-a-living-document>.

Coppa, Francesca. "Peron, Juan Domingo." *Encyclopedia of Modern Dictators: From Napoleon to the Present*. Ed. Frank J. Coppa. New York: Peter Lang, 2006. 232-34.

Crassweller, Robert D. *Peron and the Enigmas of Argentina*. New York: W. W. Norton & Company, 1996.

Curd, Patricia. "Anaxagoras." *Stanford Encyclopedia of Philosophy*. 22 Aug. 2007. <plato.stanford.edu/entries/anaxagoras/>.

Daily, Frederick W. *Stand Up to the IRS*. Berkeley, CA: Nolo, 2009.

Daniel, Frank Jack. "Food, farms the new target for Venezuela's Chavez." *Reuters*. 5 Mar. 2009. <www.reuters.com/article/topNews/idUSTRE5246OO20090305>.

Davidson, Eugene. *The Making of Adolf Hitler: The Birth and Rise of Nazism*. Columbia, MO: University of Missouri Press, 1997.

De Grand, Alexander J. *Italian Fascism: Its Origins and Development*. Third Edition. Lincoln and London: University of Nebraska Press, 2000.

"Defense-Related Employment and Spending statistics." *Allcountries.org Country information*. 04 Sept. 2009 <www.allcountries.org/uscensus/575_defense_related_employment_and_spending.html>.

Demosthenes. "Speeches." *Demosthenes with an English translation* by J. H. Vince, M.A. Cambridge, MA, Harvard University Press; London, William Heinemann Ltd. 1930. *Perseus Digital Library Project*. Tufts University. <www.perseus.tufts.edu/cgi-bin/ptext?doc=Perseus%3Atext%3A1999.01.0070;layout=;loc=1.1;query=toc>.

DeWitt, Larry. *Financing Social Security, 1939–1949: A Reexamination of the Financing Policies of this Period*. 4th ed. Vol. 67. 2007. *Social Security Bulletin*. <www.ssa.gov/policy/docs/ssb/v67n4/67n4p51.pdf>.

Di Scala, Spencer. *Italy from Revolution to Republic: 1700 to the present*. Third ed. Boulder, Colo: Westview Press, 2004.

Dickinson, John. *Death of a Republic: Politics and Political Thought at Rome 59-44 B.C.* New York: The Macmillan Company, 1963.

Diodorus Siculus. *The Library of History. Diodorus of Sicily in Twelve Volumes with an English Translation by C. H. Oldfather*. Cambridge, Mass.: Harvard University Press; London: William Heinemann, Ltd. 1989. *LacusCurtius*. Bill Thayer. <penelope.uchicago.edu/Thayer/E/Roman/Texts/Diodorus_Siculus/home.html>.

Dionysius of Halicarnassus. *Roman Antiquities*. Trans. Earnest Cary. Loeb Classical Library, 7 volumes. New York: Harvard University Press, 1937-1950. *LacusCurtius*. Bill Thayer. <penelope.uchicago.edu/Thayer/E/Roman/Texts/Dionysius_of_Halicarnassus/home.html>.

Douglass, Frederick. "A Plea for Free Speech in Boston," 1860. <classiclit.about.com/library/bl-etexts/fdouglass/bl-fdoug-freespeech.htm>.

Drew, Elizabeth. *The Corruption of American Politics: What Went Wrong and Why*. New York: Birch Lane Press, 1999.

Duggan, Christopher. *The Force of Destiny: A History of Italy Since 1796*. Boston: Houghton Mifflin, 2008.

Eatwell, Roger. *Fascism: A History*. New York: Allen Lane, 1996.

Elections in the Americas: A Data Handbook Volume 2: South America. New York: Oxford University Press, USA, 2005.

Ellul, Jacques. *Autopsy of Revolution*. New York: Knopf, 1971.

"Employment, Hours, and Earnings from the Current Employment Statistics survey (National)." *Bureau of Labor Statistics*. 27. Apr 2010. <data.bls.gov/cgi-bin/surveymost?ce>.

Engdahl, William. "The Secret Financial Network Behind "Wizard" George Soros." *Questions, questions...* 1 Nov. 1996. <www.questionsquestions.net/docs04/engdahl-soros.html>.

Engen, Darel Tai. "The Economy of Ancient Greece". *EH.Net Encyclopedia*, edited by Robert Whaples. July 31, 2004. <eh.net/encyclopedia/article/engen.greece>.

Ethics of the Fathers. *Chabad.org Library*. 13 Dec. 2009. <www.chabad.org/library/article_cdo/aid/5708/jewish/Ethics-of-the-Fathers-Translated-Text.htm>.

Euripides. *Hecuba*. Trans. E. P. Coleridge. *The Complete Greek Drama*. Ed. Whitney J. Oates and Eugene O'Neill, Jr. New York: Random House, 1938. *Perseus Digital Library Project*. Tufts University. <www.perseus.tufts.edu/hopper/text?doc=Perseus%3Atext%3A1999.01.0098>.

"Excerpts From Yeltsin's Speech to Lawmakers." *Los Angeles Times* 18 June 1992. <articles.latimes.com/1992-06-18/news/mn-936_1_united-states>.

Farley, Robert. "McCain says Obama has more czars than the Romanovs." *PolitiFact*. 12 June 2009. St. Petersburg Times Online. <www.politifact.com/truth-o-meter/statements/2009/jun/12/john-mccain/McCain-says-Obama-has-more-czars-than-Romanovs/>.

Farwell, Byron. *Over There: The United States in the Great War, 1917-1918*. Boston: W. W. Norton & Company, 2000.

"Federal Contract Awards by Major Agency." *USAspending.gov*. 30 Nov. 2009 <www.usaspending.gov/fpds/tables.php?tabtype=t1&subtype=at&rowtype=f>.

"FICA & SECA Tax Rates." *Social Security Online*. 03 Sept. 2009 <www.ssa.gov/OACT/ProgData/taxRates.html>.

Finley, Moses I. *The Ancient Economy*. Berkeley: University of California, 1999.

Franklin, Benjamin. *Memoirs of the Life and Writings of Benjamin Franklin*. Vol. 1. London: Henry Colburn, 1818.

Freeman, Philip. *Julius Caesar*. New York: Simon & Schuster, 2008.

Fromkin, David. *Europe's Last Summer*. New York: Alfred Knopf, 2004.

Fry, Michael Graham, Erik Goldstein, and Richard Langhorne. *Guide to International Relations and Diplomacy*. New York: Continuum International Group, 2004.

Fuller, J. F. C. *Julius Caesar: Man, Soldier, and Tyrant*. New York, N.Y: Da Capo Press, 1991.

Furshong, Gabriel. "What is Bolivarian Socialism? And When?" *Venezuelanalysis.com*. 4 Sept. 2005. <www.venezuelanalysis.com/analysis/1342>.

Gaddis, John Lewis. *The Cold War: A New History*. New York: Penguin (Non-Classics), 2006.

Garthoff, Raymond L. *Reflections on the Cuban Missile Crisis*. Washington: Brookings Institution, 1989.

Gellott, Laura. "Austria." *World Fascism A Historical Encyclopedia*. Ed. Cyprian Blamires. Vol. 1. Santa Barbara: ABC-CLIO, 2006. 67-71.

Gibbon, Edward. *The History of the Decline and Fall of the Roman Empire*. Ed. J.B. Bury with an Introduction by W.E.H. Lecky. New York: Fred de Fau and Co., 1906. *The Online Library of Liberty*. <oll.libertyfund.org/title/1681>.

Gormley, Michael. "Paterson: Taxing the rich backfired; the rich left the state." *The Ithaca Journal* 23 Sept. 2009. <www.theithacajournal.com/article/20090923/NEWS10/909230331/Paterson++Taxing+the+rich+backfired++the+rich+left+the+state>.

Gott, Richard. *Hugo Chavez and the Bolivarian Revolution*. New York: Verso, 2005.

Grenville, John Ashley Soames. *A History of the World from the 20th to the 21st Century.* New York: Routledge, 2005.

Hagen, Jurgen Von, and Rolf R. Strauch. "East Germany: Transition with Unification, Experiments, and Experiences." *Transition The First Decade.* New York: The MIT Press, 2002. 87-120.

Hall, Johnathan M. "Dorians." *Encyclopedia of Ancient Greece.* Comp. Nigel Guy Wilson. New York: Routledge, 2006. 240-241.

Hamerow, Theodore S. *Why We Watched: Europe, America, and the Holocaust.* New York: W. W. Norton, 2008.

Hamilton, Alexander, John Jay, and James Madison. *The Federalist Papers.* New York: J. and M. Lean, 1788. *The Constitution Society.* <www.constitution.org/fed/federa00.htm>.

Hamilton, Alexander. *The Works of Alexander Hamilton.* Ed. John C. Hamilton. New York: John F. Trow, 1850.

Hammond, N.G.L. *A History of Greece to 322 B.C.* Third ed. Oxford: Clarendon Press, 1986.

Harbottle, Thomas Benfield. *Dictionary of Quotations.* New York: Macmillan, 1906. *Internet Archive.* <www.archive.org/details/dictionaryquota02harbgoog>.

Harris, Leon A. *Upton Sinclair, American Rebel.* New York: Crowell, 1975.

Hayek, Friedrich A. von. *The Road to Serfdom.* Chicago: University of Chicago Press, 1994.

Henderson, David R. "German Economic Miracle." *Library of Economics and Liberty.* 3 Nov. 2009. <www.econlib.org/library/Enc/GermanEconomicMiracle.html>.

Herodotus. *The Histories.* Trans. A. D. Godley. Cambridge. Harvard University Press. 1920. *Perseus Digital Library Project.* Tufts University. <www.perseus.tufts.edu/cgi-bin/ptext?lookup=Hdt.+toc>.

Hershey, Robert D., Jr. "I.R.S. Staff Is Cited in Snoopings." *The New York Times* 19 July 1994, sec. D: 1. <www.nytimes.com/1994/07/19/business/irs-staff-is-cited-in-snoopings.html>.

Hershey, Robert D., Jr. "Snooping by I.R.S. Employees Has Not Stopped, Report Finds." *The New York Times* 9 Apr. 1997, sec. A: 16. Web. <www.nytimes.com/1997/04/09/us/snooping-by-irs-employees-has-not-stopped-report-finds.html>.

Hilali, A. Z. *US-Pakistan Relationship: Soviet Invasion of Afghanistan.* Burlington, VT: Ashgate, 2005.

Hirsch, Emil, W Muss-Arnolt, Wilhelm Bacher, and Ludwig Blau. "URIM AND THUMMIM." *JewishEncyclopedia.com.* 20 Nov. 2009. <www.jewishencyclopedia.com/view.jsp?artid=52&letter=U>.

"History of the U.S. Tax System." *United States Department of The Treasury.* 01 Sept. 2009 <www.treas.gov/education/fact-sheets/taxes/ustax.shtml>.

Hodge, Scott A. "U.S. Corporate Taxes Now 50 Percent Higher than OECD Average." *The Tax Foundation.* 13 Aug. 2008. <www.taxfoundation.org/news/show/23470.html>.

Hodge, Scott A. "News To Obama: The OECD Says the United States Has the Most Progressive Tax System." *The Tax Foundation.* 29 Oct. 2008. <www.taxfoundation.org/blog/show/23856.html>.

Howe, Daniel Walker. *What Hath God Wrought: The Transformation of America, 1815-1848.* New York: Oxford University Press, 2007.

Humphrey, John W. *Greek and Roman Technology: A Sourcebook.* New York: Routledge, 1997.

Humphreys, Rob. *The Rough Guide to Vienna*. 3rd ed. New York: Rough Guides, 2001.

Hurt, Charles, and Perry Chiarmonte. "Tax Chief Charlie a Tax 'Cheat,' Too." *New York Post* 27 Aug. 2009. <www.nypost.com/seven/08272009/news/regionalnews/ tax_chief_charlie_a_tax_cheat__too_186678.htm>.

Internal Revenue Service. *Fiscal Year 2008 Enforcement Results*. 8 Sept. 2009. <www.irs.gov/pub/irs-news/2008_enforcement.pdf>.

"Investigation Highlights." *U.S. Treasury Inspector General for Tax Administration (TIGTA)*. 28 Aug. 2009. <www.treas.gov/tigta/oi_highlights.shtml>.

Jacob, H. E. *Six Thousand Years of Bread Its Holy and Unholy History*. Grand Rapids: Skyhorse, 2007.

Jasina, John, and Kurt W. Rotthoff. "The Impact of a Professional Sports Franchise on County Employment and Wages." *International Journal of Sport Finance* 3.4 (November 2008): 210-27. SSRN. <ssrn.com/abstract=1151311>.

Jefferson, Thomas. *Notes on the State of Virginia*. Electronic Text Center. University of Virginia Library. <etext.virginia.edu/toc/modeng/public/JefVirg.html>.

Jefferson, Thomas. *The Works of Thomas Jefferson*. Ed. Paul Leicester Ford. New York and London: G.P. Putnam's Sons, 1904-5. <oll.libertyfund.org/1734>.

Johnson, Kenneth M. *The Changing Faces of New Hampshire: Recent Trends in the Granite State*. Carsey Institute. University of New Hampshire, 2007. <www.carseyinstitute.unh.edu/publications/Report_NH_Demographics.pdf>.

Karo, Yosef, and Moses Isserles. *Shulchan Aruch: Yoreh Deah*.

Kedward, H. R. *Fascism in Western Europe 1900-1945*. New York University Press, 1971.

Kelley, Matt, and Peter Eisler. "Lobbying a family matter: Relatives have 'inside track' in lobbying for tax dollars." *USA TODAY* 16 Oct. 2006. <www.usatoday.com/news/ washington/2006-10-16-lobbyist-family-cover_x.htm>.

Kenez, Peter. *A History of the Soviet Union from the Beginning to the End*. New York: Cambridge University Press, 1999.

Kershaw, Ian. *The "Hitler Myth": Image and Reality in the Third Reich*. New York: Oxford University Press, USA, 2001.

Kitchen, Martin. *A History of Modern Germany: 1800-2000*. Malden, MA: Blackwell, 2006.

Knoller, Mark. "Obama's $3M Chicago Olympics Pitch Falls Short of the Gold." *CBSNews*. 02 Oct. 2009 <www.cbsnews.com/blogs/2009/10/02/politics/ politicalhotsheet/entry5359359.shtml>.

Kocieniewski, David. "Rangel Tries to Explain Back Taxes on Villa." *The New York Times* 11 Sept. 2008, sec. A: 1. <www.nytimes.com/2008/09/11/nyregion/ 11rangel.html?_r=1&pagewanted=all>.

Kort, Michael. *A Brief History of Russia*. New York: Checkmark Books, 2008.

Kort, Michael. *The Columbia Guide to the Cold War*. New York: Columbia University Press, 1998.

Kort, Michael. *The Soviet Colossus: History and Aftermath*. Sixth ed. New York: M.E. Sharpe, 2006.

Laffer, Arthur B., Stephen Moore, and Jonathan Williams. *Rich States, Poor States: ALEC-Laffer State Economic Competitiveness Index*. 2nd ed. Washington: American Legislative Exchange Council, 2009. <www.alec.org/AM/Template.cfm?Section= Rich_States_Poor_States>.

Langworth, Richard, ed. *Churchill by Himself: The Definitive Collection of Quotations*. PublicAffairs, 2008.

Lav, Iris J., and Elizabeth McNichol. "New Fiscal Year Brings No Relief From Unprecedented State Budget Problems." *Center on Budget and Policy Priorities.* 23 Dec. 2009. <www.cbpp.org/cms/?fa=view&id=711>.

Lee, Stephen J. *European Dictatorships: 1918-1945.* New York: Routledge, 2008.

Levin, Mark R. *Liberty and Tyranny.* New York: Threshold Editions, 2009.

Lewis, Sian. *Ancient Tyranny.* New York: Edinburgh University Press, 2006.

Lincoln, Abraham. "Gettysburg Address." 19 Nov. 1863. *American Historical Documents, 1000–1904.* Vol. XLIII. The Harvard Classics. New York: P.F. Collier & Son, 1909–14; *Bartleby.com*, 2001. <bartleby.com/43/36.html>.

Lincoln, Abraham. *Speeches and Writings, 1859-1865.* New York, N.Y: Literary Classics of the United States, 1989.

Livy. *History of Rome.* Trans. Rev. Canon Roberts. Ed. Ernest Rhys. London: J. M. Dent & Sons, Ltd., 1905. *Bruce J. Butterfield.* <mcadams.posc.mu.edu/txt/ah/Livy/index.html>.

"Lobbying Database." *OpenSecrets.org.* 28 Aug. 2009 <www.opensecrets.org/lobbyists/>.

Lubasz, Heinz. *Fascism: Three Major Regimes.* New York: J. Wiley, 1973.

Lucretius. *Of The Nature of Things.* Trans. William Ellery Leonard. *Project Gutenberg.* <www.gutenberg.org/etext/785>.

Lustig, Robin. "Hugo Chavez: Charming provocateur." *BBC News.* 20 Oct. 2005. <news.bbc.co.uk/2/hi/americas/4359924.stm>.

Lutz, Donald. *A Preface to American Political Theory.* Lawrence: Kansas University Press, 1992.

Machiavelli, Niccolò. *Prince.* Trans. Peter Bondanella. Oxford ; New York: Oxford University Press, 2005.

Maimonides and Eliyahu Touger. *Mishneh Torah: Hilchot Ishut.* New York: Maznaim, 1994.

Maimonides and Eliyahu Touger. *Mishneh Torah: Hilchot Melachim U'Milchamoteihem.* New York: Maznaim, 1987.

Malkin, Michelle. "Obama's team is corrupt." *Today,* 29 July 2009. <today.msnbc.msn.com/id/32174484/ns/today-today_books//>.

McClellan, James. *Liberty, Order, and Justice.* Third ed. Indianapolis: Liberty Fund, 2000. <oll.libertyfund.org/679>.

McGlew, James F. *Tyranny and Political Culture in Ancient Greece.* Ithaca: Cornell University Press, 1993.

McGovern, George. *Abraham Lincoln.* New York: Times Books, 2009.

McGregor, Jena. "U.S. Companies Seek New Tax Havens." *BusinessWeek.* 28 June 2009. <www.businessweek.com/bwdaily/dnflash/content/jun2009/db20090628_851524.htm>.

Meier, Christian. *Caesar.* New York: BasicBooks/HarperCollins, 1995.

Milbank, Dana. "Family Ties Playing A Big Role On the Hill." *Washington Post* 23 Jan. 2005: sec. A: 1. <www.washingtonpost.com/wp-dyn/articles/A29415-2005Jan22.html>.

Mises, Ludwig Von. *Economic Policy, Thoughts for Today and Tomorrow.* Chicago: Regnery/Gateway, 1979. *Ludwig von Mises Institute.* <mises.org/etexts/ecopol.asp>.

Mises, Ludwig Von. *Liberalism: The Classical Tradition.* Trans. Ralph Raico. Ed. Bettina Bien Greaves. Indianapolis: Liberty Fund, 2005. <oll.libertyfund.org/title/1463>.

Mishnah: Ketuboth.

Mishnah: Sanhedrin.

Mitchell, Wesley Clair. *A History of the Greenbacks*. University of Chicago Press, 1903.

Momigliano, Arnaldo. "Freedom of Speech in Antiquity." *The Dictionary of the History of Ideas*. Vol. 2. New York: Charles Scribner's Sons, 1973-74. University of Virginia Library. <etext.virginia.edu/cgi-local/DHI/dhi.cgi?id=dv2-31>.

Montesquieu, Charles de Secondat. *Considerations on the Causes of the Greatness of the Romans and their Decline*. Trans. David Lowenthal. New York: The Free, 1965. *The Constitution Society*. <www.constitution.org/cm/ccgrd_l.htm>.

Morgan, Philip. *Italian Fascism: 1919-1945*. Second ed. New York: Palgrave Macmillan, 2004.

Morris, Warren Bayard. *Weimar Republic and Nazi Germany*. Chicago: Nelson-Hall, 1982.

Morsbach, Greg. "Venezuelan shoppers face food shortages." *BBC News*. 10 Jan. 2006. <news.bbc.co.uk/2/hi/business/4599260.stm>.

"National Accounts Main Aggregates Database." *United Nations Statistics Division*. 21 Sept. 2009 <unstats.un.org/unsd/snaama/selectionbasicFast.asp>.

"National Income and Product Accounts Table: Table 6.6D. Wage and Salary Accruals Per Full-Time Equivalent Employee by Industry." *U.S. Bureau of Economic Analysis*. 20 Aug. 2009. <www.bea.gov/national/nipaweb/TableView.asp?SelectedTable=201& Freq=Year&FirstYear=2007&LastYear=2008> and <www.bea.gov/national/nipaweb/ TableView.asp?SelectedTable=198&Freq=Year&FirstYear=1947&LastYear=1948>.

National Labor Relations Board. 04 Sept. 2009 <www.nlrb.gov/>.

Neely, Mark E. *The Fate of Liberty: Abraham Lincoln and Civil Liberties*. New York: Oxford University Press, USA, 1992.

Noguchi, Yuki. "Gates Foundation to Get Bulk of Buffett's Fortune." *Washington Post*. 06 June 2006 <www.washingtonpost.com/wp-dyn/content/article/2006/06/25/ AR2006062500801.html>.

O'Kane, Rosemary. *Paths to Democracy: Revolution and Totalitarianism*. New York: Routledge, 2004.

"OSHA's Frequently Asked Questions." Occupational Safety and Health Administration. 04 Sept. 2009 <www.osha.gov/as/opa/osha-faq.html>.

Paine, Thomas. *Common Sense*. New York: Peter Eckler Publishing, 1918.

Parkinson, Roger. *The Encyclopedia of Modern War*. New York: Stein and Day, 1977.

Paxton, Robert O. *The Anatomy of Fascism*. New York: Vintage, 2005.

Payne, Stanley G. *A History of Fascism, 1914-1945*. Madison: University of Wisconsin Press, 1995.

Payne, Stanley G. *Fascism: Comparison and Definition*. Madison: University of Wisconsin Press, 1980.

Phillips, William D. *Slavery from Roman Times to the Early Transatlantic Trade*. Minneapolis, MN: University of Minnesota Press, 1985.

Pickler, Nedra. "Fifth person pleads guilty to passport snooping." *Breitbart.com*. 17 Aug. 2009. <www.breitbart.com/article.php?id=D9A4PTO82&show_article=1>.

Pipes, Richard. *Property and Freedom*. New York: Vintage, 2000.

Plato. *Apology. Plato in Twelve Volumes, Vol. 1* translated by Harold North Fowler; Introduction by W.R.M. Lamb. Cambridge, MA, Harvard University Press; London, William Heinemann Ltd. 1966. *Perseus Digital Library Project*. Tufts University. <www.perseus.tufts.edu/cgi-bin/ptext?lookup=Plat.+Apol.+17a>.

Plato. *Republic. Plato in Twelve Volumes, Vols. 5 & 6* translated by Paul Shorey. Cambridge, MA, Harvard University Press; London, William Heinemann Ltd. 1969. *Perseus Digital Library Project.* Tufts University. <www.perseus.tufts.edu/cgi-bin/ptext?lookup=Plat.+Rep.+toc>.

Plutarch. *Parallel Lives.* Trans. Bernadotte Perrin. New York: Loeb Classical Library, 1923. *LacusCurtius.* Bill Thayer. <penelope.uchicago.edu/Thayer/E/Roman/Texts/Plutarch/Lives/home.html>.

Polybius. *The Histories.* Trans. W. R. Paton. *Loeb Classical Library, 6 volumes, Greek texts and facing English translation.* Harvard University Press, 1922 thru 1927. *LacusCurtius.* Bill Thayer. <penelope.uchicago.edu/Thayer/E/Roman/Texts/Polybius/home.html>.

Poulsen, Kevin. "Five IRS Employees Charged With Snooping on Tax Returns." *Wired News.* 13 May 2008. <www.wired.com/threatlevel/2008/05/five-irs-employ/>.

Purdum, Todd S. "Go Ahead, Try to Stop K Street." *The New York Times* 8 Jan. 2006, Week in Review sec. <query.nytimes.com/gst/fullpage.html?res=9B0CE0D61E30F93BA35752C0A9609C8B63&sec=&spon=&pagewanted=all>.

Raaflaub, Kurt. *The Discovery of Freedom in Ancient Greece Revised and Updated Edition.* New York: University Of Chicago Press, 2004.

Raddock, Charles. *Portrait of a People. Vol. I: Ancient Era.* New York: The Judaica Press, 1965.

Rich, Anthony. "Aurum Coronarium." *A Dictionary of Greek and Roman Antiquities.* London: John Murray, 1875. 182. *LacusCurtius.* Bill Thayer. <penelope.uchicago.edu/Thayer/E/Roman/Texts/secondary/SMIGRA*/Aurum_Coronarium.html>.

Roberts, Gary Boyd. "Notes on the Ancestry of Senator Barack Hussein Obama, Jr." *New England Historic Genealogical Society.* 26 Aug. 2009. <www.newenglandancestors.org/research/services/articles_ancestry_barack_obama.asp>.

Rock, David. *Argentina, 1516-1987: From Spanish Colonization to Alphonsín.* Berkeley: University of California Press, 1987.

Roosevelt, Franklin Delano. "State of the Union Address." 11 Jan. 1944. <teachingamericanhistory.org/library/index.asp?document=463>.

Roosevelt, Franklin Delano. "The Four Freedoms." 6 Jan. 1941. <www.americanrhetoric.com/speeches/fdrthefourfreedoms.htm>.

"Russia." *The World Factbook.* CIA. 11 Sept. 2009 <https://www.cia.gov/library/publications/the-world-factbook/geos/rs.html>.

Sadkovich, James J. "Isonzo, Battles of, Nos. 1-4 (1915)." *The European Powers in the First World War: An Encyclopedia.* New York: Routledge, 1999. 365-68.

Sanford, George. *Poland: The Conquest of History.* Netherlands: Harwood Academic, 1999.

Santayana, George. *The Life of Reason.* New York: America Dover Publications, 1905. *Project Gutenberg.* 14 Feb. 2005. <www.gutenberg.org/files/15000/15000-h/15000-h.htm>.

Scherman, Nosson. *Tanach: The Stone Edition.* Brooklyn: Mesorah Publications, Limited, 1996.

Scherman, Nosson. *The Chumash: The Stone Edition (Artscroll Series).* Brooklyn: Mesorah Publications, Limited, 1993.

Scherman, Nosson. *The Prophets: Kings 1 And 2: The Rubin Edition (Art Scroll Series).* Brooklyn: Mesorah Publications, Limited, 2006.

Scherman, Nosson. *The Prophets: Samuel 1 And 2: The Rubin Edition (Art Scroll Series).* Brooklyn: Mesorah Publications, Limited, 2002.

Schmid, Gerhard. "On the existence of a global system for the interception of private and commercial communications (ECHELON interception system)." *European Parliament: Temporary Committee on the ECHELON Interception System.* 11 July 2001. <www.europarl.europa.eu/sides/getDoc.do?pubRef=-//EP//NONSGML+ REPORT+A5-2001-0264+0+DOC+PDF+V0//EN&language=EN>.

Schmitz, Leonhard. "Eleutheria." *A Dictionary of Greek and Roman Antiquities.* London: John Murray, 1875. 454-55. *LacusCurtius.* Bill Thayer. <penelope.uchicago.edu/ Thayer/E/Roman/Texts/secondary/SMIGRA*/Eleutheria.html>.

Self, Robert C. *Neville Chamberlain: A Biography.* Hampshire, England: Ashgate Publishing, 2006.

Seneca, Lucius Annaeus. *Moral Epistles.* Translated by Richard M. Gummere. The Loeb Classical Library. Cambridge, Mass.: Harvard University Press, 1917-25. 3 vols.: Volume I. *www.stoics.com.* <www.stoics.com/seneca_epistles_book_1.html>.

Service, Robert. *A History of Modern Russia: From Nicholas II to Vladimir Putin.* Cambridge: Harvard University Press, 2005.

Shane, Scott A. "Are We Becoming Less Entrepreneurial?" *You're the Boss Blog.* 30 June 2009. <boss.blogs.nytimes.com/2009/06/30/are-we-becoming-less-entrepreneurial/>.

Shirer, William L. *The Collapse of the Third Republic: An Inquiry into the Fall of France in 1940.* New York: Simon and Schuster, 1969.

Shirer, William L. *The Rise and Fall of the Third Reich: A History of Nazi Germany.* New York: Simon & Schuster, 1990.

Shlaes, Amity. *The Forgotten Man: A New History of the Great Depression.* New York: HarperCollins, 2007.

"Showering With Hugo." *Investors.com.* 27 Oct. 2009. <www.investors.com/ NewsAndAnalysis/Article.aspx?id=510519>.

Skousen, Mark. *The Making of Modern Economics: The Lives and Ideas of the Great Thinkers.* Armonk, NY: M.E. Sharpe, 2001.

Smith, Adam. *The Wealth of Nations.* New York: Modern Library, 1994.

Smith, William, ed. *Dictionary of Greek and Roman Antiquities.* 1870. *The Making of America.* University of Michigan. <www.ancientlibrary.com/smith-dgra/index.html>.

Smith, William, ed. *Dictionary of Greek and Roman Biography and Mythology.* 1870. *The Making of America.* University of Michigan. <www.ancientlibrary.com/smith-bio/index.html>.

Sojo, Cleto A. "Venezuela's Chavez Closes World Social Forum with Call to Transcend Capitalism." *Venezuelanalysis.com.* 30 Jan. 2005. <www.venezuelanalysis.com/ news/907>.

Soltis, Andy. "Tax refugees staging escape from New York." *New York Post.* 27 Oct. 2009. <www.nypost.com/p/news/local/tax_refugees_staging_escape_fr

"State Lobbying Totals, 2004-2006." *The Center for Public Integrity.* 21 Dec. 2007. <projects.publicintegrity.org/hiredguns/chart.aspx?act=lobbyspending>.

"Statuto Albertino." *Encyclopædia Britannica.* 2009. Encyclopædia Britannica Online. 20 Oct. 2009 <www.britannica.com/EBchecked/topic/564286/Statuto-Albertino>.

Stearns, Peter N., ed. *Encyclopedia of World History.* Sixth ed. Boston: Houghton Mifflin, 2001.

Stenudd, Stefan. *Cosmos of the Ancients: The Greek Philosophers on Myth and Cosmology.* Grand Rapids: BookSurge, 2007.

Stone, Geoffrey. *War and Liberty: An American Dilemma 1790 to the Present.* New York: W. W. Norton, 2007.

Suetonius. *The Lives of the Twelve Caesars*. Trans. J. C. Rolfe. Loeb Classical Library, 1913-1914. *LacusCurtius*. Bill Thayer. <penelope.uchicago.edu/Thayer/E/Roman/Texts/Suetonius/12Caesars/home.html>.

Tacitus. *Annals*. Trans. Alfred John Church and William Jackson Brodribb. *Wikisource*. <en.wikisource.org/wiki/The_Annals_%28Tacitus%29>.

Talmud Bavli: Bava Basra.

Talmud Bavli: Kiddushin.

Talmud Bavli: Yoma.

Tarasulo, Isaac J., ed. *Gorbachev and Glasnost: Viewpoints from the Soviet Press*. Wilmington, Del: SR Books, 1989.

"The 25 Points of Hitler's Nazi Party." *The History Place*. 01 Nov. 2009 <www.historyplace.com/worldwar2/riseofhitler/25points.htm>.

"The Full Retirement Age is Increasing." *Social Security Online*. 03 Sept. 2009 <www.ssa.gov/pubs/ageincrease.htm>.

"The Roman Gladiator History & Origins." *Classics Technology Center*. 1 Dec. 2009. <ablemedia.com/ctcweb/consortium/gladiator1.html>.

Thomas, Brinley. *Industrial Revolution and the Atlantic Economy selected essays*. London: Routledge, 1993.

Thucydides. *The Peloponnesian War*. London, J. M. Dent; New York, E. P. Dutton. 1910. *Perseus Digital Library Project*. Tufts University. <www.perseus.tufts.edu/cgi-bin/ptext? lookup=Thuc.+toc>.

"Time Series Chart of US Government Spending." *Government Spending in the United States of America*. Ed. Christopher Chantrill. 27 Apr. 2010. <www.usgovernmentspending.com/downchart_gs.php>.

Tocqueville, Alexis De. *Democracy in America and Two essays on America*. London: Penguin, 2003.

Toland, John. *Adolf Hitler: The Definitive Biography*. New York: Anchor, 1991.

"Top 100 Recipients of Federal Contract Awards for FY 2008." *USAspending.gov*. 30 Nov. 2009 <www.usaspending.gov/fpds/tables.php?tabtype=t2&subtype=t&year=2008>.

Treisman, Daniel. *The Architecture of Government: Rethinking Political Decentralization*. New York: Cambridge University Press, 2007.

Tremoglie, Michael P. "The Facts on Halliburton." *FrontPage Magazine*. 8 Oct. 2004. <frontpagemag.com/readArticle.aspx?ARTID=11068>.

Twelve Tables. The Civil Law. Trans. Samuel P. Scott. Cincinnati: The Central Trust Company, 1932. *The Constitution Society*. <www.constitution.org/sps/sps.htm>.

Twight, Charlotte A. *Dependent on D.C.: The Rise of Federal Control over the Lives of Ordinary Americans*. New York: Palgrave Macmillan, 2002.

United States CIA. *Intelligence Memorandum: Communist Military Aid Deliveries to North Vietnam*. Nov. 1968. <www.foia.cia.gov/browse_docs_full.asp>.

"United States Federal State and Local Government Spending." *Government Spending in the United States of America*. Ed. Christopher Chantrill. 27 Apr. 2010. <www.usgovernmentspending.com/year2009_0.html>.

"Venezuela: Oil." *Energy Information Administration: Official Energy Statistics from the U.S. Government*. Jan. 2009. <www.eia.doe.gov/cabs/Venezuela/Oil.html>.

Vennochi, Joan. "Nominees and double standards." *The Boston Globe*. 18 Jan. 2009. <www.boston.com/bostonglobe/editorial_opinion/oped/articles/2009/01/18/nominees_and_double_standards/>.

Voegeli, William. "The Golden State isn't worth it." *Los Angeles Times*. 1 Nov. 2009. <www.latimes.com/news/opinion/la-oe-voegli1-2009nov01,0,825554.story>.

Vogel, Kenneth P. "Sanford had trade mission rendezvous." *Politico.* 25 June 2009. <dyn.politico.com/printstory.cfm?uuid=19217866-18FE-70B2-A8433E9A66883D89>.

Waldron, Peter. *Between Two Revolutions: Stolypin and the Politics of Renewal in Russia.* Dekalb: Northern Illinois University Press, 1998.

Wallace, Donald Mackenzie. *Russia.* London: Cassell and Company, 1912.

"Water rationing for Venezuela's capital city." *Breitbart.com.* 2 Nov. 2009. <www.breitbart.com/article.php?id=CNG.ad409ca172435301fb479b62661e070f. 361&show_article=1>.

Watson, Harry L. *Liberty and Power: The Politics of Jacksonian America.* New York: Hill and Wang, 2006.

Weerakkody, D.P.M. "Inheritance." *Encyclopedia of Ancient Greece.* Comp. Nigel Guy Wilson. New York: Routledge, 2006. 380-82.

"When governments fear the people, there is liberty...(Quotation)." *Thomas Jefferson Encyclopedia.* 21 Oct. 2009. <www.monticello.org/site/jefferson/when-governments-fear-people-there-libertyquotation>.

White, Matthew. "Death Tolls for the Major Wars and Atrocities of the Twentieth Century." *Twentieth Century Atlas.* Nov. 2005. <users.erols.com/mwhite28/warstat2.htm#North>.

White, Matthew. "Minor Atrocities of the Twentieth Century." *Twentieth Century Atlas.* July 2005. <users.erols.com/mwhite28/warstat6.htm#Cuba59>.

White, Matthew. "Secondary Wars and Atrocities of the Twentieth Century." *Twentieth Century Atlas.* Nov. 2005. <users.erols.com/mwhite28/warstat3.htm#Spanish>.

White, Matthew. "Source List and Detailed Death Tolls for the Twentieth Century Hemoclysm." *Twentieth Century Atlas.* Nov. 2005. <users.erols.com/mwhite28/warstat1.htm#WW1>.

Wiedemann, Thomas. *Emperors and Gladiators.* New York: Routledge, 1992.

Williams, Kieran. *The Prague Spring and its aftermath: Czechoslovak politics, 1968-1970.* Cambridge University Press, 1997.

Wilson, Woodrow. *War Message to Congress.* April 3, 1917. 65th Cong., 1st Sess. Senate Doc. No. 5, Serial No. 7264, Washington, D.C. <wwi.lib.byu.edu/index.php/Wilson%27s_War_Message_to_Congress>

"World's Billionaires 2009." *Forbes.* 11 Mar. 2009 <www.forbes.com/2009/03/11/worlds-richest-people-billionaires-2009-billionaires_land.html>.

"World's Billionaires 2009: #468 Marc Rich." *Forbes.* 11 Mar. 2009 <www.forbes.com/lists/2009/10/billionaires-2009-richest-people_Marc-Rich_ THOQ.html>.

Xenophanes. *Fragments and Commentary. The First Philosophers of Greece.* Trans. Arthur Fairbanks. London: K. Paul, Trench, Trubner, 1898. 65-85. *Hanover Historical Texts Project.* Mar. 2001. <history.hanover.edu/texts/presoc/Xenophan.html>.

Xenophon. *Hellenica. Xenophon in Seven Volumes, 1 and 2.* Trans. Carleton L. Brownson. Harvard University Press, Cambridge, MA; William Heinemann, Ltd., London. vol. 1:1985; vol. 2: 1986. *Perseus Digital Library Project.* Tufts University. <www.perseus.tufts.edu/cgi-bin/ptext?lookup=Xen.+Hell.+toc>.

Xenophon. *Memorabilia. Xenophon in Seven Volumes, 4.* Trans. E. C. Marchant and O. J. Todd. Harvard University Press, Cambridge, MA; William Heinemann, Ltd., London. 1979. *Perseus Digital Library Project.* Tufts University. <www.perseus.tufts.edu/cgi-bin/ptext?lookup=Xen.+Mem.+toc>.

Xenophon. *The Polity of the Athenians and the Lacedaemonians.* Trans. Henry Graham Dakyns. *Project Gutenberg.* <www.gutenberg.org/etext/1178>.

York, Byron. "Michelle Obama: It's a 'sacrifice' to travel to Europe to pitch for the Olympics. But I'm doing it for the kids." *Washington Examiner*. 30 Sept. 2009. <www.washingtonexaminer.com/opinion/blogs/beltway-confidential/Michelle-Obama-Its-a-sacrifice-to-travel-to-Europe-to-pitch-for-the-Olympics--For-Oprah-and-the-president-too--But-were-doing-it-for-the-kids-62928957.html>.

Zamagni, Vera. *The Economic History of Italy: 1860-1990 Recovery after Decline*. New York: Oxford University Press, 2003.

INDEX

Made in the USA
Lexington, KY
21 September 2012